CUBAN STUDIES 41

ADVISORY BOARD

CUBAN STUDIES 41

CATHERINE KRULL and
SORAYA CASTRO MARIÑO, *Guest Editors*
K. LYNN STONER, *Book Review Editor*
(United States)
GLADYS MAREL GARCÍA PÉREZ,
Book Review Editor (Cuba)

UNIVERSITY OF PITTSBURGH PRESS

CUBAN STUDIES

CATHERINE KRULL AND SORAYA CASTRO MARIÑO, Guest Editors

Manuscripts in English and Spanish may be submitted to Editor, *Cuban Studies,* University of Pittsburgh Press, 3400 Forbes Ave., 5th floor, Pittsburgh, PA, 15260, USA. Maximum length is forty pages, double spaced, including tables and notes. Please submit two copies, with an abstract of no more than 200 words. We prefer *Chicago Manual of Style,* 15th edition, for reference style, but MLA is also acceptable. Full manuscript preparation guidelines are available on the University of Pittsburgh Press Web site at http://www.upress.pitt.edu. *Cuban Studies* takes no responsibility for views or information presented in signed articles. For additional editorial inquiries, contact us at the address above.

Review copies of books should be sent to K. Lynn Stoner, Book Review Editor, Arizona State University, Department of History, Coor Hall 4424, P.O. Box 874302, USA. For additional inquiries about book reviews, please call 480-965-3007 or e-mail lynn.stoner @asu.edu.

Orders for volumes 16–40 of Cuban Studies and standing orders for future volumes should be sent to the University of Pittsburgh Press, Chicago Distribution Center, 11030 South Langley, Chicago, IL 60628-3893, USA; telephone 800-621-2736; fax 800-621-8476.

Back issues of volumes 1–15 of *Cuban Studies,* when available, may be obtained from the Center for Latin American Studies, 4E04 Forbes Quadrangle, University of Pittsburgh, Pittsburgh PA 15260, USA.

Articles appearing in this volume are abstracted and indexed in *Historical Abstracts* and *America: History and Life.* They are also available electronically through Project MUSE®; see http://muse.jhu.edu/publishers/pitt_press/.

Published by the University of Pittsburgh Press, Pittsburgh PA 15260
Copyright © 2010, University of Pittsburgh Press
All rights reserved
Manufactured in the United States of America
Printed on acid-free paper

Library of Congress Card Number
ISBN 13: 978-0-8229-4401-0
ISBN 10: 0-8229-4401-4
US ISSN 0361–4441
10 9 8 7 6 5 4 3 2 1

Contents

vi : *Contents*

Note from the Publisher

Volume 41 is guest edited by Catherine Krull (Queen's University) and Soraya Castro Mariño (Universidad de La Habana). The University of Pittsburgh Press is pleased to publish this volume, which continues the journal's tradition of excellence in scholarship. The press would like to thank Lou Pérez for his outstanding service. We continue to rely on his expertise and judgment during this time of transition for *Cuban Studies*. Readers may notice the absence of a bibliographic section listing recent work in Cuban studies in this volume; this was a necessary concession given the resources available at this time.

Preface

The year 2009 marked the fiftieth anniversary of the triumph of the Cuban revolution. An event with far-reaching national consequences and far-flung international repercussions, the Cuban Revolution must be considered as one of the momentous occurrences of the twentieth century. It spoke to the prevailing concerns of its time: a period of postcolonial transitions in which matters of sovereignty and self-determination and issues of social justice and economic development loomed as the overriding preoccupations of the third world.

That is why, on the fiftieth anniversary of the Cuban Revolution, the conference entitled "The Measure of a Revolution: Cuba, 1959–2009" was held from May 7–9, 2009, on the campus of Queen's University, Kingston, Ontario, Canada. Jointly organized by Catherine Krull (Queen's University), Soraya Castro (Havana University), Louis Pérez Jr. (University of North Carolina at Chapel Hill), and Susan Eckstein (Boston University), the conference assessed the revolution's achievements, analyzed its shortcomings, considered its prospects, and contemplated its legacy in the years to come. Representing over 15 countries, approximately 260 participants — including academics, writers, politicians, and artists specializing in a wide variety of themes relating to Cuba — shared their knowledge and analysis at this conference.

Now, *Cuban Studies* highlights some of the work that was presented at this conference from a variety of crucial angles. The articles in this special issue represent a variety of disciplines that study Cuba's past and present, and they provide diverse methodological approaches and multiple analytical frameworks. The coeditors have also made a concerted effort to include Cuban voices from the island — that of three contributing authors and one of the coeditors. With a range of international scholars from different disciplines — history, international relations, literature, sociology, journalism, politics, and arts and culture — the survival of Cuban revolutionary ideals and their transformation into a consequential international presence are assessed and put into the context of — including the connection among — the course of Cuban history, foreign policy, the defense of national sovereignty, solidarity, and the importance of resistance, all major issues in Cuban national identity.

We would like to thank the individuals who agreed to review papers for this issue — their expertise and insightful comments and suggestions have contributed to a stronger publication. We would also be amiss if we did not express our heartfelt thanks to Louis Pérez Jr. for coming up with the idea of featuring some of the papers from the conference in a special issue. His proficiency and dedication to this journal, his generosity to new and established scholars in the field and his overall contribution to Cuban scholarship are unsurpassed — following his example has truly been walking in the footsteps of a giant.

Catherine Krull   Soraya Castro Mariño
Kingston, Ontario   Havana, Cuba
April 2010   April 2010

CUBAN STUDIES 41

LARS SCHOULTZ

Benevolent Domination:
The Ideology of U.S. Policy toward Cuba

ABSTRACT

Washington's hostile post–Cold War policy toward Cuba is often explained as a function of domestic politics — as an effort to curry favor among Cuban American voters and campaign contributors, most of whom live in Florida, which has the fourth-largest number of votes in the electoral college. Although it does not deny the significance of domestic politics, this article argues that the bedrock of U.S. policy is an ideology of benevolent domination. Created at the time of the Spanish-American War, President Theodore Roosevelt captured this ideology perfectly in 1907 when he explained, "I am seeking the very minimum of interference necessary to make them good," and it is seen today in the 2004 report of the Commission for Assistance to a Free Cuba.

RESUMEN

La política hostil de Washington hacia Cuba en la era post-Guerra Fría es usualmente explicada como una función de la política interna de los Estados Unidos, como una resultante de los esfuerzos para lograr el favor de los votantes cubano-americanos y sus contribuciones financieras a las campañas electorales. La mayoría de ellos viven en Florida, el cual constituye el cuarto estado más importante del colegio electoral. Sin negar la significación de la política doméstica, este artículo propone que la esencia de la política de Estados Unidos hacia Cuba radica en una ideología de dominación bene-volente. Creada desde los tiempos de la Guerra Hispano-Americana, esta ideología fue perfectamente comprendida por el Presidente Theodore Roosevelt, quien en 1907 de-claró: "Estoy tratando de interferir lo menos posible para hacerles el bien", y al parecer la misma lógica se aprecia en el informe del 2004 de la Comisión para la Asistencia a una Cuba Libre.

The United States and Cuba have not had normal diplomatic relations since January 3, 1961, eleven U.S. presidents ago. In contrast, the U.S. refusal to recognize both the Soviet Union and the People's Republic of China lasted for only five presidents, sixteen and twenty-two years, respectively. And the United States has not simply declined to have normal diplomatic relations with Havana: Washington has also spent most of the past half century in an open attempt to overthrow the island's government. There is nothing like Cuba in the history of United States foreign policy. This long-standing estrangement is the product of

1

several concrete concerns related to U.S. security, to U.S. economic interests, and to U.S. domestic politics. But underlying these concerns and governing the policies of the past eleven administrations is an ideology based above all else on a belief, widespread in the United States, that Cubans, like most Latin Americans, are a stunted branch of the human species. Our euphemism for these people and their societies is "underdeveloped."[1]

This ideology is not a facade masking selfish interests and, in particular, a selfish interest in eliminating challenges to U.S. hegemony in the Caribbean. Rather, it is most useful to think of this ideology toward Latin America as the software Washington has created to take a keystroke from the environment — a revolution, for example — and process it through the policymaking computer and onto the monitor as policy. Working quietly in the background, this software is difficult to examine because it is politically incorrect to hint at its intellectual core: a firm belief that, in any hierarchy of peoples, Latin Americans are beneath the United States. Or as the minutes of a February 1959 National Security Council meeting have the CIA director warning: "Mr. Allen Dulles pointed out that the new Cuban officials had to be treated more or less like children. They had to be led rather than rebuffed. If they were rebuffed, like children, they were capable of doing almost anything." As one U.S. diplomat reported in the mid-nineteenth century, "Were it not for the civilizing influence of the United States, this country would by degrees *revert* to the aboriginal state in which Alvarado the Spaniard found it."[2]

The best way to begin — but only begin — to explain U.S. policy toward revolutionary Cuba is not with this ideology, but with a frank recognition that senior U.S. officials are extremely busy, all but overwhelmed by an endless array of pressing issues, some of them matters of life and death; it would take both time and political capital to terminate today's complex embargo that has been cobbled together over half a century. Then, after acknowledging the importance of inertia, the next step is to observe that the United States has important interests to protect in Latin America, and the estrangement that began a half century ago was largely a response to the Cuban government's reluctance to address these interests to Washington's satisfaction. Correctly or incorrectly, wisely or unwisely, the United States came to perceive Cuba's revolutionary government as a threat to its interests.

For three of the past five decades, roughly from 1960 to 1990, the most important of these interests was to protect U.S. security. Although small Caribbean nations lack the power to threaten the United States, their territory can serve other major powers as a launching pad. And so the first statement of U.S. policy toward Latin America, the 1811 No-Transfer Resolution, was aimed to stop the British from securing a toehold in Spanish Florida, and the 1823 Monroe Doctrine was based on the same bedrock principle: prudent people keep potential adversaries as far away as possible, and Cuba is close.

"We will bury you," Nikita Khrushchev boasted in 1956, just as Cuba's revolutionary leaders were planning their campaign to seize power.[3] Then in early 1960, a year after the rebels' victory, he sent the first deputy chair of the Council of Ministers of the Soviet Union, Anastas Mikoyan, to open a scientific, cultural, and technical exhibition in Havana. Before leaving the island, Mikoyan signed an agreement to purchase about 20 percent of Cuba's sugar crop for each of the following five years, and within three weeks, President Dwight Eisenhower had authorized preparation for the Bay of Pigs invasion. A Soviet-friendly government in Cuba was an unacceptable challenge to the primordial U.S. interest in security.

The Cuban Revolution also attacked substantial economic interests. The U.S. government lost some of its own property, principally Cuba's Nicaro nickel facility, which the U.S. General Services Administration had built during World War II; remaining U.S. government owned, it was operated by a private contractor, Freeport Sulphur Company, which had been developing is own nickel and cobalt mine at Moa Bay, forty miles to the east. Freeport lost that, too, and other U.S. investors suffered losses valued at about $2 billion at a time when a billion was more than pocket change. More than six thousand of those investors filed claims with the Foreign Claims Settlement Commission, and some were extremely well-connected corporate leaders, such as Robert Kleberg, the president of King Ranch in Texas, which lost its forty-thousand-acre ranch in Cienfuegos. With help from his representative in Congress, the Senate majority leader Lyndon Johnson, Kleberg promptly marched into the Oval Office, demanded President Eisenhower's help, and got it — a full-court press by U.S. diplomats.

But most investors of Robert Kleberg's generation wrote off their losses decades ago, and in the post–Cold War era, they have been replaced by a new set of powerful economic interests seeking to reopen trade with the island. Agribusiness, the single most powerful lobbying force in Washington, has been key. It took U.S. farmers almost a decade, but in 2000, they finally pushed through a law that permits the sale of food to Cuba. At first Cuba declined to buy, insisting on normal two-way trade, but then it reconsidered after a devastating hurricane in 2001; and the year ended with a boatload of U.S. poultry sailing into Havana's harbor. It was the first significant trade with Cuba since 1963.

Cubans apparently liked what they bought, and soon the invisible hand of supply and demand — combined with low shipping costs — began to work its magic. In early 2002, six House Democrats visited the island, including the Arkansas moderate Vic Snyder, touting the rice and pork his constituents produced. Then came a delegation of California producers led by Senator Barbara Boxer, and a North Dakota delegation led by Republican governor John Hoeven followed her. The North Dakotans left Havana only hours before two more members of Congress arrived with a delegation featuring a former secretary of agriculture, and this congressional delegation overlapped with a visit by Tampa's mayor Richard Greco, who was shepherding fifteen local business leaders hoping to convince Cubans to use their port for food shipments.

These visits were but a prelude to the main event in 2003: a privately organized food exhibition in Havana featuring 933 representatives of 288 U.S. vendors from thirty-three states and Puerto Rico, plus the agriculture commissioners from ten states, all eager to tap into the Cuban market. More than seventy U.S. firms signed more than $92 million in sales contracts, and North Carolina's agriculture commissioner drafted an op-ed article on her flight home: "With our economy on the skids, state budgets in shambles and our farmers going bankrupt, does it make any sense to continue a 40-year-old embargo with Cuba when there is so much to be gained by both countries? I don't think so." What was the result? In 2008, the U.S. Department of Agriculture reported that U.S. farmers had become "Cuba's largest supplier of food and agricultural products. Cuba has consistently ranked among the top ten export markets for U.S. soybean oil, dry peas, lentils, dry beans, rice, powdered milk and poultry. Cuba also has been a major market for U.S. corn, wheat and soybeans."[4]

So here we are, at a time when national security officials no longer have a significant interest in Cuba and economic interests are no longer a negative. Why does the estrangement continue? Enter the Cuban American community in Florida, which holds part — but only part — of the answer: a third interest, domestic politics or, more concretely, the interest politicians have in winning elections. As a former chief of the U.S. interests section pointed out in 2005: "Ninety-eight percent of U.S. citizens never think of Cuba; the only people who think Cuba is important are the Cubans in Miami."[5] No one would have paid these 1.2 million immigrants much attention if they had settled in Vermont, which has only three votes in the U.S. electoral college; but two-thirds chose to settle in booming Florida, which has twenty-seven votes, today's fourth-largest prize in the quadrennial electoral college sweepstakes, and after the 2010 census, Florida could move into a tie for third with New York, with twenty-nine (New York now has thirty-one but will likely lose two; Florida has twenty-seven and will probably gain two).

At first, Cuban immigrants were politically impotent, but soon they began to take out citizenship papers, and then in the 1970s, they started to elbow their way into politics, initially at the local level, where they competed for school boards and similar community councils. Then they set out to elect members of the state legislature, and they also started to form interest groups, capped in 1981 by the creation of the Cuban American National Foundation (CANF), which moved Cuban Americans up the political food chain to the national level. Primarily, CANF spoke for wealthy first-wave immigrants who were largely uninterested in the pork-barrel politics that typically characterize first- and second-generation immigrants; instead, CANF's goal was to influence U.S.

policy toward Cuba, and it did so the old-fashioned way, with campaign contributions and bloc voting.[6]

And CANF did this at a propitious moment: it had spent the 1980s honing its political skills on legislation creating Radio and TV Martí. When the Cold War ended in the early 1990s, the foundation was a recognized force in Washington, perfectly positioned to move into the vacuum left by exiting national security officials. With its focus on tightening the embargo, CANF was responsible for both the 1992 Cuban Democracy (Torricelli) Act, passed by a Democratic Congress and signed by a Republican president, and then for initiating the campaign against third-country investors in Cuba that led to the Cuban Liberty and Democratic (LIBERTAD) Solidarity Act of 1996 (the Helms-Burton Act), passed by a Republican Congress and signed by a Democratic president.[7] Helms-Burton prompted the frustrated chief executive officer of the agribusiness heavyweight Archer Daniels Midland, eager to reopen an old market, to complain that "every presidential candidate is invited to Miami to make a speech to a handful of rich Cubans, and the candidate says, 'I will never speak to Castro.' The result is that we look to the rest of the world like idiots."[8]

Then came Elián González, the five-year-old boy found clinging to an inner tube off Fort Lauderdale on Thanksgiving Day in 1999. Since his mother had drowned after their rickety boat had capsized, and sending Elián back to live with a loving father in Cuba had been the right thing to do, President Bill Clinton wrote in his memoir: "I was still concerned that it could cost Al Gore Florida in November."[9] The charges of fraud in Florida's 2000 election were multiple and centered on the exclusion of more than fifty thousand African American voters, but anyone who had followed Elián's prolonged ordeal could reasonably conclude that his return had aroused intense anger in Little Havana. And although it is important not to overstate Cuban American voting clout, one thing is certain: when the dust settled in 2000, the Democrats had lost the state by 537 votes, handing all of Florida's electoral votes to the Republicans and giving George W. Bush the presidency with a five-vote electoral college margin.

Since then, the question has been: When will Cuban Americans begin to vote their broader interests — when will they cast their ballots and distribute their campaign contributions on some basis other than which party's candidates promise to be more vigorous in their hostility toward the government of the country from which they or their forebears emigrated? Much public opinion polling and the 2008 election, when Barack Obama captured about 35 percent of Cuban American votes, have suggested that significant dispersion is already occurring; but today's politicians are still walking a very thin line, as candidate Barack Obama's Miami speech to CANF illustrated in May 2008. While promising to maintain the embargo as leverage, he argued that "the United States must be a relentless advocate for democracy." Obama also promised to "immediately allow unlimited family travel and remittances to the island."

When implemented in 2009, this relaxation of the embargo's travel and remittance provisions more than reversed a tightening in 2004, just before that year's election, when Cuban Americans were feeling neglected. In 2001, his first year as president, George W. Bush had presided over a May 20 Independence Day celebration with a party for Cuban American leaders on the White House lawn. The next year, 2002, was the hundredth anniversary of Cuban independence, and President Bush had flown to Miami to participate in the celebration. But in 2003, when the Iraq War had become a consuming focus, the president's Independence Day message had been nothing but a forty-second prerecorded restatement of what President Clinton had said a decade earlier: "My hope is for the Cuban people to soon enjoy the same freedoms and rights as we do." Then a few weeks later, the U.S. Coast Guard had intercepted a hijacked boat in the Straits of Florida and returned the hijackers to Cuba.

Enough is enough, wrote ninety-eight prominent Cuban Americans, taking out an ad in *El Nuevo Herald* on 3 August 2003, complaining in an open letter to the president that "current policy toward Cuba has not varied significantly from that of the previous administration." The Bush administration responded by creating the Commission for Assistance to a Free Cuba, chaired by Secretary of State Colin Powell. Published just before the nominating conventions in mid-2004, the commission's report recommended that President Bush tighten the embargo by reducing family visits and restricting remittances. These reductions and restrictions were not popular with many Cuban Americans, but they solidified the president's ultra-hard-line Cuban American base and probably contributed to his win in Florida.

Both George Bush and Barack Obama understood the importance of Florida's Cuban Americans, and both candidates' campaigns were guided by astute pollsters who in 2004 advised Bush to tighten the embargo but in 2008 advised Obama to relax it. The Democrats could not hope to attract the Republicans' hard-line base, but their polling indicted that a moderate Cuba policy was no longer an electoral death sentence among Cuban Americans. And the candidate's stand on Cuba was also important to many of the liberal Democrats who form that party's base. Walking an exceptionally thin line, Barack Obama promised to maintain the embargo but to lighten up on family visits and remittances. And he won Florida.

So where is U.S. policy heading? Given the torpor that has followed the Obama administration's April 2009 relaxation of restrictions on Cuban Americans, a safe hypothesis for the near term is that we may be heading toward a few more modest steps, albeit not to the full normalization of relations. But today's aging generation of Cuban revolutionaries and Cuban American counterrevolutionaries is clearly fading into the sunset. In time, the next generation of Cuban leaders will make changes on the island, and assessments of those changes by the next generation of Cuban Americans will slowly diversify. At some point, the pollsters will tell everyone it is safe to end the estrangement.

The truly interesting question is what might come after that. No one knows, of course, but it may be instructive to look at a somewhat similar situation that occurred in the early 1990s, when the Soviet Union disappeared and when Cuba no longer had the resources to promote revolution abroad, especially in Central America, which had been one of Washington's consuming concerns throughout the 1980s. With national security interests no longer part of the policy debate, a reporter asked the first President Bush in 1991 if he intended to engage Fidel Castro as he had engaged Mikhail Gorbachev. "What's the point?" he replied. "All I'd tell him is what I'm telling you, to give the people the freedom that they want. And then you'll see the United States do exactly what we should: Go down and lift those people up."[10]

We should not make too much of this off-the-cuff response, but it suggests that something more than three pedestrian interests — security, economics, and domestic politics — underlies U.S. policy. It suggests the existence of a peculiar mind-set, a way of thinking about Cuba that may point to the direction of U.S. policy in the years immediately ahead. The foundation of this uplifting mind-set is an obvious power disparity: the United States, unlike Cuba, is wealthy, and it has used a substantial portion of its wealth to create the most powerful military in the history of the human race. That raw power, in turn, has given politicians such as Richard Nixon the ability to tell voters that "the United States has the power, and Mr. Castro knows this, to throw him out of office," and it has given cabinet members such as Secretary of State Alexander Haig the ability to ask President Ronald Reagan for a simple green light: what he said to the President, according to Nancy Reagan, is: "You just give me the word and I'll turn that f—— island into a parking lot."[11]

What would seem puzzling to a visitor from another planet is why, when the Cubans refused to behave as Washington insisted, their leaders were not thrown out of office and their island was not turned into a parking lot. How have they managed to get away with it? There are several answers. Initially, Cuba balanced U.S. power by enlisting the support of a rival superpower, but that answer takes us only to about 1990, when the Soviet Union withdrew its support. Since then, much of Washington's forbearance can be attributed to the fact that no one has much time or political capital to spend on any Caribbean island. A simple list of all the other issues confronting senior officials is sufficient to explain why Nixon largely ignored Cuba when he finally claimed the presidency, why Reagan declined to endorse Haig's parking-lot solution, and why presidential adviser Arthur Schlesinger Jr. had this to say about the one president who seemed to spend more time than any other on Cuba: "Castro was not a major issue for Kennedy, who had much else on his mind."[12]

And this combination of awesome power and globe-girding responsibilities helps explain why, once Eisenhower- and Kennedy-era leaders had decided to overthrow the island's revolutionary government, they planned to do it on the cheap, with a covert operation that, like the overthrow of Guatemala's left-leaning Jacobo Árbenz government in 1954, would take only a couple of days. The CIA predicted a cakewalk, telling Kennedy that "less than 30 percent of the population is still with Fidel," and "in this 30 percent are included the negroes, who will not fight."[13] Then three months later, when Kennedy administration officials discovered at the Bay of Pigs that the Cubans would fight back, they had to decide what to do next. Certainly Cubans could be subdued, but not by a couple of thousand exiles; Washington would have to use the Marines, who might have to turn the island into a parking lot. Imagine what that would cost in the currency that might matter most: world opinion.

So what was plan B? First, there were a few years of what we today would call state-sponsored terrorism — Operation Mongoose, which focused on sabotaging power plants, torching sugar fields, and arming assassins. But when that low-cost covert activity proved unsuccessful, the consensus opinion was that Cuba was not sufficiently important to require costly, decisive action. What happened is that Lyndon Johnson, inexperienced in foreign affairs, waited only a few days after inheriting the White House to seek advice from the widely respected chair of the Senate Committee on Foreign Relations, J. William Fulbright. In their telephone conversation, Fulbright began to warn against anything dramatic but had barely completed a sentence before the new president interrupted to agree: "I'm not getting into any Bay of Pigs deal. No, I'm just asking you what we ought to do to pinch their nuts more than we're doing."[14]

Nut pinching — an embargo — has been U.S. policy ever since. During the Kennedy era, "I used to get a call from McGeorge Bundy or one of his assistants every day about something," recalled the State Department's principal Cuba officer; but "under Johnson, the calls dropped down to probably once a week, and then maybe once every two weeks or once a month."[15] Why? Because even a superpower has limited resources, and President Johnson, like every one of his successors, had better ways to spend his political capital. Instead of ramping up Operation Mongoose, Johnson initially chose to focus on domestic issues — a month after consulting with Fulbright, he went before a joint session of Congress to declare the War on Poverty and to press for passage of the Civil Rights Act of 1964. Completely absorbed in pursuing these domestic initiatives, he had little time for Cuba, especially as his administration's foreign policy eyes began to focus on Indochina. Soon, National Security Adviser McGeorge Bundy was encouraging everyone to face reality. "The chances are very good that we will still be living with Castro some time from now," he said; "we might just as well get used to the idea."[16]

But tugging U.S. policy toward greater involvement is domestic politics — Cuban American votes — augmented by a firmly established conviction that the United States is responsible for taking care of Cuba or, as the first President Bush told that reporter in 1991, if Fidel Castro would relax his grip on power, "then you'll see the United States do exactly what we should: Go down and lift those people up." This idea was close to what candidate Barack Obama told his Cuban American campaign audience in May 2008: the embargo had to be retained as leverage because "the United States must be a relentless advocate for democracy."[17] So far, Obama has given Cuba almost none of his attention, but at the April 2009 Summit of the Americas in Trinidad and Tobago, he repeated his campaign-trail commitment, emphasizing that "the Cuban people are not free. And that's our lodestone, our North Star, when it comes to our policy in Cuba." Like its predecessor, the Obama administration is committed to uplifting Cuba.

Like the two post–Cold War presidents sandwiched between them — Bill Clinton and George W. Bush — both the first President Bush and President Obama were simply continuing a century-old tradition of uplifting, which has now become a controlling component of Washington's Cuba ideology. The origin of this uplifting tradition can be traced back to the mid-nineteenth century, a time of rapid U.S. territorial expansion. But let us not expand southward, argued one member of the House of Representatives, reacting to a proposal that the United States purchase the island from Spain. His winning argument was, "We have enough of inferior races in our midst without absorbing and not assimilating the Creoles and blacks of Cuba."[18] The consensus at the time, in 1869, was that the outright incorporation of Cuba would harm rather than help the United States. But some uplifting could still occur, wrote the U.S. consul in Havana a few years later, urging a reduction of trade barriers so that American merchants could "extend to the country and its inhabitants the advantages of contact with the higher civilization, the greater energy, the purer morality of America."[19]

Today's uplifting effort, which focuses on promoting democracy, carries on a tradition established immediately after the Spanish-American War in the late nineteenth century. The congressional resolution authorizing the war said nothing about the type of government to be established in Cuba once the Spanish had been ousted, but self-rule was explicit in the war resolution's promise that the United States would "leave the government and control of the island to its people" — the demos. This suggested a democracy, but creating one was easier said than done. "We are going ahead as fast as we can," Governor-General Leonard Wood wrote President William McKinley in 1900, more than a year after the war ended, "but we are dealing with a race that has steadily been going down for a hundred years into which we have got to infuse new life, new principles and new methods of doing things. This is not the work of a day or of a year, but of a longer period."[20]

Wood's letter arrived in Washington at a moment when McKinley's thoughts were on domestic politics — reelection — and when the rival Democrats were already making political capital out of his administration's inability to pacify the Philippines, another part of the spoils seized from Spain. Seeking to balance that quagmire with progress in Cuba, the president ordered Wood to draw up the first U.S. plan for Cuba's democracy.

Wood did so. It began with the disenfranchisement of that part of the Cuban population that had gone furthest downhill. Suffrage was restricted to Cuban-born males over the age of twenty who could meet one of three requirements: the ability to read and write, the possession of property valued at $250 or more, or military service in the insurgent forces before the U.S. intervention. These restrictions eliminated two-thirds of Cuba's adult males, and Secretary of War Elihu Root was especially pleased to see that "whites so greatly outnumber the blacks" in the electorate: "When the history of the new Cuba comes to be written the establishment of popular self-government, based on a limited suffrage, excluding so great a proportion of the elements which have brought ruin to Hayti and San Domingo, will be regarded as an event of first importance."[21]

But then, when given their opportunity to vote — for Cuba's first constituent assembly — Cubans elected the wrong individuals. "The dominant party in the Convention to-day contains probably the worst political element in the Island," Wood reported. Because this was the body that would write Cuba's first constitution, and because the U.S. election was over, Wood's first reaction was to press for a delay, promising "that at the next municipal elections we shall get hold of a better class of people." He also reopened the issue of keeping the island, citing the concerns of local property owners who, he reported, "are very reluctant to see a change of government, unless it be annexation to the United States."[22]

But the Republicans had made an unambiguous campaign commitment to Cuban independence, and so they turned to their fallback position — the Platt Amendment, named after Connecticut Senator Orville Platt, chair of the Senate Committee on Relations with Cuba, who worried that Cubans were too juvenile for complete independence: "In many ways they are like children."[23] Platt's 1901 amendment to the army appropriations bill prohibited the withdrawal of U.S. troops until Cubans had amended their new constitution to authorize the United States the right to intervene for "the maintenance of a government adequate for the protection of life, property, and individual liberty."[24] Once Cubans had agreed — they were told they had no choice if they wanted their independence — Wood handed over power to Tomás Estrada Palma, a naturalized U.S. citizen who had lived in the United States for three decades. Uncontested on the ballot, he won Cuba's first U.S.-supervised presidential election without leaving his home in upstate New York. Estrada Palma's election ended Washington's first effort to promote democracy in Cuba.

A second effort began four years later, in 1906, when a substantial number of Cubans rebelled in response to that year's fraudulent election. "I am so angry with that infernal little Cuban republic that I would like to wipe its people off the face of the earth," an exasperated President Theodore Roosevelt confided to a friend. "All we have wanted from them was that they would behave themselves and be prosperous and happy so that we would not have to interfere. And now, lo and behold, they have started an utterly unjustifiable and pointless revolution." Roosevelt invoked the Platt Amendment, and U.S. forces took over the island once again. Asked to explain his purpose, the president told to a Harvard audience, "I am doing my best to persuade the Cubans that if only they will be good they will be happy. I am seeking the very minimum of interference necessary to make them good."

Forced to the defensive after retaking a country only recently granted its independence, Roosevelt's provisional governor of Cuba, Secretary of War William Howard Taft, reminded readers of *National Geographic* that "the record of the nine years since the beginning of the Spanish War, looked at from an impartial standpoint, is on the whole an unblemished record of generous, earnest effort to uplift these people"; and he said the same thing directly to Cubans: "We are here only to help you . . . with our arm under your arm, lifting you again on the path of wonderful progress." And he continued in the manner of a caring Dutch uncle to an audience celebrating the reopening day of the University of Havana: "perhaps you will pardon me if I invite your attention, as an educated and intelligent audience, to some of the difficulties of your people." These difficulties were many, but the most significant problem was that "the young Cubans who are coming forward into life are not sufficiently infused with the mercantile spirit." To Taft, it boiled down to a simple thing: "What you need here among the Cubans is a desire to make money."[25]

As did Leonard Wood before him, Taft understood that the uplifting would not be easy. He told Roosevelt that the insurrection "could not have occurred in a country in which the common and ignorant people are not as easily aroused"; he wrote his wife that "the whole thing demonstrates the utter unfittness of these people for self govt." Nonetheless, this second U.S. intervention was also intended to be brief — Roosevelt instructed the War Department, "Our business is to establish peace and order on a satisfactory basis, start the new government, and then leave the island."[26] These instructions were handed to a new governor-general, Charles Magoon, who agreed that Cuba's fiery culture was the underlying problem: "Like all other people of Spanish origin they are hot blooded, high strung, nervous, excitable and pessimistic." Uplifting would therefore be slow, for "we cannot change these racial characteristics by administering their Government for two years or twenty years."[27]

As an alternative to a time-consuming attempt to de-Hispanicize Cuban culture, Magoon tried to constrain the excitable Cubans by strengthening their institutions. He created the Advisory Law Commission composed of nine carefully chosen Cubans and three U.S. citizens, and chaired by Colonel Enoch Crowder, an army attorney; it prepared an array of administrative reforms, including a thoroughly revised electoral code that expanded suffrage to nearly all adult males and established proportional representation to encourage the loyal participation of minority parties. Magoon then supervised a clean election, and in early 1909, he sailed for home.

Although U.S. forces returned in 1912 to quash a complex Afro-Cuban labor dispute in eastern Cuba, it was not until several years later that the United States launched its third effort to promote democracy in Cuba. It began during the Wilson administration, which still today is the record holder for Caribbean Basin interventions. President Wilson is said to have characterized his policy as an effort "to teach the South American Republics to elect good men," and before Cuba, he had already ordered the invasions of the Dominican Republic, Haiti, Honduras, Mexico, Nicaragua, and Panama. All of these nearby countries were fortunate, argued Wilson's assistant secretary of state, who noted in 1916 that "nature, in its rough method of uplift, gives sick nations strong neighbors." Three months later, the United States sent several hundred soldiers to maintain order around U.S.-owned sugar estates in central Cuba, where they stayed for five years.[28]

It was during this partial occupation that the Wilson administration pressured President Mario García Menocal to invite Enoch Crowder to take another crack at improving Cuba's democracy; it also sent a new uplift-oriented ambassador, Boaz Long, who believed that "extending our influences over these less favored people with the idea of educating them and regulating and improving their agricultural and commercial development, and making them good citizens of a democracy, involves a colossal task, but one not unworthy of an enlightened American policy." Acting Secretary of State Frank Polk warned Cubans that more troops would be sent unless "President Menocal assumes a receptive attitude in respect to the advice and just recommendations which the President has instructed General Crowder to convey to him."[29]

Two days later, Crowder sailed into Havana's harbor aboard a battleship, the USS *Minnesota*, which would serve as his home for a year. Because he was already familiar with the island, Crowder wasted no time before producing a stream of memoranda directing García Menocal and his successor, Alfredo Zayas, to enact essential reforms. Memorandum 8 demanded "the immediate removal from office of every official who . . . ," and then follow seven separate categories of behavior indicative of "Graft, Corruption and Immorality in the Public Administration." Memorandum 10 required "an immediate reform of the Lottery which is the source of widespread graft."[30] This type of uplifting is inherently slow, but by 1926, the State Department felt sufficiently satisfied with Cuba and the series of other Caribbean interventions to pause for a "mission accomplished" moment: "If the United States has received but little gratitude, this is only to be expected in a world where gratitude is rarely accorded to the teacher, the doctor, or the policeman, and we have been all three. But it may be that in time they will come to see the United States with different eyes, and to have for her something of the respect and affection with which a man regards the instructor of his youth and the child looks upon the parent who has molded his character." Two years later, when the Senate began debating how to handle equally obstreperous Nicaragua, Senator William Bruce asked his colleagues to "think of our intervention in Cuba. This is absolutely one of the finest things in human history."[31]

But it was ultimately unsuccessful, and soon backsliding prompted the fourth attempt to promote democracy in Cuba. It occurred in the 1940s, and by that time, Cubans had learned how to handle the insistent Yankees. Arriving in Havana a month after Pearl Harbor, a new U.S. ambassador was astounded by the government's apparent willingness to cooperate. "The American Ambassador here is in a completely unique position," reported Spruille Braden, "and if I breathe out of one nostril harder than the other it may provoke a political crisis." Unlike his previous posting in Bogotá, Braden found that "here we can ask for things and get them practically over the telephone." To show his appreciation for Cuba's cooperation with the war effort, Braden encouraged Franklin Roosevelt's administration to invite Cuban President Fulgencio Batista to pay a state visit to Washington, where a highlight of his 1942 speech to the House of Representatives emphasized the two nations' "common ideals of democracy."[32]

Batista had used force to seize office in 1933–1934 but had been fairly elected in 1940. Once Braden looked beneath the surface, however, he could see that "democracy, as it has been experienced in Cuba, is far from the real thing. On the contrary its workings have been filled with corruption, abuse and inefficiency." But, he continued, "We can assist in bringing about a tremendous betterment." Braden's uplifting focused on preventing the Cuban leader's reelection in 1944, because "Batista and his gang would like to free themselves from such few shackles as the Cuban creole democracy imposes, and which prevent their unbridled acquisition of even more complete power and greater wealth."[33] Always in perfect pitch with U.S. policy, Batista yielded to the constitutional prohibition of immediate reelection and supervised a contest everyone considered fair — his handpicked successor lost.

An elated Braden informed Washington that Cuba's new president, Ramón Grau San Martín, was determined "to exercise the powers of the government as a public trust for the good of the Cuban people." The honeymoon was brief: it took less than a month for Braden to see that Grau "simply does not have what it takes to succeed." The principal problem was the new Cuban leader's "egolatric stubbornness" — a fuzzy term that seems to have meant that Grau was disinclined to accept the ambassador's advice — "to ignore wise counsels and to stand on his opinion once formed, irrespective of how faulty it may be."[34]

The 1944 election nonetheless cast Braden as a democracy maker, and soon Washington sent him to handle Argentina's Juan Perón. His replacement in Havana, Henry Norweb, an experienced career diplomat, could see almost immediately that Cubans "possess the superficial charm of clever children, spoiled by nature and geography — but under the surface they combine the worst characteristics of the unfortunate admixture and interpenetration of Spanish and Negro cultures — laziness, cruelty, inconstancy, irresponsibility and inbred dishonesty." Cuba had been dealt a poor hand during the era of European colonization, and Norweb reported, "It is idle but not irrelevant to speculate what might have been the status of this bountiful island community had it been settled by colonists from the British Isles, Scandinavia, French Canada or even China." Instead, settlers from Spain and slaves from Africa had combined to produce an uplifter's nightmare: "It seems less than honest to report that there appears to be anything either in the Cuban character or in our present policy towards Cuba and the other Caribbean peoples that would augur the future establishment of an honorable and constructive member of the family of nations in this rich island."[35]

This pessimistic evaluation then combined with the onset of the Cold War to shelve Washington's fourth attempt to strengthen democracy in Cuba. With the notable exception of the Carter administration, for the next several decades, Washington partnered with any Latin American strongman, however undemocratic he might be, so long as he was anticommunist. As President Eisenhower's Treasury secretary insisted, the National Security Council should "stop talking so much about democracy, and make it clear that we are quite willing to support dictatorships of the right if their policies are pro-American."[36] Two years earlier, in 1952, Batista had seized power once again, and the U.S. embassy had sloughed off his military coup as par for the course: "Until Cubans learn that discipline and sacrifice are a necessary part of democracy, then upsets such as just occurred will be inevitable. . . . Whether the new group under Batista will be any better is a question. Governments in Cuba are made up of Cubans."[37]

After holding power for most of the 1950s, Batista fled from Cuba's revolutionary forces in the predawn hours on January 1, 1959. Although the United States criticized the Castro government's early decision to postpone competitive elections, for the next three decades, Washington's principal concern was Cuba's alliance with Moscow. Then, with the end of the Cold War, the United States launched its fifth concerted effort to install democracy in Cuba. It began with the 1992 Cuban Democracy Act, which focused on tightening the embargo by prohibiting third-country subsidiaries of U.S. firms from trading with

Cuba. From its beginnings in 1962, the embargo has sought to make life on the island so miserable that Cubans would force a change in their government, and the Cuban Democracy Act simply took one more step in that direction: subsidiary licenses had risen to an all-time high of $728 million in 1992 but promptly dropped to $1.6 million in 1993 and zero in 1994.

But the Cuban government did not fall, and so the United States gave another twist to tighten the noose in 1996 with the Cuban Liberty and Democratic Solidarity Act (Helms-Burton). In addition to putting substantial roadblocks in the way of non-U.S. foreign investment in Cuba, Helms-Burton also codified the embargo, most of which had until 1996 been created by presidential directive, not legislation. Helms-Burton prohibited ending the embargo until the president certified that Cuba has a democratic government that is defined, inter alia, as one that is "moving toward a market-oriented economic system." Helms-Burton also takes a step unprecedented in the annals of U.S. legislation: it identifies specific individuals whom Cubans are not allowed to select as their leaders. "It is difficult to see how Castro can sensibly continue to hope that his dictatorship can survive the rough provisions of this legislation," commented Senator Jesse Helms. "Castro's days are indeed numbered."[38]

When that prediction proved erroneous, in mid-2003, President George W. Bush created the Commission for Assistance to a Free Cuba, which pledged "to help the Cuban people put Castro and Castroism behind them forever." The commission's 423-page report first defines what Washington means by "a Free Cuba" and then explains in careful detail how Cubans can — and must — reach that goal, beginning with regime change. And what if Cubans continue to balk at accepting Washington's plan for their uplifting? Then the United States has a plan for that, too: "Hastening Cuba's Transition" is the title of chapter 1 of the report, forty-eight pages listing sixty-two steps the United States intends to take to trigger regime change, with President Bush promising at the report's unveiling that "we're not waiting for the day of Cuban freedom; we are working for the day."

Once Cubans concede and agree to an acceptable transition from their current government, it will be on to the uplifting: chapter 2 "Meeting Basic Human Needs"; chapter 3, "Establishing Democratic Institutions"; chapter 4, "Establishing the Core Institutions of a Free Economy"; chapter 5, "Modernizing Infrastructure"; and chapter 6, "Addressing Environmental Degradation." And because some of the island's residents might be reluctant to watch quietly while the United States sets everything straight, the 2006 updating of the plan contains a still-classified security appendix. The gist of this appendix is probably captured by an unclassified sentence in the 2004 report recommending that some part of the U.S. government — the Pentagon? — should be standing by if requested "to keep all schools open during an emergency phase of the transition in order to keep children and teenagers off the streets."[39]

And so what began as an attempt to improve Cuba during the U.S. occupation in 1898 continues to this day. The embargo has to be kept as leverage, argues Barack Obama, because "the United States must be a relentless advocate for democracy." So far, this fifth U.S. attempt to promote democracy in Cuba has not been successful. Yet from the perspective of U.S. foreign policy, the most interesting aspect of this current effort is not its success or its failure but how oblivious Washington seems to be to the way that Cubans have received its efforts. In their wildest reveries, no one in Washington appears to have thought about how everyone in that city — absolutely everyone — would react if some foreign country were to create the Commission to Improve the United States, especially if this imagined commission were to begin its report by listing sixty-two steps it intended to take to overthrow the current U.S. government. Citizens of the United States would be outraged, but Washington assumes no such outrage on the part of Cuban nationalists because it is blinded by an ideology that assumes the need for U.S. assistance; without it, Cubans will remain underdeveloped. A century ago, Leonard Wood put his pro-consular finger on today's problem: "No one wants more than I a good and stable government here, but we must see that the right class is in office."[40] Some might find this comparison unfair, but the Obama administration, like all three of its post–Cold War predecessors, has selected its class — it wants the democratic class in office and has promised to continue the embargo until Cubans concede. In 1978, Fidel Castro put his finger on what has always been the central problem for Cuban nationalists, telling two U.S. envoys, "It is difficult to talk to you, a powerful, rich and highly developed country with a mentality of arrogance."[41]

Eventually the United States might find the right combination of carrots and nut pinching to convince the next generation of Cubans to accept a little uplifting. Then a modest army of contractors and grantees from U.S. Agency for International Development and the National Endowment for Democracy will begin helping Cubans construct a new and improved country. Perhaps it will work this time, but history warns us not to be optimistic. Indeed, if history tells us anything, it is that Cubans do not want to be uplifted by the United States of America. For better or for worse, as Leonard Wood told Theodore Roosevelt more than a century ago, "it is next to impossible to make them believe that we have only their own interests at heart."[42]

NOTES

1. A full elaboration of this ideology is in Lars Schoultz, *Beneath the United States: A History of U.S. Policy toward Latin America* (Cambridge, MA: Harvard University Press, 1998).

2. Minutes of Discussion of the 396th Meeting of the National Security Council, 12 February 1959, National Security Council Series, Whitman File, box 11, Eisenhower Papers, Dwight David Eisenhower Library, Abilene, Kansas; Henry Savage to James Buchanan, 5 February 1848, "Des-

patches from U.S. Ministers to Central America, 1824–1906," Record Group (RG) 59, National Archives (NA), Washington, D.C.

3. Khrushchev's comment to Western diplomats in Moscow, on 18 November 1956, was reported in the *London Times*, 19 November 1956, 8.

4. Meg Scott Phipps, "Lift Ban on Trade with Cuba," *Charlotte Observer*, 24 October 2002, 19A; U.S. Department of Agriculture, Foreign Agricultural Service, Office of Global Analysis, *Cuba's Food and Agriculture Situation Report* (Washington, D.C.: Department of Agriculture, March 2008), 1. Agricultural exports from the United States to Cuba dropped from $695.2 million in 2008, the peak year in the first decade of the twenty-first century, to $527.7 million in 2009.

5. Personal interview with John Ferch, retired Foreign Service Officer, Fairfax, Virginia, 17 February 2005.

6. Of the nation's 1,254,439 Cuban Americans, the 2000 U.S. census indicated that two-thirds (833,120) lived in Florida, and of those, a rough estimate was that 425,000 were registered to vote, making them account for 4 percent of the state's 10.8 million registered voters. On the creation of CANF, see Patrick J. Haney and Walt Vanderbush, "The Role of Ethnic Interest Groups in U.S. Foreign Policy: The Case of the Cuban American National Foundation," *International Studies Quarterly*, 43 (1999): 341–46; Patrick J. Haney and Walt Vanderbush, *The Cuban Embargo: The Domestic Politics of an American Foreign Policy* (Pittsburgh: University of Pittsburgh Press, 2005).

7. On CANF's role as champion of this key component of Helms-Burton, see U.S. Congress, House Committee on International Relations, Subcommittee on the Western Hemisphere, *Hearings on Cuba and U.S. Policy*, 104th Cong., 1st Sess. (23 February 1995), especially 88–90.

8. CEO Dwayne Andreas interview in 1996 with Patrick J. Kiger, in Patrick J. Kiger, *Squeeze Play: The United States, Cuba, and the Helms-Burton Act* (Washington, D.C.: Center for Public Integrity, 1997), 40. I am indebted to Kiger for sharing his interview notes with me.

9. Bill Clinton, *My Life* (New York: Knopf, 2004), 906.

10. George H. W. Bush Press Conference, 19 December 1991, *Public Papers 1991* (Washington, D.C.: White House, 1992), 1647.

11. Nixon speech to the Veterans of Foreign Wars, Detroit, 24 August 1960, reprinted in Senate, *Freedom of Communications: Final Report of the Committee on Commerce, United States Senate*, part 2, *The Speeches, Remarks, Press Conferences, and Study Papers of Vice President Richard M. Nixon, August 1 through November 7, 1960*, 87th Cong., 1st Sess., Report 994 (1961), 30 and 219; Nancy Reagan quoting Alexander Haig in Nancy Reagan (with William Novak), *My Turn: The Memoirs of Nancy Reagan* (New York: Random House, 1989), 242.

12. John Ferch, "Fencing with Fidel and Other Tales of Life in the Foreign Service: A Selective Memoir" (unpublished typescript), 161–65; Arthur J. Schlesinger Jr., *Journals, 1952–2000* (New York: Penguin, 2007), 596.

13. Central Intelligence Agency, "Increasing Opposition to Castro/Shortage of Consumer Goods/Lack of Currency," Report No. 00-A3177796, n.d. [late January 1961], Thomas Paterson Collection, *The United States and Castro's Cuba, 1950s–1970s* (Wilmington, DE: Scholarly Resources, 1998), microfilm, reel 13, frame 211.

14. Telephone conversation, 2 December 1963, "December 1963 [1 of 3] Chrono File" folder, box 1, JFK Series, Johnson Papers, Lyndon Baines Johnson Library, Austin, Texas.

15. Association for Diplomatic Studies and Training, *The U.S. Foreign Affairs Oral History Project*, CD-ROM (Arlington, VA, 2000), "John Crimmins Oral History," 10 May 1989.

16. Bundy memorandum of conversation with the president, 19 February 1964, in U.S. Department of State, *Foreign Relations of the United States 1964–68* (hereafter *FRUS*) (Washington, D.C.: Government Printing Office, 1999), 31:11.

17. Speech by Barack Obama, Miami, 23 May 2008, http://www.barackobama.com/2008/05/23/remarks_of _senator_barack_obam_68.php.

18　：　Lars Schoultz

18. *Congressional Globe*, 9 April 1869, appendix, 18–30.

19. Adam Badeau, Confidential Memorandum, 23 October 1883, Consular Despatches from Havana, RG 59, NA.

20. Wood to McKinley, 12 April 1900, Wood Papers, Manuscript Division, Library of Congress (hereafter LC).

21. Wood to Roosevelt, 8 February 1901, and Root to Wood, 20 June 1900, both in Wood Papers; Root to Paul Dana, 16 January 1900, Root Papers, all LC.

22. Wood to Platt, 6 December 1900; Wood to Root, 8 February 1901; Wood to Root, 30 May 1901 — all in Wood Papers, LC; Wood to Root, 19 January 1901, Root Papers, LC; Wood to Root, 16 June 1901, General Classified Files, 1898–1945, RG 350, NA.

23. Orville H. Platt, "The Pacification of Cuba," *Independent*, 27 June 1901, 1467.

24. The Platt Amendment is 31 Stat. 897, 2 March 1901.

25. Roosevelt to Henry L. White, 13 September 1906, Roosevelt Papers, LC; Speech to the Harvard Union, 23 February 1907, in Theodore Roosevelt, *Presidential Addresses and State Papers* (New York: Review of Reviews, 1910), 6:1178–79; William H. Taft, "Some Recent Instances of National Altruism," *National Geographic*, 18 (July 1907), 438; Speech of Provisional Governor William Howard Taft, opening-day exercises of the National University of Habana, 1 October 1906, in U.S. War Department, *Annual Reports of the War Department for the Fiscal Year Ended June 30, 1906* (Washington, D.C.: Government Printing Office, 1906), 541–42.

26. "Report of William H. Taft," 11 December 1906, in U.S. War Department, *Annual Reports*, 456; Taft to Helen Taft, 20 September 1906, Taft Papers, LC; Roosevelt to Taft, 22 January 1907, in *Letters of Theodore Roosevelt*, ed. Elting E. Morison (Cambridge, MA: Harvard University Press, 1954), 5:560.

27. Magoon to Roosevelt, 16 April 1908, Roosevelt Papers, LC.

28. President Wilson's "good men" comment, which may be apocryphal, comes to us fourth-hand from Burton Hendrick, the biographer of Wilson's ambassador to Britain, Walter Hines Page. Page told Hendrick that a British envoy, William Tyrrell, had heard Wilson's comment (i.e., Wilson to Tyrrell to Page to Hendrick). See Burton J. Hendrick, ed., *The Life and Letters of Walter Hines Page* (Garden City, NY: Doubleday, Page, 1923), 1:204. A follow-up letter expressing the same idea is Wilson to Tyrrell, 22 November 1913, Wilson Papers, LC. The "sick nations" comment is by Assistant Secretary of State Huntington Wilson; see Huntington Wilson, "The Relation of Government to Foreign Investment," *Annals of the American Academy of Political and Social Science* 68 (November 1916): 301.

29. Boaz Long to Robert Lansing, 15 February 1918, RG 59, 711.13/55, NA; Norman Davis to Crowder, 31 December 1920, RG 59, 837.00/1952b, NA; Norman Davis to Boaz Long, 4 January 1921, RG 59, 837.00/1949, NA. For a memorandum acknowledging Acting Secretary of State Polk's verbal instructions of 10 January 1919, see Ambassador William Gonzales to Polk, 4 February 1919, William Gonzales Papers, University of South Carolina.

30. Division of Latin-American Affairs, "Synopsis of General Crowder's 13 Memoranda," 14 November 1923, RG 59, 123 C 8812/51, NA.

31. Stokely W. Morgan, "American Policy and Problems in Central America," Lecture to the Foreign Service School, Department of State, 29 January 1926, RG 59, entry 623, inventory 15, NA; Senator Bruce, *Congressional Record*, 20 January 1928, 1787.

32. Braden to Gerald Keith, 24 August 1942, "Correspondence Diplomatic 1942 I-L" folder, box 8, Spruille Braden Papers, Columbia University; Batista, *Congressional Record*, 8 December 1942, 9429.

33. Braden to Secretary of State, "Comments Concerning the Cuban Political Situation," May 29, 1943, RG 59, 837.00/9298, NA.

34. Braden to Secretary of State, "Recent Political Developments," 19 December 1944, RG 59, 837.00/12-1044, NA; Braden, "Agenda for Washington," 20 January 1945, RG 59, 837.00/

1-2045, NA; Braden to James H. Wright, Department of State, 20 July 1942, "Correspondence Diplomatic 1942 Wr-Z" folder, box 9, Spruille Braden Papers. See also Braden to Secretary of State, "Comments Concerning the Cuban Political Situation," 29 May 1943, RG 59, 837.00/9298, NA; Braden to Secretary of State, "Fundamental Conditions in Cuba and Their Effect on Our Relations," 22 November 1943, attached to "Cuban Governmental Corruption and United States Aid," 30 November 1943, RG 59, 837.00/9398, NA.

35. Norweb to Secretary of State, "Year-End Political Summary," 14 January 1946, RG 59, 837.00/1-1446, NA.

36. National Security Council Meeting, 21 December 1954, *FRUS*, 2:838.

37. Embassy to Department of State, 11 March 1952, RG 59, 737.00/3-1152, NA.

38. *Congressional Record*, 5 March 1996, 3598.

39. U.S. Commission for Assistance to a Free Cuba, *Report to the President* (Washington, D.C.: U.S. Department of State, 2004), xxi.

40. Wood to Senator Foraker, 11 January 1901, box 30, Wood Papers, LC.

41. Memorandum of Conversation, Peter Tarnoff and Robert Pastor, "U.S./Cuban Relations, December 3–4, 1978, Havana," in "Cuba: President Carter's Trip, May 12–17, 2002," vertical file, Jimmy Carter Library, Atlanta, Georgia.

42. Wood to Roosevelt, 12 April 1901, Roosevelt Papers, LC.

MAYRA ESPINA PRIETO

La política social cubana para
el manejo de la desigualdad

RESUMEN

El texto describe los diferentes momentos y rasgos de la política social que ha caracterizado la reforma económica cubana de los noventa y su etapa actual, valora el estado de la desigualdad y las perspectivas para el fortalecimiento de las estrategias de promoción de equidad en el país. Incluye una síntesis de propuestas elaboradas desde las ciencias sociales para elevar la capacidad de la gestión estatal de reducción de las desventajas sociales, la pobreza y potenciar la equidad, entre las que destaca un nuevo enfoque de política social que combina focalización y universalidad (políticas universales espacialmente focalizadas o direccionadas), que permitiría mayores avances en la superación de brechas de equidad que aún permanecen y han tendido a fortalecerse con la crisis y la reforma (de género, raza, clase y territorio, fundamentalmente).

ABSTRACT

This article focuses on the different moments and characteristics of Cuban social policy since the economic reforms of the 1990s until today to try to evaluate the inequalities and the perspectives of trying to enforce strategies that promote equity. Special attention is paid to the so-called universal focused or directed policies" with an aim to close the gaps between classes, gender, and race.

La lógica de la política social en la Revolución Cubana

Cuando analizamos la manera en que se ha diseñado y puesto en práctica la política social en la experiencia de la Revolución Cubana esta puede calificarse como una política integradora, que opera con una lógica de unicidad, al combinar en una estrategia única prevención, compensación y redistribución.

Los rasgos generales de esta política han sido: centralidad de la equidad, como instrumento de avance hacia la igualdad; perspectiva clasista de la inequidad que implica la alteración de la matriz de propiedad sobre los medios de producción y la eliminación de las posiciones estructurales que generan posibilidades de apropiación excluyente del bienestar por unos grupos sociales sobre otros; carácter universal, de cobertura total, centralizado, unitario y planificado de la política social; la absolutización del estado como coordinador y gestor de la política social; la consideración como derecho de ciudadanía de las

20

necesidades básicas (trabajo, servicios de salud, amparo y educación gratuitos); prioridades macroeconómicas que privilegian el gasto de inversión social, baja (casi nula) presencia del mercado como mecanismo de distribución; servicios sociales unitarios y universales.

En esta perspectiva la equidad es definida como la integración de tres principios básicos: el de igualdad absoluta (expresa la exigencia ético-jurídica de completar un espacio de derechos universales básicos inalienables y oportunidades reales para que todos los ciudadanos puedan desarrollar sus capacidades sin exclusión alguna); el de solidaridad (incluye la atención preferencial diferenciada a las desventajas y necesidades especiales de individuos y grupos sociales particulares, por motivo de discapacidad, ancianidad o desventajas de naturaleza socioeconómico históricas); el de igualdad relativa o proporcional (acepta la presencia de desigualdades legítimas, asociadas al monto, la calidad y la utilidad de aportes laborales o servicios de otro tipo individuales y colectivos).[1]

Se parte de que la equidad y la justicia social no son función de la distribución de ingresos monetarios a escala individual y familiar, que no es este el factor decisivo para asegurarlas y que ellas dependen directamente de la acción redistributiva estatal a través de los gastos sociales, con énfasis en las transferencias por servicios que promocionan desarrollo y amparo a través de espacios de igualdad.

Espacio de igualdad define un mecanismo de distribución a través de los fondos sociales de consumo, que se caracteriza por la universalidad, masividad, gratuidad o facilidad para el acceso, condición de derecho legalmente refrendado y carácter público centralizado de su diseño y de la garantía para acceder a él, participación social, preponderancia de las soluciones colectivas sobre las individuales, homogeneidad, calidad creciente, opción de integración social en igualdad de condiciones para todos los sectores sociales, independientemente de sus ingresos y aspiración a la igualdad de resultados.

En el caso cubano el estado, a través de una extensa red pública de cobertura total, es el protagonista hegemónico y decisivo, de estos espacios distributivos, no existen otras alternativas (privadas o extraestatales en general) para acceder al bien que se distribuye en el espacio de que se trate, o estas son de muy bajo perfil y no pueden competir con la opción estatal.[2]

Tomando el gasto social como expresión concentrada de las estrategias de intervención sobre el cambio social, y analizándolo en una perspectiva dinámica, observamos que la política social cubana, desde el inicio de la experiencia socialista en la década de los sesenta, se caracteriza por una alta prioridad macroeconómica de la esfera social, por gastos crecientes y por la prioridad de las áreas de educación y salud y asistencia social como los ámbitos centrales de esta política (ver Tablas 1 y 2).

Aunque se aprecian variaciones en los años ochenta con relación al peso

22 : Mayra Espina Prieto

TABLA 1. Cuba: Gasto social, período 1975–1986
(años seleccionados, millones de pesos, precios corrientes)

Año	Total	Porcentaje de variación (con relación al año anterior)
1975	817,5	—
1978	1.398,5	30.2
1981	2.010,2	22.3
1986	2.762,0	3.0

Fuente: Cálculos propios a partir de Comité Estatal de Estadísticas 1987.

TABLA 2. Cuba: Estructura del gasto social en áreas seleccionadas, período 1975–1986

Año	Total	Educación	Servicios personales y comunales	Cultura y arte	Salud, asistencia social, y deporte	Ciencia y técnica
1975	100	46,56	18,18	7,94	24,90	2,42
1976	100	47,12	18,87	7,34	24,22	2,45
1977	100	46,83	18,04	8,12	24,39	2,62
1978	100	46,32	18,77	7,41	24,80	2,69
1979	100	47,13	17,14	7,89	25,02	2,82
1980	100	47,09	20,37	8,14	22,45	1,93
1981	100	43,73	23,95	7,46	21,98	2,88
1982	100	42,65	24,47	8,36	21,48	2,77
1983	100	40,98	26,49	9,37	20,08	3,08
1984	100	39,43	28,02	9,03	20,16	3,36
1985	100	38,64	28,19	8,73	20,94	3,50
1986	100	37,76	26,89	8,07	23,19	4,09

Fuente: Cálculos propios a partir de los datos del Oficina Nacional de Estadísticas.

porcentual de los servicios educacionales y de salud, que tiende a disminuir a favor, fundamentalmente de los servicios personales y comunales, no se trata de un cambio de prioridades, pues educación y salud conservan sus lugares establecidos en el conjunto de gastos, sino de un reacomodo interno del destino de las erogaciones para, una vez asegurada las cobertura en esos dos ámbitos, favorecer elementos del bienestar familiar.

La política social de la reforma

La crisis de los años noventa tuvo entre sus numerosos efectos, un impacto negativo sobre la oferta de servicios y prestaciones sociales estatales, especialmente en una disminución de la calidad de la oferta de todos los servicios, una disminución de la cantidad y calidad de la oferta en al ámbito de los productos

TABLA 3. Cuba: Gastos sociales, período 1989–2000 (años seleccionados)

Año	Gastos en servicios sociales (millones de pesos)	Porcentaje de variación (con relaciónal año anterior)
1989	3.750,1	—
1991	3.743,0	−1.9
1992	3.811,2	1.8
1993	4.008,0	5.1
1994	4.021,6	0.3
1995	4.179,7	3.9
1996	4.439,0	6.2
1999	6.279,1	32.8
2000	6.363,9	1.3

Fuente: Togores (2003b).

de la alimentación básica subvencionada y en la caída de la capacidad real de consumo y aseguramiento de las necesidades básicas de los salarios y las prestaciones monetarias de la seguridad y la asistencia social.[3]

La reforma diseñada para el manejo de esta crisis conserva la concepción estratégica general anteriormente descrita de la política social, pero introdujo algunas modificaciones que se expresan en dos momentos diferenciados.

Un primer momento, de carácter reactivo ante la crisis, se dirige a la creación de condiciones para el restablecimiento económico y el amortiguamiento de los costos sociales y abarca acciones como la disminución de la oferta de empleo estatal y la ampliación del trabajo por cuenta propia y otras opciones privadas, la implementación de mecanismos que eleven la articulación entre la retribución por el trabajo y los resultados productivos individuales y colectivos; implementación de sistemas de remuneración en divisas en actividades y ocupaciones seleccionadas; aumentos salariales para actividades seleccionadas, que generan divisas o por su rol social prioritario (personal de la salud, la educación, la ciencia y el orden interior); garantía de protección a trabajadores de actividades económicas cerradas o reestructuradas; legalización de las remesas familiares y despenalización de la tenencia de divisas; creación de una red pública comunitaria de alimentación subvencionada para personas de bajos ingresos; jerarquización, dentro del conjunto de servicios públicos, de la educación y la salud, como forma de optimizar el uso de los recursos.

Aún en la década de los noventa, en condiciones de crisis y de reforma económica, la proporción del gasto público social con relación al producto interno bruto (PIB) se mantuvo por encima del 20 por ciento, situación sólo similar a la de Uruguay y Brasil en América Latina y recupera su dinámica ascendente en muy poco tiempo (ver Tablas 3 y 4).[4] El incremento de los gastos sociales en el año 1993, aún en un momento muy grave de la crisis, se explica

TABLA 4. Cuba: Características del gasto público social

Período	Porcentaje del PIB	Porcentaje del gasto público total
1990–1991	23,1	28,4
1994–1995	21,9	31,9
1998–1999	22,8	41,6
1989–2000	23,3	34,3

Fuente: Togores (2003a).

fundamentalmente por los gastos adicionales en prestaciones para pago a trabajadores temporalmente cesados de su trabajo, que dejaron de devengar sus salarios.

Un segundo momento, iniciado hacia finales de los años noventa, se orienta a recuperar la acción proactiva estatal en la inversión social de cara al desarrollo, el rol de la equidad y de los espacios de igualdad y se sustenta en la implementación de nuevos programas sociales dirigidos a la modernización y el rescate de los servicios públicos, especialmente en salud, asistencia social y educación y una política de subsidios a la oferta (ver Tabla 5), la elevación del protagonismo de lo local comunitario como escenario de la política social (implementación del Programa de Trabajo Comunitario Integrado, creación de un extenso movimiento de trabajadores sociales a escala comunitaria), programas de masificación de la cultura y atención focalizada a necesidades especiales y sectores vulnerables y pobres, aumentos de las pensiones y de los salarios en general y en grupos ocupacionales seleccionados, ampliación de la capacidad de construcción de viviendas por mecanismo estatales y esfuerzo familiar. Ese nuevo momento de la política social explica el notable aumento de los gastos sociales a partir de 1999 que se muestra en la Tabla 3.

Los cambios actuales se ubican dentro de esa lógica general de política social proactiva de desarrollo, con la novedad de un énfasis en la retribución y el acceso al bienestar con mayor diferenciación de acuerdo al aporte laboral de cada grupo.

Encontramos también que esta estrategia ha logrado una alta estabilidad en el tiempo de sus montos generales y de su estructura de prioridades, con un fuerte peso en la inversión social (salud, educación) y en los subsidios, acentuando el rol del consumo social en la distribución, por encima del de los ingresos individuales y familiares.

Como promedio, los gastos de inversión social hacia finales de la década del noventa e inicios de la actual década, en su conjunto, sobrepasan el 47 por ciento del total de gastos sociales, marcando con ello la tónica de la política social cubana orientada al desarrollo, su énfasis preventivo y la relevancia de los espacios de igualdad y del consumo social frente al mercan elemento tan

TABLA 5. Cuba. **Estructura de los gastos sociales por áreas, período 1998–2004**

Gastos	1998	1999	2000	2001	2002	2003	2004
Total	100.00	100.00	100.00	100.00	100.00	100.00	100.00
Educación	21.50	22.17	22.59	25.92	27.20	28.90	30.01
Cultura y arte	2.40	2.31	2.52	3.40	3.91	4.17	4.75
Salud pública	19.15	18.82	18.16	19.66	19.01	17.78	17.41
Ciencia y técnica	1.48	1.55	1.66	1.79	1.66	2.00	1.76
Deportes	1.79	1.70	1.73	1.79	1.94	1.95	2.02
Seguridad social	24.28	21.64	19.26	20.34	19.62	18.01	18.10
Asistencia social	2.07	1.94	1.92	2.36	3.93	4.22	4.97
Vivienda y servicios comunales	8.05	8.29	8.23	9.05	8.63	8.42	8.88
Subsidio a diferencias de precio	19.28	21.58	23.93	15.70	14.09	14.55	12.10

Fuente: Cálculos propios a partir de Oficina Nacional de Estadística, 2005.

relevante del acceso al bienestar en el plano familiar, como la vivienda, ha quedado sistemáticamente en un plano muy rezagado con respecto a otras esferas atendidas por la intervención pública (ver Tabla 5).

El ascenso en los gastos en educación se debe a dos factores: la expansión de los programas educativos y al aumento de los salarios que devengan los maestros y profesores de todos los niveles de enseñanza, medida tomada con la intención de retenerlos en este sector, toda vez que uno de los problemas que desde los noventa a afectado la educación ha sido la fluctuación de sus especialistas hacia otras actividades de mayores incentivos económicos, como el turismo, por ejemplo. Por su parte, los gastos en seguridad social tienden a crecer por una política de aumento de las jubilaciones mínimas.

Valorando la política social cubana en su conjunto y trayectoria en términos de manejo de las dimensiones sociales del desarrollo y de la promoción de equidad en una sociedad periférica, se aprecia que la universalización de los derechos sociales de ciudadanía a través de una amplia intervención estatal y de su regulación en todas las esferas, ha resultado una fórmula adecuada para proveer rápidamente integración social a las más amplias mayorías, mejorando su acceso al bienestar, aun en condiciones de poco crecimiento económico. Prueba de ello es el mejoramiento sostenido de los indicadores sociales mas relevantes (esperanza de vida, mortalidad infantil, escolarización, ingresos), lo que se sintetiza en los favorables resultados alcanzados por Cuba en la medición del Índice de Desarrollo (ver Tabla 6).

TABLA 6. Lugar de Cuba en las mediciones del Índices de Desarrollo Humano
con relación al total de países en que se ha medido

Informe	Lugar de Cuba
1990	39/130
1991	62/160
1992	61/160
1993	75/173
1994	89/173
1995	72/174
1996	79/174
1997	86/175
1998	85/174
1999	58/174
2007–2008	51/177

Fuente: Martínez et al. (2000) y PNUD (2008).

Algunos rasgos de las desigualdades en la Cuba actual

Los claros avances en términos de equidad e igualdad social que han caracterizado la transición socialista cubana y que continúan siendo una guía estratégica de su política social, aun en la reforma, están colocados ahora ante un escenario de ensanchamiento de las diferencias socioeconómicas. Diversos estudios sobre los impactos de la crisis y la reforma han identificado tendencias que indican la apertura de un proceso de reestratificación social,[5] que incluye rasgos como:

*Diferenciación de ingresos y consumo y reemergencia de
situaciones de pobreza y vulnerabilidad*

Véase que el coeficiente Gini, calculado para finales de los noventa, se elevó a 0,38, en contraste con el 0,24 encontrado en los ochenta, y aunque aún es bajo con relación a la situación de la gran mayoría de los países de América Latina, este incremento da cuenta de un proceso de concentración de ingresos que supone una interrupción de la lógica desconcentradora anterior.[6]

Por otra parte, algunas áreas de necesidades básicas (al menos el 50 por ciento de los requerimientos alimentarios, el vestuario, productos de aseo, materiales para reparación y equipamiento de la vivienda, según mis propias observaciones) sólo encuentran una parte importante de sus satisfactores en el mercado de precios libres, en el mercado en peso cubano convertible (CUC) o en el negro, lo que, junto a la caída de la capacidad adquisitiva del salario real de los trabajadores y de los ingresos en general, asociada a la crisis y al incremento de los precios de productos de primera necesidad y no recuperada

TABLA 7. Cuba: Canasta básica calculada a partir de información referente al año 2006

	Canasta básica en pesos cubanos			
Partida	*1 asal. + 1 menor + 1 pensionado*	*2 asal. + 1 mayor sin pensión*	*2 asal. + 1 menor*	*2 asal + 1 pensionado*
Alimentos (3,356 kcal/día)	693,17	748,13	685,43	748,13
Productos no alimenticios	175,30	174,47	175,30	174,47
Ropa y calzado	92,50	91,67	92,50	91,67
Higiene y aseo	82,80	82,80	82,80	82,80
Servicios básicos	65,34	65,34	65,34	65,34
Otros servicios	3,70	3,70	3,70	3,70
Total de gasto mensual	937,51	991,64	929,78	991,64
Ingreso mensual	583,74	796,00	796,00	981,74
Déficit de ingresos para acceder a la canasta	398.77	195.64	133.78	9.9

Fuente: García y Anaya (2006).

aún, y al incremento de los precios al consumidor, ha reconstituido a los ingresos y al mercado como elementos de alta fuerza diferenciadora.

Aunque hacia el año 2005 se había producido un considerable incremento de los ingresos, por la vía de una política de aumento salarial y de pensiones, que hizo que el salario medio mensual de los trabajadores ascendiera a 398 pesos (de 203 en 1996, o de 282 en el 2004) y el salario mínimo se elevó a 225 pesos en ese año y las pensiones y asistencia social mínima llegaron a 164 y 122 pesos, respectivamente, ello no ha significado una recuperación significativa del salario real ni del poder adquisitivo de las pensiones, puesto que la tendencia alcista de los preciso de artículos de primera necesidad se ha mantenido.[7]

Un estudio reciente de García y Anaya que construyó una canasta básica en la que se incluyen alimentos y otros bienes y servicios indispensables para el desarrollo de los seres humanos indica que a pesar de que en el ingreso medio de la población se ha incrementado notablemente por la acumulación de los resultados de un conjunto de medidas que favorecieron los aumentos de salarios, pensiones por jubilación y de la asistencia social, éste continúa siendo deficitario para amplios grupos poblacionales (Tabla 7).[8]

El análisis anterior se refuerza con el hecho de que atendiendo a pobreza de ingresos y necesidades básicas insatisfechas, se aprecia un cambio en la magnitud de la población urbana bajo esta situación que va desde 6,3 por ciento, en 1988, a 20 por ciento, hacia el año 2000.[9]

Obviamente, estas magnitudes indican la estructuración de mecanismos distributivos excluyentes, cuyo efecto negativo fundamental es la colocación de la desigualdad social a nivel de la posibilidad de satisfacción de necesidades básicas.

Territorialización de las desigualdades

Puede decirse que con la crisis y la reforma, estamos asistiendo en Cuba a un proceso de selectividad territorial, que se monta sobre un escenario diferenciado anterior, reforzándolo y añadiéndole nuevos matices.

Una visión integrada de estos procesos de conexión territorio-desigualdad nos la ofrece un estudio sobre las reconfiguraciones espaciales que identifica como los factores más poderosos a los que se asocia la heterogenización territorial desigualitaria los siguientes: la expansión de formas de propiedad no tradicionales (mixta, externa); la amplitud de la presencia territorial de los mecanismos de mercado en la distribución; la jerarquización de sectores y actividades económicas como turismo, minero-metalurgia y energético, agroindustria no cañera; la prioridad de la producción agropecuaria; y el fortalecimiento de la propiedad cooperativa o individual en la agricultura no cañera y la gestión individual y familiar que fomentan intenso mercado formal e informal. Aún cuando cada uno de estos factores no expresen por sí solos necesariamente niveles superiores de desarrollo, sí constituyen elementos que potencian o limitan la inserción de los grupos sociales en los procesos de producción-consumo, entrando el espacio geográfico como oportunidad en las determinaciones de nuevas desigualdades y como inequitativo regulador de oportunidades.[10]

Para ilustrar las diferencias espacializadas en Cuba, también resulta muy útil un Índice de Desarrollo Humano Territorial (IDHT), calculado considerando los desempeños socioeconómicos provinciales en indicadores seleccionados, sobre la base de documentación de quince años, entre 1985 y 2001, a partir del cual se agruparon todas las provincias del país en tres niveles del IDHT:[11]

- Nivel alto (de 0,600 y más): Ciudad de La Habana y Cienfuegos
- Nivel medio (entre 0,462 y 0,599): La Habana, Matanzas, Villa Clara, Sancti Spíritus, Ciego de Ávila e Isla de la Juventud
- Nivel bajo (inferior a 0,462): Pinar del Río, Camagüey, Las Tunas, Holguín, Granma, Santiago de Cuba y Guantánamo

De aquí se desprenden cuatro inferencias sobre la relación territorio-desigualdad: la baja presencia de territorios que logran los niveles más altos de IDHT, la mayor concentración de provincias en el nivel más bajo, el peso de factores de naturaleza económica aun cuando se instrumenten políticas sociales con fuerte acción modificadora, la preferencia del patrón de configuración de desventajas por territorios históricamente ubicados en situaciones desventajosas (la dificultad para vencer situaciones heredadas y condiciones de partida desiguales).

Fortalecimiento de brechas de equidad de clase, género y raza

Considerando los resultados de diversos estudios de corte cuantitativo y cualitativo, es posible llegar a una caracterización de rasgos personales y familiares asociados a la pobreza y a las desventajas sociales en general, como un patrón de preferencia para los mecanismos de exclusión:[12]

- Familias que tienen un tamaño superior al promedio nacional;
- Presencia de ancianos y niños en el núcleo familiar
- Familias monoparentales con mujeres jefas de hogar que no trabajan establemente
- Altos niveles de fecundidad y de maternidad adolescente sin apoyo paterno
- Ancianos viviendo solos y sin apoyo de otros parientes
- Trabajadores del sector estatal tradicional en ocupaciones de baja remuneración y de baja calificación
- Acceso nulo o muy bajo a ingresos en divisas
- Sobrerrepresentación de negros y mestizos
- Personas que no trabajan por discapacidad o ausencia de condiciones diversas para hacerlo
- Nivel escolar relativamente inferior a la media nacional
- Precariedad de la vivienda y de su equipamiento
- Repertorio de estrategias de vida reducido, de bajo nivel de solución
- Importante peso de migrantes desde territorios de menor desarrollo socioeconómico comparativo, que se asientan en barrios improvisados sin la infraestructura y la cobertura de servicios públicos necesarios
- Mayor frecuencia de abandono o interrupción de estudios
- Utilización de los niños para apoyar las estrategias de los adultos (cuidado de hermanos más pequeños, venta en el barrio de artículos elaborados o conseguidos por los adultos, realización de tareas domésticas y otros encargos)
- Ubicación espacial preponderante en barrios marginales o de situaciones precarias del entorno
- Presencia cualitativamente significativa del origen social obrero y de empleados, de baja calificación
- Reproducción generacional de las desventajas
- Alta presencia en territorios de la región oriental del país
- Situación de desventaja para las zonas rurales, en cuanto a características educacionales y de calificación de la población, carga de dependencia de los hogares y servicios de agua, transporte y electricidad

En los datos del censo de 2002, puede comprobarse la presencia de diversos ámbitos de diferencias asociadas al color de la piel, como por ejemplo, y el patrón de preferencia racial hacia negros y mestizos en las desventajas socioeconómicas:[13]

- La población desocupada alcanza una proporción de 2,9 por ciento para la población blanca, 3 por ciento en la población negra y 3,3 por ciento la mestiza, mientras que el 64 por ciento del total de la población ocupada es blanca y 36 por ciento no blancos.
- En relación al acceso a cargos de dirección, de empleados de oficinas y de profesionales, científicos e intelectuales los blancos aparecen sobrerrepresentados en 4,9, 4,5 y 4 puntos porcentuales por encima de la media de la ocupación respectivamente, mientras los no blancos se sitúan a una misma distancia por debajo.
- Entre los obreros calificados y trabajadores no calificados los no blancos aparecen sobrerrepresentados en alrededor de 5 puntos porcentuales.
- Entre los trabajadores autoempleados, cuyos ingresos suelen ser superiores a los de ocupaciones equivalentes en el sector estatal, la proporción de blancos representa 8,3 puntos por encima de la media.
- En relación con el acceso a estudios superiores, los blancos culminan más estos estudios que los no blancos (4,4 puntos).
- En lo que respecta a la vivienda, alrededor del 44 por ciento de la población cubana vive en viviendas en estado regular o malo, pero los no blancos aparecen sobre representados en ambas categorías.

También diversas investigaciones de carácter cualitativo, realizadas entre los años noventa y la primera década del presente siglo, develaron aristas significativas de las brechas de equidad racializadas:

- Las desventajas de ingresos y bienestar aparecen asociadas, entre otros elementos, a la mayor presencia de trabajadores blancos en actividades que concentran posiciones económicamente ventajosas y, como correlato, al predominio de negros y mestizos en actividades de la industria y la construcción del sector tradicional; la mayor presencia de blancos en los grupos ocupacionales calificados en actividades revitalizadas por la reforma; el aumento de la proporción de dirigentes blancos en la medida que se asciende en la jerarquía de dirección; la concentración de las remesas familiares en la población blanca; la sobrerrepresentación de la población negra y mestiza en las peores condiciones de vivienda y habitacionales en general.[14]
- En un estudio realizado con el universo de los alumnos que ingresaron en la educación superior durante el año 2004, se comprueba igualmente la sobrerrepresentación que acusa el ingreso de los estudiantes blancos en esta enseñanza.[15]

En lo que respecta al perfil femenino de las desventajas encontramos una marcada subrepresentación de las mujeres en cargos de dirección en relación con su proporción en el empleo y en la fuerza de trabajo calificada; la disminución del peso de las mujeres a medida que se asciende en el nivel de jerarquía de la dirección; la asimétrica distribución del poder en la dirección de los procesos productivos, esfera donde se advierte casi una exclusión de las mujeres de la dirección.[16]

Ellas representan sólo el 30 por ciento de los directivos, en diferentes niveles, de todos los ocupados en actividades de dirección en la economía nacional. En relación con la dirección política, las mujeres constituyen aproximadamente un 28 por ciento del total de parlamentarios y un 14 por ciento de los miembros del Concejo de Estado.[17]

Se infiere de todo ello la existencia de mecanismos de "segregación ocupacional"[18] y un déficit de empoderamiento, en el sentido de que la estructura de la división social del trabajo y de la organización de la participación política reservan posiciones para ellas y les clausura otras, aquellas relacionadas con la toma de decisiones económico-empresariales y estratégicas de alto nivel.

A estos hallazgos podemos añadir los resultados de un estudio cualitativo reciente de movilidad social que corrobora las brechas de equidad ya identificadas de raza, género y territoriales, a las que añade un relevante elemento: que la reproducción de desventajas suele tener un carácter de transmisión generacional de déficits de activos y capitales en el ámbito familiar y se asocia al origen clasista. Tal hallazgo cualitativo alerta que una parte de la pobreza y la vulnerabilidad tienen un carácter estructural y no coyuntural.

Comentario de cierre

Es justo reconocer que aun cuando la crisis de los noventa afectó la calidad de los servicios públicos y obligó a una reforma que implicó el traspaso hacia el mercado de una proporción considerable del consumo familiar, no se ha producido en Cuba una disminución de la cobertura creada y los gastos sociales han tendido a recuperarse. Se trata de una reforma económica con apertura de mercado y ciertos grados de descentralización, pero que conserva y amplía una política social de equidad, de corte universal y unitaria, donde el estado es el máximo responsable y actor.

Sin embargo, aun con los avances de equidad y acceso mayoritario al bienestar que Cuba ha logrado, se conservan y reproducen brechas de equidad que conservan viejas desigualdades y las traspasan de una generación a otra. La inferencia obvia desde estas reflexiones es que se necesita introducir cambios que posibiliten mayores avances en la superación de estas brechas.

Desde mi punto de vista la persistencia de brechas de equidad y la dificultad para remover los mecanismos reproductores de la pobreza no sólo se explica por la carencia de recursos, sino que se asocian también a fallas en el modelo y la aplicación de la política social. Entre esas fallas pueden señalarse las siguientes:[19]

- Débil sustentabilidad económica y débil retorno de la inversión social hacia la economía (reflejado en un bajo efecto de la elevación de la instrucción y la calificación sobre los niveles de productividad y la innovación tecnológica)

- Baja articulación entre los resultados del trabajo y el acceso al bienestar
- Predominio de las estrategias sectoriales, que obstaculiza la concepción integradora del desarrollo social
- Excesivo énfasis en el consumo social estatalmente normado, en detrimento de la esfera familiar autónoma de elección de satisfactores de necesidades
- Absolutización del estatalismo, excesivo centralismo y tecnoburocratización en la formulación de las estrategias de desarrollo, lo que disminuye la posibilidad de participación en la toma de decisiones de los actores locales (gubernamentales y no gubernamentales) y la consideración de la diversidad territorial y grupal de las necesidades y sus satisfactores
- Universalismo identificado con homogenismo distributivo, que minimiza el papel de la diversidad estructural y cultural en la expresión de las necesidades y en la elección de satisfactores
- Fallas de focalización y poco uso de políticas de acción afirmativa, lo que tiene como efecto la reproducción de desventajas de grupos históricamente desfavorecidos que no pueden aprovechar en paridad las condiciones favorables generales creadas (p. ej., negros, mujeres, ancianos, comunidades en territorios de mayor retraso relativo)
- Desbalance en las asignaciones del gasto social para diferentes dimensiones, que genera déficits acumulados en áreas relevantes asociadas a la situación familiar (fundamentalmente en lo relacionado con el acceso a una vivienda y un hábitat familiar adecuados y empleos con ingresos suficientes)

Antes de ofrecer alternativas es imprescindible introducir tres matices: el primer matiz se refiere a la ambivalencia del estado de las desigualdades en Cuba hoy. Si bien estas se han ensanchado y lacerado aspectos de la equidad lograda, en otro sentido la ampliación de las desigualdades no puede considerarse como una tendencia negativa en su totalidad, puesto que ese proceso está ligado a mayor efectividad económica y a la necesidad de ampliar fuentes de empleo, de producción y de ingresos y, hasta cierto punto o para determinadas formaciones socioclasistas, ha supuesto una mayor correspondencia entre aporte y acceso al bienestar material, mientras que, en otro sentido, refuerza desigualdades injustas.

El segundo matiz rescata la presencia de un estado de cambio y una cierta provisoriedad imperante. La sociedad cubana está colocada en un escenario interno de cambio de múltiples aristas y fuentes y de una sostenibilidad en el tiempo. Por una parte tenemos los efectos de la reforma de inicios de los noventa, con sus vaivenes y su trayectoria en zigzag, que aún están en curso, por otra, el cambio generacional en la dirección política y en todas las esferas de la vida por razones demográficas inapelables y, aun más, el inicio de una nueva etapa reformadora vinculada a los dos elementos anteriores (que podríamos considerar macroestructurales) y presionados por una corriente de mudanza que proviene, con mayor o menor conciencia o grado de explicitación, de las prácticas cotidianas de escala micro, descentralizadas y flexibles, con un patrón de transformación que vincula caos y orden y que son en sí mismas una reforma desde abajo.

Estos factores de naturaleza interna se articulan con el cambiante entorno internacional en el que estamos inmersos, con las alteraciones climáticas y sus consecuencias para la economía, la sociedad y la cultura, las modificaciones de las relaciones económicas y políticas internacionales y la reconfiguración de bloques y alianzas en el plano geopolítico.

Por supuesto que dos factores externos de elevada importancia para la situación nacional, que desbordan las posibilidades analíticas de este texto, son los posibles cambios en la política norteamericana hacia Cuba y los efectos de la crisis económica internacional. Rodeados ambos factores de incertidumbres acerca de sus derroteros futuros y la fuerza de su impacto sobre la economía y la sociedad cubana, una primera conjetura que puede adelantarse, obviando un escenario de levantamiento rápido del bloqueo económico que no me parece muy cercano, es que en cualquier variante podría esperarse un aumento de las desigualdades al menos por la vía de la interconexión de dos procesos simultáneos contradictorios; la caída de los ingresos reales de diversos grupos poblacionales (por ejemplo aquellos vinculados en diversas modalidades y grados al turismo, los servicios gastronómicos y de ocio, el arrendamiento de habitaciones y viviendas, el transporte privado, cuya demanda suele bajar en tiempos de crisis) y la elevación de los ingresos de los receptores de remesas y de los que se conecten con los servicios, estatales y privados que demandaría el eventual restablecimiento de un nivel estándar de visitas al país de la comunidad cubano americana.[20]

El tercer matiz especifica algunas características del nuevo momento reformador, abierto formalmente por el discurso de Raúl Castro el 26 de julio de 2007, y con sucesivas explicitaciones, en sus discurso posteriores del 24 de febrero de 2008 y de clausura del sexto pleno del PCC en abril de este año. Este momento parece tener como ejes principales de su plataforma el reforzamiento del rol directivo del partido en la economía y la sociedad; la desburocratización del aparato estatal, por achicamiento de sus estructuras, personal y poder de restricciones en las gestiones personales (permisos de viajes, de compras y ventas, de permutas, entre otras); restauración de derechos de ciudadanía y propiedad personal y familiar; ampliación de franjas de mercado para bienes y servicios suntuosos (según el estado del consumo en Cuba: equipos de computación, telefonía celular, DVD y videos, acceso a hoteles y centros turísticos, etc.); reorganización agropecuaria a favor del cooperativismo y de la pequeña producción mercantil familiar, de la descentralización de la política de producción de alimentos a escala local y de la ampliación del mercado; ampliación de los espacios para el debate y la crítica pública y la participación ciudadana.

Una de las primeras preguntas que han surgido con relación a esta plataforma es su impacto sobre las desigualdades. Considero que el principal impacto será (es ya) de visibilización de desigualdades ya existentes al concretar formas legales de satisfacer una demanda de bienes y servicios que requieren alto poder adquisitivo, y el reforzamiento de las tendencias mencionadas de la reestratificación.

En este contexto algunas investigaciones sociales han elaborado propuestas para elevar la capacidad de la gestión estatal para reducir las desventajas sociales, la pobreza y potenciar la equidad, entre las que se encuentran.[21]

Definición y puesta en práctica de una estrategia de dotación de sustentabilidad económica a la política social

Esa estrategia debería tener varias escalas espacio-temporales y su primer elemento se relaciona con la mejoría de la inserción de Cuba en el sistema mundo económico, en la cadena de extracción del valor, restricción que un país periférico no puede variar sustantivamente (menos aun Cuba, sometida a la hostilidad de la superpotencia mundial), pero al menos es posible intentar colocarse más favorablemente en ella. En esta línea encontramos la propuesta de transitar definitivamente desde el modelo de sustitución de importaciones a uno de sustitución de exportaciones basado en la exportación de manufacturas tecnológicamente intensivas, lo cual no excluye, más bien se complementa, con procesos de sustitución de importaciones y de exportaciones de recursos naturales.

Esta sería una opción selectiva encomendada a la economía estatal, que requiere también de un mercado interno de apoyo y necesariamente debe articularse con una reestructuración económica que amplíe las actividades productivas de las más diversas escalas y variantes en el uso de la tecnología, la calificación y las formas de propiedad.

La complementación de sujetos socioeconómicos estatales y extraestatales

Apela a la aceptación de un esquema clasista múltiple, típico de la transición socialista, y a una posibilidad de ampliación de la propiedad no estatal en diferentes variantes, reforzando sus aristas complementarias y bajo hegemonía de la propiedad social, con la intención de descargar al estado de actividades y tareas que lo desbordan, de concentrarlo en lo esencial y de diversificar las posibilidades de generación de ingresos adecuados y de productos y servicios.

Las posibilidades de reconstruir el esquema de organización de la propiedad sobre los medios productivos, sin alterar su núcleo duro de socialización y colectivización, son variadas: propiedad colectiva de pueblos y municipios, propiedad comunitaria, cooperativas urbanas de productores y proveedores de servicios, propiedad profesional y de asociaciones, propiedad mixta (estatal-privada, estatal-cooperativa) en pequeñas y medianas empresas, pequeñas y microempresas privadas, diversificación y expansión de las posibilidades del autoempleo.

El tema es complicado y lleva siempre a la interrogante de si se trata de un problema de propiedad formal o de poder real, cuya solución se acercaría más a la implementación de procesos autogestivos, de base usufructuaria, que a la diversificación y desestatalización de la propiedad.

Seguramente la solución no podría ser única, y debería combinar, según sea más conveniente en casos concretos, el usufructo autogestionario y la copropiedad con formas de propiedad individuales y colectivas en diferentes grados, también sometidas o controladas de forma indirecta a mecanismos de gestión social, pero sin que ello invalide, como ha sucedido con la experiencia de la cooperativización agropecuaria, la autonomía imprescindible.

Desplazamiento desde una concepción de política social que enfatiza en la homogeneidad social hacia otra que asume una norma socialista de desigualdad que establece un sistema de prioridades básicas para manejar la tensión entre equidad e inequidad

Los elementos generales de esta norma son la ausencia de desigualdades asociadas a relaciones de explotación o dominación de cualquier tipo, que enajene y ponga en situación de inferioridad a cualquier grupo social; la ausencia de la condición de pobreza y la garantía del acceso a la satisfacción de las necesidades básicas para todos los grupos sociales; el aseguramiento de espacios de igualdad que no pueden ser objeto de distribución mercantil para todos los grupos sociales y la utilización del mercado como mecanismo indirecto de distribución que admite diferencias; el reconocimiento de la legitimidad de las desigualdades asociadas al trabajo y a la atención a desventajas sociales, y de la expresión de las diferencias que no ponen en desventaja o afectan el derecho a la igualdad de otros individuos y grupos; el derecho y el deber de contribuir individualmente al bien común en dependencia de la magnitud de los ingresos personales y de la capacidad productiva.

Fortalecer la complementación de políticas universales con acciones focalizadas o direccionadas de base territorial, centradas en la articulación educación-trabajo-hábitat

Plantea la necesidad de accionar prioritariamente sobre espacios deprimidos, considerando que las brechas de equidad (especialmente las vinculadas a la raza, el género y el origen social) suelen tener una concentración territorial, sin clausurar los instrumentos de universalidad, sino de complementarlos a través de una focalización integrada territorialmente.

Asumir la concepción del territorio como factor de desarrollo

Esto implica la potenciación al máximo del desarrollo local endógeno, incluyendo elementos de economía local, y de sus actores socioeconómicos como agentes de cambio; la construcción de fórmulas de enlace a través de la creación de redes de relaciones sinérgicas interterritoriales, que permitan corregir los desbalances espaciales que no pueden ser solucionados localmente; el trazado de estrategias centradas en la sustentabilidad, entendiendo esta cualidad como el uso intensivo de la riqueza natural, cultural, calificacional e histórica que garantice su regeneración, el respeto a las tradiciones junto a la potenciación de la innovación y la instalación de una capacidad perdurable de autogestión y auto-organización participativa de las sociedades locales.

Complementación centralización-descentralización en la gestión de la política social

Esto otorga mayores responsabilidades al Poder Popular Territorial, las comunidades y las familias en las decisiones de política social y el control de las actividades, conservando el papel protagónico del estado y de una estrategia social centralizada y universal.

Introducir modificaciones en las prioridades estratégicas del gasto social, a favor del fortalecimiento de la capacidad de definición de satisfactores en la esfera doméstico-individual-familiar

Entre otros aspectos, conceder mayor prioridad a la política de empleo que asegure ingresos suficientes para cubrir las necesidades básicas y modificación de la política de vivienda que considere fórmulas variadas y flexibles para su construcción y mantenimiento (cooperativas, esfuerzo propio, créditos familiares, entre otras).

Ampliación de los contenidos y límites de la participación en la construcción de la agenda social, priorizando sus elementos de cogestión, formulación estratégica y control popular del proceso y sus resultados

Se trata de una propuesta de cambio colocada en el nivel de líneas estratégicas generales que, obviamente, son insuficientes para la toma de decisiones y el diseño de políticas concretas y su valor estriba en la intención de proponer, desde la investigación social, a decisores y a la sociedad civil, una plataforma preliminar de debate sobre transformaciones posibles y necesarias.

NOTAS

El texto es una síntesis revisada de la ponencia de igual título presentada en la conferencia internacional "The Measures of a Revolution: Cuba, 1959–2009", celebrada en Queen's University, Kingston, Canadá, en mayo de 2009.

1. Tratamientos más amplios de estos temas pueden encontrarse en M. Espina, "Políticas de atención a la pobreza y la desigualdad. Examinado el rol del Estado en la experiencia cubana" (Buenos Aires: Consejo Latinoamericano de Sciencias Sociales y Comparative Research Programme on Poverty [CLACSO-CROP], 2008) 144–45; y en J. Santana, "Justicia social vs. incentivo al trabajo con alta productividad," Ponencia presentada en el *Taller Justicia social, creci-*

miento y desarrollo sostenible (La Habana: Fundación F. Ebert y Sociedad Económica de Amigos del País, 2009) 4–5, donde aparece una definición de estos principios.

2. Espina, "Políticas de atención a la pobreza y la desigualdad. Examinado el rol del Estado en la experiencia cubana", 144–45

3. Para el tema de la crisis consultar Julio Carranza, "La crisis: un diagnóstico. Los retos de la economía cubana", en *Cuba: Apertura y reforma económica; Perfil de un debate*, ed. Bert Hoffmann (Caracas: Nueva Sociedad, 1995); Comisión Económica para América Latina y el Caribe, *La economía cubana: Reformas estructurales y desempeño en los noventa* (México, D.F.: Fondo de Cultura Económica, 2000).

4. Comisión Económica para América Latina y el Caribe, *Panorama social de América Latina 1994* (Santiago de Chile: Naciones Unidas, 1994), ha utilizado una clasificación de países que los agrupa, de acuerdo con la prioridad macroeconómica asignada al gasto social, en la escala siguiente: (1) grupo de países de gasto social alto (más de diez puntos del PIB); (2) grupo de gasto social medio (entre cinco y diez puntos del PIB); (3) grupo de gasto social bajo (inferior a cinco puntos del PIB).

5. Para una caracterización del proceso de reestratificación social, ver Espina, "Viejas y nuevas desigualdades en Cuba: Ambivalencias y perspectivas de la reestratificación social", en *Nueva Sociedad* 216 (Buenos Aires, 2008).

6. Como en Cuba los datos de ingresos no son públicos, no me es posible elaborar un cálculo propio del Gini. Para algunos analistas este cálculo oficial subvalora el grado de concentración real de los ingresos, especialmente por las dificultades para captar ingresos informales diversos y el acceso real a la moneda dura CUC. El Gini calculado para los ochentas lo he tomado de C. Brundenius, *Crecimiento con equidad: Cuba, 1959–1984* (Managua: Cuadernos de Pensamiento Propio INIES-CRIES, no. 11, 1984); y el de los noventas de L. Añé, "La reforma económica y la economía familiar en Cuba" en de M. Miranda (comp.), *Reforma económica y cambio social en América Latina y el Caribe*, (T/M Ediciones Cali, 2000).

7. Oficina Nacional de Estadísticas Anuario Estadístico (La Habana, 2006).

8. A. Ver García y B. Anaya, "Política Social en Cuba, nuevo enfoque y Programas recientes". Ponencia presentada en el Seminario, Fondos del Centro de Estudios de la Economía Cubana del Centro de Estudios de la Economía Cubana (La Habana, 2006)

9. Ver A. Ferriol, "Explorando nuevas estrategias para reducir la pobreza en el actual contexto internacional", ponencia presentada al seminario internacional "Estrategias de reducción de la pobreza en el Caribe: Los actores externos y su impacto" (La Habana: CLACSO-CROP, 2002).

10. L. Iñiguez y O. Pérez, "Territorio y espacio en las desigualdades sociales de la provincia Ciudad de La Habana" en *15 Años del Centro de Estudios de la Economía Cubana*, Editorial Feliz Varela, (La Habana, 2004).

11. El índice se calculó delimitando las privaciones que sufre cada territorio (provincia) en seis variables básicas (mortalidad infantil, índice de ocupación, volumen de inversiones, tasa de escolarización, salarios medios devengados y mortalidad materna), en una escala de clasificación que va de uno a cero. Tomado de E. Méndez y M. C. Lloret, "Índice de Desarrollo Humano a nivel territorial en Cuba: Período 1985–2001", *Cubana de Salud Pública* 31, no. 2 (2005): 2–4.

12. Espina, "Políticas de atención a la pobreza y la desigualdad: Examinado el rol del estado en la experiencia cubana", 182–84.

13. Este procesamiento por color de la piel de los datos censales ha sido tomado Grupo Reducción de Desigualdades, "Propuesta para la elaboración de políticas tendentes a la reducción de las desigualdades raciales" (La Habana: Polo de Ciencias Sociales y Humanidades, 2008).

14. R. Espina y P. Rodríguez, "Raza y desigualdad en la Cuba actual." *Temas* 45 (La Habana, 2006).

15. N. González, "Familia, racialidad y educación," Trabajo de Diploma. Departamento de Sociología (Universidad de La Habana, 2006)

38 : MAYRA ESPINA PRIETO

16. D. Echevarría, "Mujer, empleo y dirección en Cuba: algo más que estadísticas". En *15 Años del Centro de Estudios de la Economía Cubana*, ed. Félix Varela (La Habana, 2004).

17. M. Álvarez, "Mujer y poder en Cuba". En *Cuba construyendo futuro*, eds. Manuel Monereo, et al., (Madrid: El viejo Topo, 2000).

18. Echevarría, "Mujer, empleo y dirección en Cuba: algo más que estadísticas", 155.

19. Para profundizare en estas fallas consultar "Políticas de atención a la pobreza y la desigualdad: Examinado el rol del estado en la experiencia cubana", 202–15.

20. Para ampliar sobre los impactos de estos factores y posibles escenarios que generarían en su interrelación, pueden consultarse I. Peña, J. Triana, y S. M. Sánchez, participación en el pánel "La crisis económica en América Latina y el Caribe: ¿El fin del neoliberalismo?" Jornadas internacionales crisis económica global y su impacto en América Latina (La Habana: Fundación por la Europa de los Ciudadanos, Consejo Latinoamericano de Ciencias Sociales, Cátedra de Estudios del Caribe y Centro de Investigaciones de la Economía Internacional de la Universidad de La Habana, 2009).

21. En Espina, "Políticas de atención a la pobreza y la desigualdad: Examinado el rol del estado en la experiencia cubana", puede encontrarse un análisis amplio de estas propuestas y sus fuentes.

JEAN STUBBS

El Habano *and the World It Has Shaped:* Cuba, Connecticut, *and Indonesia*

ABSTRACT

In the half century since the 1959 Cuban Revolution, *El Habano* remains *the* premium cigar the world over; but both before and since 1959, the seed, agricultural and industrial know-how, and human capital have been transplanted to replicate that cigar in a process accentuated by upheavals and out-migration. The focus here is on a little-known facet of the interconnected island and offshore Havana cigar history, linking Cuba with Connecticut and Indonesia: from when tobacco was taken from the Americas to Indonesia and gave rise to the famed Sumatra cigar wrapper leaf; through the rise and demise of its sister shade wrapper in Connecticut, with Cuban and Sumatra seed, ultimately overshadowed by Indonesia; and the resulting challenges facing Cuba today. The article highlights the role of Dutch, U.S., British, and Swedish capital to explain why in 2009 the two major global cigar corporations, British Imperial Tobacco and Swedish Match, were lobbying Washington, respectively, for and against the embargo on Cuba. As the antismoking, antitobacco lobby gains ground internationally, the intriguing final question is whether the future lies with *El Habano* or smokeless Swedish *snus*.

RESUMEN

En el medio siglo que ha transcurrido desde la Revolución Cubana en 1959, El Habano sigue siendo globalmente el puro de lujo, pero tanto antes como después de 1959, la semilla, el conocer agrícola e industrial, y el capital humano se han trasplantado para replicarlo, en un proceso acentuado por eventos y movimientos migratorios. El enfoque aquí es sobre una faceta poco conocida de la historia de El Habano tanto fuera como dentro de la isla, que vincula Cuba con Connecticut, Estados Unidos e Indonesia: desde cuando el tabaco se llevó de las Américas a Indonesia, dando lugar a la capa afamada de la hoja Sumatra; pasando por el auge y declive de la hermana capa tapado — *shade* — en Connecticut, de la semilla cubana y la de la Sumatra, pero que fue eclipsada finalmente por Indonesia; y los desafíos resultantes Cuba enfrenta hoy día. Se pone de relieve el papel del capital holandés, estadounidense, británico y sueco para explicar porqué en 2009 las dos corporaciones mayores globales del puro, British Imperial Tobacco y Swedish Match, estuvieron presionando en Washington a favor y en contra, respectivamente, del embargo contra Cuba. En la medida en que se fortalezca la campaña internacional en contra del humo y del tabaco, la intrigante pregunta final es si el futuro está con El Habano o con el *snus* sueco, sin humo.

In 2009, the two major international cigar conglomerates, Swedish Match and British Imperial Tobacco, were on opposite sides of the Washington lobby for maintaining and lifting the United States' fifty-year trade embargo on Cuba. Ten years earlier, in 1999, the U.S. glossy *Cigar Aficionado* ran a feature by its European editor James Suckling on East Java, Indonesia, titled "Tobacco Mecca."[1] Suckling celebrated the quality of top cigar leaf from both Java and Sumatra and reported that, in 1996, Swedish Match had opened a premium cigar factory in Pandaan, near Surabaya, with the help of Cuban rollers from Havana's Partagas factory. Indonesian workers were described as meticulous by project manager Sander Van Hattem, who had previously run a small factory in the Dominican Republic. According to Suckling, "If you have ever wondered what a modern, well-financed Cuban factory would look like, the Swedish Match operation is it." What is the connection between these two developments? How are they to be framed in the broader tobacco histories of the United States (Connecticut, in particular) and Indonesia (Sumatra and Java) in connection with Cuba? And what are the contemporary implications for all three, given the major international shifts in tobacco in response to the growing international antismoking lobby?

Those are questions I seek to explore here, in the context of how, in the fifty years since the Cuban Revolution of 1959, *El Habano* has continued to be not only *the* world premium handmade cigar but also one much imitated the world over.[2] Since the late nineteenth century, by which time *El Habano* had made its mark, the seed, agricultural, and industrial know-how, and human capital have all been transplanted abroad in an attempt to replicate the quality product. The upheavals of two landmark political events in Cuba — the late-nineteenth-century wars of independence from Spain and the 1959 revolution — exacerbated this process. Each brought waves of out-migration and growing overseas competition, involving Cuban agronomists, growers, manufacturers, and workers.[3]

What follows first draws on earlier work to outline the broader island and offshore Havana cigar history as a backdrop to documenting the history that links Cuba with Connecticut and Indonesia. It moves on to the late-nineteenth-century development of tobacco, originally from the Americas, as a cash crop in Indonesia with Dutch capital in the latter part of the nineteenth century, which gave rise to the famed Sumatra wrapper leaf. It then traces Connecticut tobacco history and the development by U.S. capital — and fleetingly British capital — of a leaf to undercut Sumatra, creating a hybrid out of Cuban and Sumatra seed: the equally famed Connecticut shade wrapper (shade tobacco also is grown across the Florida-Georgia border area). It subsequently turns to Java towering over Connecticut and Cuba in tobacco, leading up to the late-twentieth-century opening, with Swedish capital, of the Havana cigar factory in Pandaan. Finally, it signals how *El Habano* highlights the need to conceptualize a global historical approach, and it concludes by posing, though not answering, a key question as to the future of *El Habano* in the context of global antismoking and the growing popularity of smokeless Swedish *snus* (moist snuff). With or without the U.S. embargo on Cuba, will the future lie with *El Habano* or *snus*?

Transnationalizing the History of the Havana Cigar

Fernando Ortiz grounded his classic concept of transculturation in the *contrapunteo* of tobacco and sugar, fashioning the two commodities as metaphorical constructs and highlighting the fetish power of the commodities and a counterfetish interpretation that challenged "essentialist understandings of Cuban history."[4] Both the fetishism and the counterfetishism are of particular significance when it comes to understanding Havana cigar history. The cigar, more than any other product of Cuba, has come to symbolize Cuban nationalism and sovereignty, and yet the cigar equally lies at the heart of a highly interconnected island-offshore history.[5]

Crucial to "de-essentializing" Havana's cigar history is documenting the transnational history of its agriculture and industry; agricultural science; and technology, peasantry, and labor. Cigar leaf tobacco was grown and cigars manufactured in Cuba for marketing across the world, but in particular to Europe and to the United States until, in response to the 1959 revolution, the United States imposed its trade embargo on Cuba. Over time, however, both before and since the revolution, interlocking economies and communities have been created in neighboring Caribbean islands and surrounding mainland territories — Dominican Republic, Jamaica, Honduras, Mexico, Nicaragua, and Puerto Rico, as well as Brazil (Bahia), the United States (Connecticut, Florida, Georgia, New York), Europe (the Canary Islands, in particular), and beyond (the Philippines and Indonesia).

The lifting of the Spanish monopoly on Cuban manufacture in 1817 heralded *El Habano*'s coming of age as the world's luxury tobacco product of the nineteenth century, taking over from pipe and snuff. With Spanish, German, British, and French capital, it conquered European, North American, and world markets, notably London, Amsterdam, Bremen, Madrid, Paris, Lisbon, and New York. Out-migration, mainly north to the United States but also to the Caribbean and Central America, as well as in-migration from the Canary Islands, marked Cuba's First and Second Wars of Independence from Spain — 1868–1878 and 1895–1898. From the Florida-Georgia tobacco towns of Key West, Tampa, Marti City (today's Ocala), Quincy, Havana, Sumatra, and Amsterdam — to New York and Connecticut, as well as in Jamaica and Mexico, Cuban tobacco interests came together in the settler territories, providing a familiar means of livelihood for the displaced migrant community and an economic and political mainstay for the independence struggle at home.[6]

Early-twentieth-century U.S. occupation opened Cuba to mass U.S. investment in major leaf and manufacturing concerns, undercutting other foreign investment; in its carving up of the world, the cartel formed by the American Tobacco Company and British Imperial Tobacco agreed Cuba would be the former's domain.[7] Yet rival economic and political interests to Cuba built up abroad — with trading and other advantages over the home country in turmoil — and returnee Cuban cigar workers found themselves without jobs, only to leave again. A second wave of Canary Islander settler, return, cyclical, and relief migration contributed to the Canary Islands' own emergent tobacco agriculture and industry, and the 1930s Depression and labor unrest culminated a process whereby U.S.-owned manufacturing withdrew production from Cuba to the United States. By then, mass-mechanized cigarette production was fast overshadowing the cigar, and relocation north was to undermine successful Cuban opposition to the introduction of the cigar machine. The Cuban industry was not to regain its former glory, but independents held out — small family firms, producing the premium handmade Habano, which predominated right up until the 1959 revolution.

The revolution reaccentuated the migratory phenomenon. Smaller manufacturers, dealers, growers, and workers sought fertile ground for overseas business, profiting from upheavals linked to insurrection, agrarian reform, and nationalization, plus the U.S. trade embargo that — with U.S. pressure — extended to most of the Americas, Canada and Mexico being the only early exceptions. Prior to the embargo, the U.S. Department of Agriculture (USDA) commissioned a report to document the extent to which the U.S. cigar industry relied on Cuban leaf imports and to advise on sourcing alternative supplies.[8] The report's recommendations were to seek these in neighboring Caribbean and Central American territories, whereby agronomists, growers, and manufacturers would experiment in the Dominican Republic and Nicaragua in particular. Over time, Western markets became a battleground for disputed Havana cigar brands from island-offshore parallel production and marketing systems, and Eastern European socialist bloc and some third-world countries emerged as new Havana cigar partners.

Thirty years on, the fall of the Berlin Wall in 1989 signaled the beginning of the end of the special Soviet bloc trade and aid that had built up in the vacuum left by U.S. hostility and embargo. At the same time as the U.S. response to Cuba's ensuing crisis was to tighten and extraterritorialize the embargo in the 1991 Torricelli and 1996 Helms-Burton acts, a U.S. cigar revival was in full swing, engineered in part by the New York glossy *Cigar Aficionado*, created in 1992. The then two U.S. cigar giants Consolidated Cigar and General Cigar and émigré Cuban tobacco interests were in all-out competition with island Cuba. Cuba, in turn, courted non-U.S. trade and investment, and cigars became part of its crisis structural adjustment strategy. In 1994, landmark credit-for-tobacco deals were struck between the Cuban state tobacco enterprise, Cubatabaco, and its French and Spanish parastatal tobacco counterparts, Societé Nationale des Tabacs (SEITA) and Tabacalera Española; a new holding company, Habanos, S.A., was set up to handle overseas marketing ventures; and a European cigar-marketing deal was struck in Britain, with Hunters and Frankau.

In 1999, as the cigar revival peaked, Tabacalera Española and SEITA formed Alianza de Tabacos y Distribución (Altadis), which bought 50 percent shares in Habanos. Tabacalera Española had earlier that year bought Consolidated and was in both the Havana and the clone Havana cigar business through Altadis and Altadis USA. In 2007, Altadis was sold to the British Imperial/Gallaher group and General Cigar to Swedish Match, which was the backdrop to the lobbying efforts of each in Washington regarding the U.S. embargo. In what ways do Connecticut and Indonesia fit into this larger picture?

Sumatra Wrapper and the Deli

"Horticulturalist's quest for perfect tobacco spans globe" was the lead for a 1988 article by Linda Hirsh in Connecticut's *Hartford Courant*,[9] featuring seventy-seven-year-old Henry Nienhuys, who had managed plantations in Indonesia, Cuba, and the Connecticut Valley. His grandfather Jacobus Nienhuys was reported as having been the first to take Sumatra tobacco to Holland in 1860 and as having formed the Deli — Deli Maatschappij Company. Hirsh quoted *The Dictionary of Tobacco* on the Sumatra strain having first been imported to America in 1883, and from then until 1910, U.S. cigar manufacturers used 4.5 million pounds a year.[10] In 1899, the USDA first experimented with nets, to simulate the natural cloud coverage of Sumatra; and by 1911, when Nienhys was born, their use for growing tobacco under cloth — shade tobacco — was gaining momentum.

Nienhuys grew up in Haarlem, in the Netherlands, and studied tobacco at the agricultural University of Wageningen, where he wrote his doctoral thesis comparing Sumatra wrapper and Connecticut shade. He traveled to Hartford, Connecticut, where he grew tobacco on the Brewer family farm in 1936, and he joined the Deli in 1937. In pre–World War II years, the Nienhuys family belonged to a close-knit community of Dutch families, who then became prisoners of war. After the war, from 1946 to 1949, the Deli sent Nienhuys back to Connecticut to work on the tobacco farms and bring his experience and knowledge back to Indonesia to rehabilitate tobacco plantations from wartime neglect.

Allegedly disenchanted when the company began dictating from Amsterdam what kind of fertilizer to use on the crops, Nienhuys responded to a call from Henry Duys, the owner of Connecticut tobacco farms, telling him that blue mold had decimated his crop and asking whether he would return to work with him. He joined Duys in 1952, and Hirsh reported, "Between managing Duys' South Windsor farms and the Hartford warehouse, he would spend part of the season in Cuba. There he studied the climate to monitor when blue mold spores were in the air, then dusted the leaves to control the spots." At the time, local wrapper was harvested only by those whom Nienhuys called diehards, because "it is cheaper to grow the tobacco in Honduras and Guatemala, where labor is right around the corner." Nienhuys left tobacco in 1970, as did many others, to set up horticultural nurseries.

The Indonesia story as told by Hirsh is ratified in the official history of what later became Deli Universal Company.[11] Despite early efforts to grow tobacco in the mid-1850s on Java, which yielded only low grades, Dutch entrepreneurs firmly believed the region's climate could produce higher quality tobacco. The arrival of Nienhuys heralded the start of the colony's growth in tobacco. In 1867, Nienhuys and his partner P. W. Janssen secured financial backing, half of which came from the Nederlandsche Handel-Maatschappiji, and in 1869, they established the Deli Maatschappij, with a concession to produce cigar tobacco along Sumatra's Deli River.

The initial Dutch commercial attention to East Sumatra is said to have derived from an 1863 delegation sent from Java, which included Nienhuys, who had already been growing tobacco in Java.[12] The delegation's report was unfavorable, yet Nienhuys stayed; arranged land concessions; and secured financing for the Deli, which within twenty years had increased cultivation tenfold on twenty-one estates. When Nienhuys returned to the Netherlands in 1871, Jacob Theodore Cremer took his place; and though other companies followed the Deli — such as Deli Batavia (1875), Tobacco Company Arendsburg (1877), and Senembah Company (1889) — by 1883, the year Cremer himself returned to the Netherlands, the Deli's exports had soared to nearly 7.6 million pounds. By 1900, the company had bought up most other plantations, and the Deli reigned supreme, controlling not only the Sumatra tobacco industry, with a monopoly on tobacco exports and acting as broker for tobacco growers, but also the East Sumatra rubber and palm oil plantation belt, all worked with Javanese, Chinese, and other migrant labor.[13]

Sumatra leaf was by then renowned worldwide as cigar wrapper, as its thin central vein and thin flexible texture meant that it could be used to wrap up to four times as many cigars as other leaf. Growers in the United States lobbied hard for protectionist high duties to keep Sumatra imports down, but companies were to establish plantations in Sumatra for their own supply, and by the outbreak of World War I, more than 90 percent of all U.S.-imported wrapper came from Sumatra.

The U.S. cigar history was to be fast overshadowed in the twentieth century by that of Indonesia, in the context of the different colonial and postcolonial systems that emerged.[14] London and Amsterdam had been established as European twin pillars of the international circulation of tobacco in the seventeenth century as the British and Dutch expanded their empires. Tobacco became big business, with Crown and state playing a central role. European states such as Spain, Portugal, and France all established monopolies purchasing and processing tobacco, whereas German states enforced all-important taxation. There were no such monopolies in Britain, the Netherlands, or the United States, but whether via monopoly or market, the state was heavily involved.

After 1800, the United States rose to preeminence, partly because its competitors were few — only Brazil and Cuba in the Western Hemisphere, and Holland and Germany in Europe — and partly because the colonial system ensured global segmentation. The Dutch Culture System of the 1830s and 1840s in the Netherlands East Indies was designed to foster export crops: sugar, coffee, and indigo first, and then others, including tobacco. After 1866, when tobacco was allowed to be cultivated on a private basis, production grew, and it was the Deli that accounted in large part for Sumatra exports soaring from 17 million pounds in the late 1860s to nearly 170 million pounds by World War I. The Deli region was by then producing one-third of the Sumatra crop, and East Sumatra was reputed to have Indonesia's greatest concentration of agricultural estates. Tobacco dominated the area around the capital Medan, beyond which were rubber and palm oil plantations.

By the outbreak of World War I, the Dutch East Indies was the world's second-largest exporter of leaf, accounting for 18 percent of the market. Sumatra and Java supplied the international market via Amsterdam and Rotterdam in the Netherlands and Bremen in Germany, competing with Algeria, the Philippines, the United States, and Cuba. After World War I, France was second to the United States as a buyer of Sumatra tobacco, and Belgium and France joined Germany as main purchasers of Java tobacco, which continued to dominate the Netherlands market. There were also growing numbers of Chinese and Javanese traders. In contrast, whereas in 1840 the United States exported 87 percent of the world's leaf, with the breakup of the colonial system and the opening of new regions to the international market, especially the Dutch East Indies, Brazil, and Cuba, the U.S. share of world output had dropped to 30 percent by 1884 and, by 1984, a century later, to only 13 percent.

The Deli's enormous profits were invested in turn-of-the century railroad construction in Indonesia, the United States, and elsewhere. By the 1920s, however, the company's fortunes began to decline. Cigar smoking had dominated the tobacco market, but in 1927, sales of cigarettes surpassed cigars, and in the 1930s, cigar sales plummeted during the Depression. World War II and Japanese occupation brought Sumatra's tobacco exports to a virtual standstill, and the Deli was cut off from its Dutch financial backers. The end of the war saw the Deli reenter a dramatically changed Dutch East Indies and a global market dominated by tobacco giants; and in Indonesia's subsequent struggle against the Dutch for sovereignty, which it attained in 1949, the Deli was in turmoil, from squatters' illegal land occupations, strikes, and labor organizing to the so-called Indonesianizing of estate personnel. In early 1958, when all Dutch economic interests were nationalized, the Deli, almost exclusively Dutch owned, lost its estates. Remaining Dutch personnel left soon thereafter, and the operation transferred to Indonesian nationals.

The Deli relocated greatly reduced operations to the Netherlands and took over the U.S. American Sumatra Tobacco Corporation,[15] whose origins dated back to 1891, when A. Cohn and Company purchased fourteen thousand acres in the Florida-Georgia belt for tobacco cultivation. The company's tobacco plantation, named Amsterdam, claimed at the time to be the largest tobacco plantation in the world under single ownership. In 1907, seven of the larger growers and packers in the area merged to form the American Sumatra Tobacco Company, with a division in Amsterdam, by then a small company town. It became the American Sumatra Tobacco Corporation in 1910 and grew during and after World War II into one of the world's largest sources of wrapper, linking New York–based financial partners with farmers in the South. The Deli bought American Sumatra in 1955 but shut down its leaf operations in 1965, continuing the production of only the new homogenized tobacco sheets (also known as reconstituted tobacco), in which it became a major player in Italy, Greece, and the fast-growing Brazilian market.

The Deli's involvement in the import-export market for flue-cured and burley tobaccos brought partnership with the Universal Leaf Tobacco Company in the mid-1960s, followed by merger in 1986. Universal, which had been founded in 1918, had grown by the 1960s into one of the world's largest leaf tobacco distributors and had restructured after the merger, combining tobacco interests in Universal Leaf Tobacco and grouping diversified trading acquisitions under Deli Universal.[16]

Of significance here is that the Deli's advantage over competitors and enormous profits derived in no small part from what U.S. and Dutch reports decried as coolie slave labor. The Deli may have been renowned among cigar smokers for growing and curing the world's most prized wrappers, but it was also reviled for making other Dutch colonial ventures look benevolent. Its labor and living conditions were infamously compared to those of slavery, and peasant laborers' burning of its barns became a constant worry for both the Deli and the colonial government.[17] The Deli legacy was what Ann Laura Stoler, in her late-twentieth-century fieldwork for *Capitalism and Confrontation in Sumatra's Plantation Belt, 1870–1979*, referred to as one of "brutalities alternatively whispered and shouted," ever present in peasant-laborer discontent, which still saw the burning of tobacco barns, and in the postcolonial state's "maneuvers and menaces," open to foreign business and ruthless in stamping out oppositional political and labor organizing.[18]

Connecticut and Shade

Contrary to Indonesia's contemporary tobacco preeminence, the history of Connecticut's Tobacco Valley — so intimately linked to that of Nienhuys, the Deli, American Sumatra, Universal Leaf, and Cuba — is one little in evidence today. Margaret Buker Jay, in her "Historical Perspective," in *Changing Landscape through People: Connecticut Valley Tobacco,* began thus:

Anyone driving an automobile in the summertime through the fields and hills of the picturesque Connecticut Valley to the north of Hartford is struck by the great number of tobacco tents constantly coming into view, covering acres of land, running up the hillsides and stretching over the valleys. . . . The visual landscape of the Connecticut Valley has changed dramatically from the view which prompted this observation in 1917. Tobacco production dominated the landscape of many communities for most of this century. This *was* "Tobacco Valley."[19]

In and among suburban and small-town residential areas are now only small expanses of tent-covered shade tobacco land, alongside disused tobacco barns and derelict seasonal farmworker camps. Valley tobacco acreage was at its height in 1921, with almost thirty-one thousand acres, having grown from fewer than forty acres in 1839. Linked with Cuba's fortunes, the 1960s and the 1990s would witness ephemeral revival. However, neither revival was on a scale to stem the steady tide of long-term decline that had begun with the 1950s introduction of homogenized binder and wrapper, compounded by the U.S. Report of the Surgeon General in 1964 on the hazards of smoking and sealed by offshore relocation.

Escalating costs — taxes, labor, fertilizer, fuel, and interest rates — all reduced profit margins, and acreage fell as land was sold for industrial, commercial, and suburban residential development. Hartford County's population increased 28 percent over the decade from 1950 to 1960; many towns (e.g., East Granby, Granby, Windsor, East Windsor) grew by more than 50 percent; and four towns (Enfield, Simsbury, South Windsor, and Windsor Locks) more than doubled in population.

In 1960, there had been some 9,000 acres under tobacco, and during the decade this stabilized to around 6,000 acres, but by 1979, it had declined to 3,000 acres and was at a low of 720 acres in 1992. Acreage increased only slightly to 910 in 1994 before dwindling again. At the turn of the twenty-first century, tobacco was still a cash crop for some, but many had given up the crop altogether. Companies had stopped buying from contract growers, had liquidated land holdings, and had gone out of business. What was once the heart of the old shade district are today's Buckland Mall, Bradley International Airport, technology business parks, and suburban subdivisions.

James F. O'Gorman, in his 2002 *Connecticut Valley Vernacular: The Vanishing Landscape and Architecture of the New England Tobacco Fields*, describes how "tobacco sheds remain the most characteristic example of agricultural vernacular architecture in the Connecticut River Valley . . . common relics of a vanishing episode of Valley life."[20] Accompanying the text are the U.S.–Puerto Rican photographer Jack Delano's haunting visual images of a fading way of life: the shade tents and wooden sheds; shifting immigrant populations; long, hot hours laboring in summer fields, the autumnal curing process, and stripping rooms.

What was often recounted in its heyday as a proud New England story of twentieth-century tobacco family dynasties was, in O'Gorman's words, "a high risk, labor intensive, controversial but potentially rewarding occupation for owners if not for laborers. Cultivation demands constant attention, backbreaking hard work in the fields and under the tents, and knowledgeable adherence to detail in the curing sheds and stripping and sorting rooms."[21] The story was also laced with cutthroat tobacco business and labor practices, as narrated in snapshot detail almost half a century earlier by the local writer Mildred Savage, whose 1958 best-selling novel *Parrish*, made into a 1961 Hollywood movie of the same name, was described at the time as a scenic, tobacco-road soap opera.[22]

The late-twentieth-century end of that heyday would see relocation to the Dominican Republic and Central America, Brazil, and Ecuador in search of alternatives not only to outcast post-1959 Cuba but also — in a cost-cutting, profit-making drive — to outcast Connecticut itself.

From Havana "Segars" and Seed . . .

As related in *Connecticut and Tobacco: A Chapter in America's Industrial Growth*, "It is a curiosity of history that the original Dutch and English settlements in Connecticut were in the very areas that some two and half centuries later were to become the heart of Connecticut's valuable tobaccoland."[23] The first tobacco growers were Native Americans, but the tobacco was said to be bitter in taste, and early colonists replaced it with a West Indian variety brought to Connecticut from Virginia. By the early 1700s, tobacco, centered around Windsor, became an important article of trade between valley towns and the West Indies. It declined in the late 1700s, as a result of increased competition from Virginia and England's refusal to allow trade with the West Indian colonies, but it was to come into its own with cigars in the late 1700s and early 1800s with a Cuban connection:

Colonel Israel Putnam is generally credited with the introduction of the cigar into Connecticut in 1762, on his return from an expedition against Havana. . . . [W]ithin a generation of his time, there was a swing in the taste of Connecticut smokers to cigars. West Indian cigars were coming into the state by 1791, the year in which an advertisement offering "segars" first appeared in the *Connecticut Courant*.[24]

These were Cuban-manufactured imports. The first advertisement for "segars" of domestic manufacture was published in the *Connecticut Courant* of 1799.

As the story goes, farmers' wives began home rolling cigars for barter in Windsor, and this spread through the valley. The first cigar making on a commercial basis is also credited to a woman. Little attention was paid to quality, and the cigars were known as paste or barnyard segars, sold to storekeepers for a dollar or two per thousand and retailed at a cent a piece. The shortest — twofers — sold two for a cent. The Viets brothers set up the first cigar factories in Suffield and East Windsor in 1810: "Samuel Viets had by chance come upon a wandering Cuban who understood the art of cigar rolling. He engaged him to teach his craft to a dozen or more women in a newly opened factory at Suffield."[25]

Peddlers traveled the New England countryside selling short sixes and long nines — so named from the size and bundle — made with all-Connecticut leaf or Connecticut filler and Cuban or Maryland wrapper. After factory operations were well established, Havana filler with a Connecticut wrapper began to be used. What became known as the half-Spanish cigar had a favorable effect on local markets, and as manufacturers began to blend Cuban and Brazilian with native leaf, demand for quality Connecticut leaf created warehouses for packing and shipping to New York and other cigar-manufacturing centers.

Larger cigar manufacturers began to emerge after an experimental transplant of Maryland broadleaf resulted in 1830s Connecticut broadleaf, which had an elegant, light-bodied, fine finish, for binder and wrapper. Then:

Sometime in the early 1870's, under the supervision of state and federal soil and plant specialists, experiments were again undertaken with carefully selected Havana seeds. . . . The leaf obtained after a few crops was . . . not only excellent as a binder but was far superior to any of domestic growth as a wrapper. . . . Seeds were imported for each new sowing and the plants obtained from them for the first three years were known as "Spanish" or "Havana." After a necessary cultivation of four years in Connecticut soil the type acquired certain desired characteristics and was then called "Havana Seed" [and later] became generally known as "American" as distinct from "Spanish."[26]

Writing almost a century later, in the 1950s, P. J. Anderson, an agronomist with the Connecticut Agricultural Experiment Station, recorded that the name of the man who imported the seed was not known:

[But p]robably he hoped to duplicate in Connecticut the aroma and other qualities for which the tobacco of Cuba is famous. Although the seed evidently came from Cuba, today there is no district in that island which grows tobacco like it. . . . By generations of selection and acclimatization here, the size and shape of the leaf have so changed that we fail to recognise the Cuban ancestor.[27]

After the Civil War, competition from Pennsylvania and Wisconsin's dark leaf halted New England expansion, then the development of the new Havana seed tobacco and the return to light-colored cigars restored the competitive advantage that Connecticut had over other U.S. growers. However, they faced a strong new foreign competitor.

European manufacturers had, since the 1860s, been using Dutch East Indies Sumatra wrapper; a sample shipment reached New York manufacturers in 1876, and by the 1880s, it was being imported there. In 1883, alarmed farmers formed the New England Tobacco Growers Association, which petitioned Congress for tariff restrictions, as a result of which duties increased from $0.35 to $0.75 per pound, and again to $2 in 1890. They were reduced to $1.50 in 1894 for three years, after which they increased to $1.85, yet this did not stop imports increasing, as domestic cigar consumption rose, such that annual U.S. purchases of Sumatra tobacco in the 1890s approached $6 million. In 1900, 5 million pounds of leaf were still being imported, and only the high tariff levels enabled Connecticut growers to survive economically. The long-term solution was to develop a leaf that could compete in quality with the Sumatra wrapper.

Experiments in 1898, supervised by the U.S. Bureau of Plant Industry, resulted in just such a leaf, destined to become Connecticut shade: U.S. Type 61. The first experiment, in 1900, in the small town of Poquonock, was carried out by Dr. E. H. Jenkins, director of the Connecticut Agricultural Experiment Station, with Marcus Floyd, of the USDA's Division of Soils, who had experience in Florida shade and chose soil comparable to that of Florida.[28] The story is recounted thus:

From one field a superior crop developed from Cuban seeds. Unlike its richly flavoured parent, it was completely bland in taste. Experimentally, some of the wrappers were entered in an exhibition at St. Louis in 1904 and won a prize. . . . The seeds of numerous varieties continued to be planted, a specific seed to each separate acre. Of the many specimens that finally evolved, four types were found to have merit. Among these were Uncle Sam Sumatra and Hazlewood Cuban.

It was the latter that received approval as best for growing under shade in Connecticut soil, and potentially the most profitable. . . . Seed selection among Connecticut Valley farmers became so expert and so precise that experienced Cuban farmers turned to buy tobacco seeds from the Yankees.[29]

Anderson's 1950s account concurs:

In the original tests, seed was imported from Sumatra. The experiment proved this variety was unsuited to shade culture and seed from Cuba was tried. After a few years of selection, the Cuban type became established and its culture spread until it reached about 9,000 acres. . . . The variety is identical to the tobacco grown generally in Cuba today but has been more carefully selected for uniformity. . . . Its only competitor is the imported Sumatra wrapper. . . . The common Cuban strain was for many years the only one grown under cloth but in recent years new higher-yielding strains have been developed and are rapidly replacing the old Cuban. . . . Connecticut 15, Connecticut 49, and Fowler Special are now grown on more acres than common Cuban.[30]

After additional experiments with seed, curing, and fertilizer, shade dramatically changed the Connecticut landscape.[31] Whereas thousands of small, independent farmers had grown broadleaf and Havana seed outside tobacco in combination with other crops, shade required substantial investment in poles, wires, and netting beyond the resources of the average farmer. Because of the high initial investment required, increased production costs, and greater financial risks, shade was dominated by a small number of large companies, some owned outside the state with investments in other cigar leaf areas, cigar manufacture, or tobacco trading.

The Connecticut Tobacco Company, formed in 1901 by Marcus Floyd and a group of Connecticut growers, was one of the first. In 1917, it merged with American Sumatra, with its extensive holdings in Florida-Georgia, and by the mid-1930s, American Sumatra was the largest single producer of cigar tobacco in Connecticut, owning six thousand acres and sorting and packing facilities in Bloomfield and East Hartford. Other leading corporations were Cullman Brothers (subsequently Culbro), Consolidated, General, Imperial, and Hartman (formed in 1928 as a result of the consolidation of several smaller companies). Prominent growers included Windsor Shade, formed in 1937 by a group of independents, though shade land was mostly owned and rented out under a variety of leasing arrangements. Growers formed cooperatives in an attempt to maintain fair prices for their product, the first recorded being the warehouse system in Hartford in 1852, which was disbanded in 1862 and only briefly reorganized in 1870. In the early twentieth century, a major cooperative was the Connecticut Valley Tobacco Growers Association (CVTGA), and others followed.[32]

After being hard hit in the 1920s and 1930s with the drop in cigar consumption, cigar mechanization, and the demand for smaller and cheaper cigars, the onset of World War II saw concerns that unfair competition from abroad was approaching crisis level:

Tobacco is imported into this country that is grown and produced by indentured labor — coolies who received but a few cents a day and are forced to work for a given period of time or suffer the consequences. This ever-increasing tendency to use tobacco that is produced by almost slave labor, that employed foreign capital, foreign material and equipment, is slowly piling on the last few straws which tend to break the camel's back. . . . Only in the last few years under trade agreements, the import duty has been cut from $2.35 a pound to $1.50 a pound, on Sumatra tobacco.[33]

In 1940, Dr. Boyd, an economist at Storrs Agricultural Station, demonstrated that Connecticut alone could supply wrapper for the 2.5 billion cigars then wrapped with imported tobacco. He called for the state to foster this project and end the decreasing duties on imports from low-wage or no-wage countries — the last cut of nearly 40 percent having resulted in a drastic drop in acreage — and for a campaign to smoke valley-wrapped cigars.[34] Nothing, however, would stem the tide of late-twentieth-century decline.

To Homogenization, Migration, and Relocation

In 1954, homogenized binder was introduced, whereby scrap filler, stems, and leaves that would otherwise be rejected were reduced to powder; mixed with water and cellulose adhesive; and formed into thin, paperlike sheets cut to the desired width. This reconstituted tobacco, classified as "manufactured binder sheet" and fed automatically from a spool into cigar-making machines, with substantially reduced labor and raw materials manufacturing costs, was a technological development that salvaged up to 40 percent of what had before been scrap or at best converted to nonbinder use. As reported in a spate of articles in the local *Hartford Courant* and *Hartford Times*, this was to exacerbate a dramatically imposed reduction in acreage and was subsequently compounded with the introduction of processed cigar wrapper as well.[35]

By the early 1960s, the annual cost of equipment, maintenance, materials, supplies, and services required in Connecticut tobacco production was estimated at around $23 million, and a visual cost-cutting change came when shade growers switched from white to orange cloth — the color came from the lead chromate that impregnated the cloth to make it last longer.[36]

The local press reported more dramatic downturns in the late 1960s and 1970s, and more federal price-support policies, as well as the 1966 Federal Crop Land Adjustment Program, provided subsidies to growers while they experimented with new crops or found new jobs. The climate was one of downturn for even major companies such as Consolidated and Bayuk Cigars; and the Connecticut-Massachusetts Tobacco Cooperative, the receiving agency for tobacco under the government price-support program, was taking about two-thirds of binder tobacco.[37]

By the 1940s, more than half the grading and sizing of wrapper was being done in Puerto Rico. Some of the wrapper went into cigars made on the island, but most returned for machine manufacture on the U.S. mainland. During World War II, special wartime shade labor arrangements were made, and in 1942, the Shade Tobacco Growers Association (STGA) was set up to help underwrite the expense of housing, food, medical care, and transportation for seasonal workers.

Growers had long met their labor requirements in various ways, some more savory than others. They employed child labor, until this was legislated against, and then local high school students during their summer holidays.[38] Many of those who worked the tobacco as students reminisced in *Windsor Storyteller* how hard and dirty the work was but also how welcome the money was for them and their families, and the fun they had in what for the community was almost a "rite of passage."[39]

Growers turned further afield for their main sources of labor, and the successive waves of migrant labor appear to have had less fun. In the 1920s and 1930s, students were bused up from black colleges of the U.S. South.[40] They, too, welcomed the work for the money but met with racial hostility, as did the Jamaicans subsequently brought up during World War II under agreement with the British colonial government.[41] From the 1950s to the 1970s, the growers flew in Puerto Ricans under agreement with the Puerto Rican Migration Division. Specially created to meet agricultural labor needs along the Eastern Seaboard, the division functioned as an escape valve in the areas of Puerto Rican tobacco that collapsed when U.S. companies pulled out. The conditions Puerto Rican migrant workers faced came in for heavy criticism, and the program was finally brought to an end in 1974.[42] Since then, reduced numbers of day laborers have been bused in, many of them Central American, Mexican, and Chicano, as well as Hartford-resident descendants of Jamaicans and Puerto Ricans.

Only Consolidated Cigar — then a subsidiary of Gulf and Western and the largest grower in the area, accounting for 45 percent of acres planted — and General Cigar's Culbro division increased growing. Hartman, like many others, had switched to vegetable farming, reducing tobacco to 75 of its 1,289 acres and leasing its Windsor Tobacco Farm to Consolidated.[43]

Although the antismoking crusade following the 1964 Report of the Surgeon General was directed mainly against cigarettes, it did affect cigars: airlines, for example, while introducing smoking and no-smoking sections, banned cigar and pipe smoking. By 1979, U.S. cigar sales had dropped 50 percent from the 9.1 billion units sold in 1964.[44] Two years later, in 1981, Consolidated launched a $5 million advertising campaign for Backwoods, a "wild 'n mild" cigar, in an attempt to lure younger smokers, but within months, it, too, had cut half of its 1,800 acres of tobacco land.[45]

By then, only half of the tobacco crop grown by Hartford County's eighty independent farmers was sold commercially, and farmers were forced to sell to the government at break-even prices.[46] As the *New York Times* reported, in Connecticut, "Shrinking markets, rising prices, a decrease in cigar smoking and an increase in foreign competition — as well as torrential rains and flooding in the wettest June in memory — have hastened the atrophy of the once muscular industry."[47]

Connecticut made a limited comeback in response to a new generation of cigar smokers as the late 1980s revalidated a get-rich, conspicuous-consumption culture of socializing with fine liquors and cigars. Then 1990s health research findings extended to mouth and throat cancer associated with cigar smoking as well as the lung cancer associated with cigarette smoking, and new health warnings were introduced on packaging. In the early 1960s, the Connecticut tobacco industry may have optimistically estimated that business would not suffer unduly from government findings on smoke and health, because cigarette smoking was the villain,[48] but by the 1990s, the antitobacco lobby had gained significant ground.

The Boston-based Tobacco Divestment Project targeted three Hartford-area insurance firms — AETNA, Travelers, and Cigna — to divest their tobacco stocks: City University New York and Harvard were the first two universities to eliminate their stock holdings; in 1991, the Yale–New Haven Hospital announced it would sell its tobacco stocks, and Yale University was considering divestment; and in 1992, West Hartford Beth Israel Synagogue became the first Reform Jewish Congregation in North America to divest its stocks.[49]

When the early 1990s cigar revival came, with the newly founded New York glossy *Cigar Aficionado* embarking on its anti-antismoking quest, a Connecticut feature was prominent: "That tobacco is grown in Connecticut is certainly a surprise to the uninitiated," said Daniel Nuñez, director of Culbro Tobacco's Connecticut and Dominican Republic operations.[50] Many top producers of cigars, especially from the Dominican Republic, fought to get best-quality Connecticut wrappers for their cigars, because they were among the best to buy, the article declared. Davidoff cigars, once made in Cuba, also used the best-available Connecticut wrapper on Dominican-produced cigars. "A nice Connecticut wrapper," declared Christophe Kull, president of Davidoff of Geneva's U.S. operations, "is like the skin on a baby's bottom, very silky, very fine. From a marketing point of view, it is considered at the moment to be one of the best tasting and looking wrappers available."

The high price of Connecticut tobacco, it was explained, reflected high labor, land, and other costs of running a U.S.-based operation. "Connecticut wrapper is very expensive," agreed Carlos Fuente, president of Tabacalera A. Fuente y Compañía, the Tampa-based firm that relocated to the Dominican Republic to produce handmade premium cigars:

But the producers of Connecticut wrapper run first-class operations, and, additionally, the sorting has been very good. You can always count on high quality, and aside from being expensive, it sells. . . . Though wrapper leaf tobacco seed varieties developed in the valley have been planted in Costa Rica, the Dominican Republic, Honduras, Mexico, Panama and other places, no one has yet been able to duplicate the color, flavour and texture of the Connecticut Valley leaf.

Yet by the early 1990s, Consolidated, General, and other smaller companies had relocated operations offshore, and only a handful of farms remained. Culbro, which a decade previously had operated seven farms on 1,300 acres, had only four farms on 400 acres in 1992 and only 200 acres planted with tobacco, having cut production by half in 1991. Culbro's Ed Cullman explained:

We are growing a lot less tobacco than we used to grow, but these things tend to go in waves. The valley as a whole is growing about 1,200 acres. In 1970, there were nine billion cigars being consumed; now there are just over two billion. That's a huge change that occurred in the cigar business, and it has to be reflected in the growing of wrappers in Connecticut.

The other remaining leaf processor was Windsor Shade, then a cooperative of twelve farmers, working about a thousand acres between them. In 1998, as the 1990s cigar boom peaked, Consolidated cultivated a modest 150 acres, while Enfield Shade farmed 400 acres supplying wrapper to Altadis USA.

Java and Besuki Leaf

Although Sumatra, Connecticut, and Cuba may have attained preeminence for quality leaf, Java's central principalities and residency of Besuki overtook all of them in volume. In Besuki, George Birnie, a Dutch agricultural extension worker, was convinced that tobacco could grow well in Bondowoso and Jember. Together with C. Sandenberg and A. D. van Gennep, in 1859, he established De Landbouw-Maatschappij Oud-Djember (LMOD). Other pioneers were J. D. Franssen van de Putte (De Landbouw-Maatschappij Soekowono) and Ry van Beest Holle and Geertsema (De Cultuur Maaatschappij Djelboek). In the Klaten regency of the central principality of Surakarta, the Dorrepaal family, backed by strong financial connections, formed Cultuur Maatschappij, CM-Wedi-Birit (CM) and competed with Deli and Besuki.

Ratna Saptari's comparative work on tobacco regimes in Dutch-colonial Sumatra and Java links the emergence of Nienhuys in Sumatra with Birnie and Dorrepaal in Java to 1860s increased demand for leaf tobacco as the Dutch Culture System was reaching its end and state intervention was giving way to a larger and stronger role for private enterprise.[51] All formed estates according to different local arrangements. The apanage system, which was in Java unique to the central principalities, gave benefits to companies through local village heads, but the Dutch never applied it to the directly ruled parts. There, the 1856 Landrental Law enabled investors to hire land for twenty years. This was subsequently replaced by *erfpacht* for up to seventy years, later reduced to fifty years, but otherwise unchanged until nationalization in 1958.

In Besuki, short-lease farmland was initially restricted to dry lands, but diminishing yields led to its extension to irrigated lands as well from the mid-1870s. After 1875, *erfpacht* was granted on extensive uncultivated areas of Jember, where tobacco became the primary crop. By 1883, LMOD leased 5,700 hectares (14,000 acres) of irrigated lands and 4,300 hectares (10,600 acres) of dry land. By 1908, the figures had risen to 16,000 hectares (40,000 acres) and 11,000 hectares (27,000 acres), respectively, and LMOD controlled 11,400 hectares (28,000 acres) of *erfpacht* land. In the early 1900s, Amsterdam-Besoeki Tabak Maatschappij (ABTM) established estates in Jember. Planters set up the Besoeki Immigration Bureau, bringing in mainly Madurese and later Javanese, from densely populated areas of Central and East Java, as a result of which Besuki had the highest migrant population.

Dutch companies also purchased cigar tobacco that local peasants grew under conditions that conceded peasants weak rights over the land they cultivated but exacted heavy labor obligations. In 1917, peasant rights were increased and company rental rights reduced, but the strong influence of companies over local rulers and the Dutch authorities enabled production with very low costs and very high profits, especially from 1890 to 1915 and in the 1920s.

In the early twentieth century, there were two major types of tobacco — Kedu, for cigar binder and filler, and Deli, wrapper — grown primarily on lowland Jember. But in the 1920s, a hybrid of Deli and Kedu gradually expanded, such that hybrid and Kedu became the types grown. Tobacco exports through the main Besuki port of Panurukan accounted for 20 percent of total tobacco exports from Java, on par with Semarang, the main port for Central Java Province. In its heyday, from 1926 to 1930, Besuki supplied 25 percent of Java exports, exceeding any other region of Java.

Tobacco was grown on both dry and wet land leased from peasants on relatively short five-year leases and on *erfpacht* land, made possible because it was still relatively sparsely populated in comparison with other parts of Java, especially the hinterland of Besuki, the Bondowoso, Jember, and Banyuwangi regencies. Smallholder farmers (*vrimantabak*) were also important, their share of exports and acreage often exceeding plantation tobacco.

Two regional studies by Indonesian scholars on Besuki Residency are illuminating. Writing in the 1990s, Soegijanto Padmo traced the transition from small-scale development from the 1860s to the 1890s, with several individually owned estates producing tobacco and other cash crops, to corporatization in the 1880s, with more specialized production by fewer and larger companies from 1890 to 1920.[52] During the final years of Dutch rule, the degree of consolidation was such that the Klaten and Besuki regencies were each basically under the control of one major corporation, the Klaten Estate Company and LMOD, and after 1958, under the new state tobacco company regional groupings Pusat Perkebunan Negara Baru (PPN-Baru or PPN).

S. Nawiyanto critiqued what he saw as the negative bias of Dutch and Indonesian historiography on the devastating effects of Japanese occupation.[53] He documented how the Dutch, anticipating war in 1939, were already turning export cash-crop plantations over to food production, in effect starting what has been described as the Japanization of rice farming in Indonesia. Besuki Residency, which had become the leading center of twentieth-century Indonesian agricultural production, was then targeted for the highest quota of forced rice delivery imposed by the Japanese, to feed the troops and for wartime self-sufficiency.

Tobacco was at the time the most important export crop, run by large-scale companies, on both farm and plantation, drawing in waves of Madurese and Javanese migration. Cultivation restriction policies — of up to 60 percent for large plantations — during the Depression had taken their toll, but there were signs of recovery in the years before the Japanese invaded. Under the occupation, however, producers lost their Dutch and other international markets, and tobacco fields were converted to meet each residency's quota of rice. In June 1943, it was decided that Hatabako Company buy all tobacco exclusively, buying was concentrated in six store houses, and farmers were allowed to produce tobacco only for domestic consumption and some export to the other Indonesian islands as part of mutual exchange for nonmilitary commodities.

The collapse of the plantation economy weighed heavily on the peasantry, whose income derived mainly from the plantation sector, and Jember was one area where parts of estate lands were redistributed to produce food. This was a time bomb when plantation owners came to reclaim their *erfpacht* rights and came into conflict with squatters, who were strongly supported among Indonesian nationalist circles. In effect, Nawiyanto argues, the profound reorientation of commodity production during the Japanese period helped cement the foundations for independence and nationalization.[54]

Fast-forward to 2009 and James Suckling's *Cigar Aficionado* article with which I opened: "Listen to the tobacco. The massive warehouse is silent except for the sound of tobacco leaves in motion. Hundreds of young women build and dismantle piles of tobacco that have just arrived from the fields located around the city of Jember, in Indonesia's East Java province."[55] They worked in silence. "We forbid our workers to speak while they work. Otherwise, they may make a mistake. They must work meticulously. The tobacco must be handled with respect," said Sin Teguh Wanamarta, a Dutch-trained physician working with his father, Eddy Dharsan Wanamarta, processing and trading tobacco at their company, PT Ledokombo. Chinese Indonesians, the Wanamartas were two of a handful of key tobacco men in and around Jember buying, processing, packing, and shipping tobacco around the world in the boom 1990s.

Suckling celebrated the Sumatra wrapper leaf that had spawned the Sumatra-seed cigar tobacco grown in many regions of the Americas, mainly for use in machine-made cigars. However, he explained, Java tobacco was cheaper and more readily available; and although tobacco grown in East Java, particularly near Jember, was important to premium cigar makers, a lot of poor tobacco was also grown and shipped to manufacturers supplying the U.S. cigar market. "People could see the money," said Jan Meskens of the Netherlands-based Indoco International, which marketed and sold tobacco from Indonesian processor PT Tempu Rejo. "You had just about anyone setting up and trading in tobacco. It was bananas. We just kept supplying our regular customers, but plenty of people wanted tobacco from us. We did not speculate; but others around us certainly did."

In the mid-1990s, Jember tobacco dealers were receiving visits from U.S. buyers who had never set foot in Indonesia before. Although the boom lasted for only two or three harvests, companies took advantage of the situation and just about anything passing for cigar tobacco was sold, mostly to European manufacturers such as the French SEITA, Swedish Match, Dutch Agio, and Swiss Burger Group, which together accounted for close to half the global cigar market. "No one could keep up with the demand," Meskens commented.

Wrapper was grown mostly south of Jember, and to the north filler, on which European manufacturers had a monopoly. One U.S. company that maintained its supplies of quality tobacco from Java during the boom was Consolidated. In the early 1990s, Tempu Rejo and PT Perkebunan Nusantara had developed a premium version of *tembakau bawah naungan* (TBN, "tobacco under sheet," or shade grown).[56] The TBN was a cross between what had come to be known as Besuki tobacco and Connecticut shade. A lot of tobacco sold as TBN, however, was either shade-grown Besuki or an inferior tobacco grown outside the region resembling TBN, called *vorstenlanden bawah naungan* (VBN), grown in central Java. Consolidated first used TBN on machine-made cigars for several years, before using it on some key handmade brands; and many cigar manufacturers today use Indonesian binder and wrapper.

Driving around Jember in 1999, Suckling reported that it was difficult to see a house without tobacco drying in the sun. Most was for cigarette production, as cigar production was small and of uneven quality. The only premium cigar factory was in Pandaan, near Surabaya, which Swedish Match had opened three years earlier. Heralding what a "modern, well-financed Cuban factory might look like," Suckling quoted the project manager Van Hattem celebrating its workers: "It's not just money here that motivates workers like it is in the Caribbean. They have pride in their work. They are slower than rollers in other countries, but their quality is excellent." Contrast this with a Jember tobacco worker who commented, "It's amazing that more people do not riot considering their situation." That worker also added that a few tobacco-drying barns had been burned that September in protest: "It is so difficult for us to survive."[57]

El Habano or *Snus?*

In 1995, four years before Suckling's Java article, as the U.S.-engineered cigar boom of the 1990s was gathering momentum and Cuba was seeking ways out of the depths of its early 1990s crisis, Suckling reported for *Cigar Aficionado* on Connecticut-seed tobacco for shade wrapper being grown in the Partido tobacco district of Havana province.[58] Not as prestigious as El Corojo tobacco grown in the Vuelta Abajo tobacco district of Pinar del Río province, destined for the handmade Habano, the Connecticut seed was mostly destined for small, European, machine-made cigars. It was a Cuban joint venture with Lippoel Leaf BV in the Netherlands, which described the leaf as "Cuban-grown shade tobacco of the Connecticut type," meeting the demand for light-colored shade tobacco.

In the words of Adriano Martínez, of Habanos S.A., "It has an important place in the market, and we want a part of the action. I can't see how any of the growers or manufacturers of cigars with Connecticut wrapper should care. Most of them have made a point of growing Cuban seed tobacco; so it's the same thing." The Cubans hoped to tap into the European market with better-quality Connecticut at a lower price. The small cigars could also be sold as 100 percent Havana leaf, which would be a plus in many European countries, especially France.

The Cubans did not expect to sell their Connecticut wrapper tobacco to makers of handmade cigars in the Dominican Republic or Honduras, because it would be illegal to sell cigars with Cuban-grown wrappers in the United States. Nor did they see Cuba as an option: "We could use the Connecticut wrapper grown here, but we won't," declared Martínez. "We will never do that, since it would change the character of the cigars. Our cigars have a unique character and this has not included Connecticut wrapper."

Suckling quoted a tobacco expert familiar with the Cuban project and the global market for tobacco as saying, "It doesn't taste like Cuban leaf and it doesn't taste like Connecticut. If you want to do Connecticut, why do it outside [the state]? There is so much land out there still to be planted in Connecticut, but everybody around the world is copying Connecticut. You can find it in Ecuador or wherever, even in Indonesia." He also reported General Cigar President Austin McNamara's comment: "The most generous thing I can say is that it is an honor and privilege having the Cubans recognize Connecticut as an important tobacco by planting it themselves."

Potentially, the Cubans could plant up to two thousand acres of Connecticut tobacco — nearly the total shade-leaf planting in the Connecticut Valley. But Cuban Partido's enterprise manager, Rafael Collazo, said, "It all depends on the demand in the market. . . . It is a commodity. This whole thing is totally commercial. It is clear, given the economic situation that we are in, that we need to find new sources for hard currency."

Forward again to 1999 and *Cigar Aficionado* veteran reporter David Savona penned a feature on Connecticut shade.[59] Nothing, he wrote, seems to draw cigar smokers like oily, golden-brown Connecticut shade. Savona quoted Theo W. Folz, president and chief executive officer of Consolidated Cigar, as saying, "I would estimate that 50 percent of the handmade cigars sold [in the United States] are made with Connecticut-shade tobacco." He wrote of Connecticut growers proudly recounting Connecticut inventions, like the automated sewing machine stitching tobacco leaves together for hanging in the barns, which elsewhere is done slowly, by hand — and more cheaply, one might add. Tobacco barns elsewhere can be built for a fraction of the cost of those in Connecticut, which have to withstand the cold and snow of winter and need gas burners to create tropical conditions for curing.

In the drive to push down costs, the quest for cheap labor was clearly a prime determinant in the demise of Connecticut and the rise of Indonesia. Cuba's 1959 revolution aimed to break with this, but Cuba's proud export product, *El Habano,* still had to navigate these international waters. Historians tend to study developments in a particular nation, but the nation-state is not always the logical unit of analysis, nor does the world consist solely of interacting national communities. Rather, by reason of commodity flows, migration, wars, and such, people create their own cross-national systems,[60] themselves "de-essentialising" national history, as Don Fernando Ortiz has so evocatively suggested.

But where and with what does the future lie? Swedish Match was the leading premium cigar manufacturer in the United States, with substantial machine-made cigars businesses in both the United States and Europe and main markets in the United States, France, Spain, Benelux, Germany, and Australia. It had played an important role in the industrial and commercial sector in Sweden since the early twentieth century. Its tobacco operations began with AB Svenska Tobaksmonopolet, a monopoly founded in 1915, and Svenska Tändsticks AB, in 1917. The two merged in 1992 as the Procordia Group, and in 1994, they were joined under the company name Swedish Match, whose U.S. and European foothold came through buying and selling acquisitions. In 2007, for example, the company acquired Bogaert Cigars, which had been producing machine-made cigars since 1937 in Jabbeke, Belgium, and in Pasuruan, for France, Germany, the Netherlands, and Belgium, and PT Java cigar manufacturing in Indonesia. In 2009, it had ten production plants, the main ones in the United States, Dominican Republic, Honduras, Belgium, and Indonesia — the others were in Brazil, Bulgaria, the Netherlands, the Philippines, and Sweden. The company distributed third parties' tobacco products on the Swedish market, and it derived more than half its sales and two-thirds of operating profits from cigars and from *snus.*[61]

Snus is the company's landmark product. It is claimed that when more than 1 million Swedes emigrated across the Atlantic from 1846 until 1930, they took with them their tradition of *snus*, such that it became an identity mark for Swedes, and main streets of Swedish American districts came to be called *snus* boulevards. *Snus* began to regain popularity in the late 1960s, after the documented health risks associated with smoking. By 2006, 220 million cans of *snus* were sold to about 1 million users in Sweden — nearly one-fifth of whom were women — and in 2010, Swedish Match promoted itself as the market leader in smoke-free tobacco, especially *snus*, its fastest-growing product in both Sweden and the United States.

In 2010, Indonesia, one of the world's largest tobacco producers, was the only Southeast Asian country not to have ratified the World Health Organization's Framework Convention on Tobacco Control. Pressure on government not to sign came from the tobacco sector, the livelihood of whose 600,000 workers and 3.5 million farmers would be hit.[62] The fate of Connecticut, by contrast, appeared to be sealed, and that of Cuba, in the balance. Cuba had stepped up its health-related domestic antismoking campaign, and in late 2009, it announced a 30 percent reduction in growing, as international markets for both leaf and cigars were down. The 2009–2010 harvest, however, was good, and sales were better than expected. That is a story beyond the confines of this article, but the question is whether, with or without the U.S. embargo, *El Habano* will continue to hold its own. Or is *snus* the future?

NOTES

This article is derived from a paper presented at the International Workshop of the Netherlands-funded Plants, People, and Work Project, held in Yogyakarta, Java, Indonesia, in August 2009. My research has been made possible by Rockefeller Scholarships at the University of Florida's Center for Latin American Studies, Florida International University's Cuba Research Institute, and the University of Puerto Rico's Caribbean 2000 Programme; funding from London Metropolitan University's Caribbean Studies Centre and the Commodities of Empire British Academy Research Project, a collaboration between the Open University's Ferguson Center for African and Asian Studies and the University of London's Institute for the Study of the Americas; and the many colleagues who over the years have so generously facilitated my field and archival research.

1. James Suckling, "Tobacco Mecca: Indonesia's East Java Continues to Produce Fine Tobacco Despite Its Troubled Economy," *Cigar Aficionado*, January/February 2009, http://www.cigaraficionado.com/Cigar/CA_Archives/CA_Show_Article/0,2322,381,00.html. Since it was founded in 1992, *Cigar Aficionado* has been an invaluable source of feature articles, reportage, and news on the Havana cigar and the global cigar world, and its entire archive is available online.

2. There is a considerable body of work on the significance of Cuban tobacco, especially the Havana cigar: the Cuban ethnographer Fernando Ortiz's classic *Cuban Counterpoint: Tobacco and Sugar* (1940; repr., Philadelphia: Temple University Press, 1995); former cigar maker Gaspar Jorge García Galló's *Biografía del tabaco habano*, 2nd ed. (1959; repr., Havana: Comisión Nacional del Tabaco Habano, 1961); Cuban historian José Rivero Muñiz's *Tabaco: Su historia en Cuba*, 2 vols. (Havana: Instituto de Historia, Comisión Nacional de la Academia de Ciencias de Cuba, 1965), as

well as studies such as Jean Stubbs, *Tobacco on the Periphery: A Case Study in Cuban Labour History, 1860–1958* (London: Cambridge University Press, 1985). Recent promotional publications include those by Cubans Eumelio Espino Marrero, *Cuban Cigar Tobacco: Why Cuban Cigars Are the World's Best* (Neptune City, NJ: T. F. H. Publications, 1996); Enzo A. Infante Urivazo, *Havana Cigars, 1817–1960* (Neptune City, NJ: T. F. H. Publications, 1997); and Antonio Núñez Jiménez, *The Journey of the Havana Cigar* (Neptune City, NJ: T. F. H. Publications, 1998). They all have a national focus but make reference to the many falsifications at home and abroad. See also Charles Del Todesco, *The Havana Cigar: Cuba's Finest* (New York: Abbeville Press, 1997); Gerard Pere et Fils, *Havana Cigars* (Paris: Seul, 1995; repr., Edison, NJ: Wellfleet Press, 1997).

3. Little work connects the various offshore economies and communities, but a recent landmark exception is Araceli Tinajero, *El lector de tabaquería: Historia de una tradición cubana* (Madrid: Editorial Verbum, 2007), which links the institution of reading in Cuba, New York, Tampa, Puerto Rico, Mexico, and Spain. Evan M. Daniel is working on a transnational cigar worker history: "Rolling for the Revolution: A Transnational History of Cuban Cigar Makers in Havana, South Florida and New York City, 1850s–1890s," paper presented at the 2006 Latin American Studies Association Congress, San Juan, Puerto Rico.

4. See the introduction by Fernando Coronil in Ortiz, *Cuban Counterpoint*, xxviii.

5. For a discussion, see Jean Stubbs, "Tobacco in the Contrapunteo: Ortiz and the Havana Cigar," in *Cuban Counterpoints: The Legacy of Fernando Ortiz*, ed. Mauricio Font and Alfonso Quiroz (Lanham, MD: Lexington, 2004), 105–23; Jean Stubbs, "Havana Cigars and the West's Imagination," in *Smoke: A Global History of Smoking*, ed. Sander L. Gilman and Zhou Xun (London: Reaktion Press, 2004), 134–39. Juan José Baldrich highlights the strong connections among Cuba, Puerto Rico, and the United States in "From Handcrafted Tobacco Rolls to Machine-Made Cigarettes: The Transformation and Americanization of Puerto Rican Tobacco, 1847–1903," *Centro Journal* 17 (Fall 2005): 144–69; Juan José Baldrich, "Cigars and Cigarettes in Nineteenth Century Cuba," *Revista/Review Interamericana* 24 (Spring/Winter 1994): 8–35.

6. The best-known Cuban émigré local histories are on Key West and Tampa: A. Stuart Campbell, *The Cigar Industry of Tampa* (Tampa, FL: University of Tampa, 1939); L. Glenn Westfall, *Don Vicente Martínez Ybor, the Man and His Empire: Development of the Clear Havana Industry in Cuba and Florida in the Nineteenth Century* (New York: Garland, 1987); L. Glenn Westfall, *Key West: Cigar City U.S.A.* (Key West, FL: Historic Key West Preservation Board, 1984). Historical overviews include Gerald E. Poyo, "The Cuban Experience in the United States, 1865–1940: Migration, Community and Identity," *Cuban Studies* 21 (1991): 19–36. Louis A. Pérez Jr. pioneered cigar-worker histories of Tampa in "Reminiscences of a *Lector*: Cuban Cigar Makers in Tampa," *Florida Historical Quarterly* 53 (1975): 443–49. Others more recently include Nancy A. Hewitt's exploration of labor, gender, and race in *Southern Discomfort: Women's Activism in Tampa, Florida, 1800s–1920s* (Urbana: University of Illinois Press, 2001); Robert P. Ingalls and Louis A Pérez Jr., *Tampa Cigar Workers: A Pictorial History* (Gainesville: University Press of Florida, 2003). For the interconnections with race, see Susan D. Greenbaum, *Afro-Cubans in Ybor City: A Centennial History* (Tampa, FL: Tampa Printing, 1986); Susan D. Greenbaum, *More Than Black: Afro-Cubans in Tampa* (Gainesville: University Press of Florida, 2002); Evilio Grillo, *Black Cuban, Black American: A Memoir*, introduction by Kenya Dworkin y Méndez (Houston, TX: Arte Público Press, 2000); Winston James, "From a Class for Itself to a Race on Its Own: The Strange Case of Afro-Cuban Radicalism and Afro-Cubans in Florida, 1870–1940," in *Holding Aloft the Banner of Ethiopia: Caribbean Radicalism in Early Twentieth-Century America*, ed. Winston James (London: Verso, 1998), 232–57. There is a far more voluminous literature on Puerto Rican émigré communities in the United States, and there is reference to nineteenth-century Cuban cigar makers alongside Puerto Ricans in New York in the celebrated memoirs of Puerto Rican émigré cigar maker Bernard Vega, in César Andreu Iglesias, ed., *Memoirs of Bernardo Vega* (1977; repr.,

New York: Monthly Review Press, 1984). They also feature in the forthcoming work of Lisandro Pérez, *Cubans in Gotham: Immigrants, Exiles, and Revolution in Nineteenth-Century New York* (New York: New York University Press, 2010). For the lesser-known histories of Cuban tobacco in Jamaica and the Dominican Republic, see Jean Stubbs "Political Idealism and Commodity Production: Cuban Tobacco in Jamaica, 1870–1930," *Cuban Studies*, 25 (1995): 51–81; Jean Stubbs "Reinventing Mecca: Tobacco in the Dominican Republic, 1763–2007," Commodities of Empire Working Paper No. 3, Open University (October 2007), http://www.open.ac.uk/Arts/fergusoncentre/commodities-of-empire/working-papers/index.html

7. For the broader picture, see Maurice Corina, *Trust in Tobacco: The Anglo-American Struggle for Power* (London: Michael Joseph, 1974); for Cuba, see Stubbs, *Tobacco on the Periphery.*

8. A copy of the 1960 USDA Report is housed in the Special Collections Library of the University of Florida and provides statistical and qualitative evidence on the history and juncture at the time of the U.S. cigar industry, as well as the significant impact of the embargo on Cuban leaf imports. President John F. Kennedy famously ensured he had his supply of Havana cigars before signing the embargo into law.

9. Connecticut State Library, Hartford, holds a valuable Newspaper Clipping Files collection (CSL NCF) from which this and other features and reportage are taken.

10. Raymond Jahn, *The Dictionary of Tobacco* (New York: Philosophical Library, 1954).

11. Deli Universal N.V., available at http://www.deli-universal.nl.

12. See Lim Kim Liat, "The Deli Tobacco Industry: Its History and Outlook," in *Prospects for East Sumatran Plantation Industries: A Symposium*, ed. Douglas S. Paauw, South East Asian Studies Monograph Series No. 3 (New Haven, CT: Yale University Press, 1962), 1–19.

13. For general Indonesian economic history, see P. Creutzberg, ed., *Changing Economy in Indonesia: A Selection of Statistical Source Material from the Early 19th Century up to 1940*, 15 vols. (1975; repr., The Hague: M. Nijhoff, 1996); J. Th. Lindblad, ed., *Historical Foundations of a National Economy in Indonesia, 1890s–1990s* (North Holland: Koninkliijke Nederlands Akademie van Wetenschappen, 1996); J. Th. Lindblad, *New Challenges in the Modern Economic History of Indonesia* (Leiden: Programme of Indonesian Studies, 1993). For Sumatra plantation history, see Thee Kian-Wie, *Plantation Agriculture and Export Growth: An Economic History of East Sumatra, 1863–1942* (Jakarta: Indonesian Institute of Sciences [Leknas Lembaga Ilmu Pengetahuan Indonesia], 1977), and Ann Laura Stoler's excellent *Capitalism and Confrontation in Sumatra's Plantation Belt, 1870–1979*, 2nd ed. (Ann Arbor: University of Michigan Press, 1995).

14. For a discussion of the different colonial systems, see Jordan Goodman, *Tobacco in History: The Culture of Dependence* (London: Routledge, 1993).

15. Julius Lichtenstein, then president of American Sumatra Tobacco Company, is credited with bringing together six independent cigar manufacturers competing for sales in local markets with regional brands in 1918. In 1921, Consolidated Cigar Corporation, later Altadis USA and then Imperial, officially formed. One of the original six manufactured a brand called Dutch Masters, which became the new corporation's flagship brand and one of the biggest-dollar-volume cigar brands in the United States. The signature brand today is Montecristo.

16. See Maurice Duke and Daniel P. Jordan, eds., *Tobacco Merchant: The Story of Universal Leaf Tobacco Company* (Lexington: University Press of Kentucky, 1995). All major tobacco companies were diversifying in response to the growing antismoking lobby. Deli Universal moved primarily into lumber from the 1980s and, from the 1990s, into wood products for the burgeoning do-it-yourself sector in the Netherlands, Belgium, and Germany.

17. Ratna Saptari, "The Politics of Land, Labour and Leaf: Tobacco Regimes in Colonial Java and Sumatra (Late 19th–Early 20th Century)," paper presented at the workshop "Plants, People, and Work," Yogyakarta, Java, Indonesia, August 2009. Saptari highlights early-twentieth-century debates regarding working conditions coming to a head with a 1902 report and 1903 government-

commissioned investigation of conditions in East Coast Sumatra plantations and the Labor Inspectorate established in 1908. Yet Deli expansion continued unabated, and by 1912, more than two hundred plantations had 150,000 workers and 35,000 to 50,000 new recruits arriving each year.

18. Stoler, *Capitalism and Confrontation*, refers to silences as the quiet menace of a colonial past casting its shadow over the present. See also K. L. Pelzer, *Planters against Peasants: The Agrarian Struggle in East Sumatra, 1947–1958* (The Hague: Martinus Nijhoff, 1982); K. L. Pelzer, *Planter and Peasant: Colonial Policy and the Agrarian Struggle in East Sumatra, 1863–1947* (The Hague: Martinus Nijhoff, 1978); and Jan Breman, *Taming the Coolie Beast* (New York: Oxford University Press, 1989).

19. Margaret Buker Jay, "Historical Perspective," in *Changing Landscape through People: Connecticut Valley Tobacco, a Documentary of Photographs and Writing for the 1980s*, ed. Anadel Schnip and Katya Williamson (N.p.: n.d.). This volume is one of several nostalgic photographic books.

20. James F. O'Gorman, *Connecticut Valley Vernacular: The Vanishing Landscape and Architecture of the New England Tobacco Fields*, with photographs by Jack Delano (Philadelphia: University of Pennsylvania Press, 2002), 3.

21. Ibid., 5.

22. Mildred Savage, *Parrish* (New York: Simon & Schuster, 1958).

23. *Connecticut and Tobacco: A Chapter in America's Industrial Growth* (Washington, D.C.: Tobacco History, n.d.).

24. Ibid., 26. Iain Gately, *La Diva Nicotiana* (New York: Simon and Schuster, 2001), 172, in referring to Cuban tobacco flourishing with free trade after the end of the Spanish monopoly in 1817, states that although Havana cigars had a ready market in Europe, the main market was the United States. This dominance had existed ever since General Abe Putnam had participated in the British sack of Havana in 1762: "Putnam had loaded three donkeys with Havana cigars as his share of the plunder, which he sold singly to customers of a tavern he owned in Connecticut."

25. Ibid., 30.

26. Ibid., 35–38.

27. P. J. Anderson, "Growing Tobacco in Connecticut," *Connecticut Agricultural Experiment Station Bulletin*, 564 (January 1953): 10.

28. See Randall R. Kincaid, "Shade Tobacco Growing in Florida," *Quincy North Florida Experimental Station Bulletin* 136 (May 1960 [1956]): 3–43. Shade wrapper was an important crop in the Florida-Georgia area in the first half of the twentieth century. According to Kincaid, "About 1898, tests conducted at Quincy showed that leaves grown under artificial shade were of fine quality comparable to wrapper tobacco imported from Sumatra" (4). This was U.S. Type 62, which increased in acreage in the area from three thousand in 1921 to six thousand in 1960 (though there was a drop in the 1930s). Some three-quarters of this was in Florida, with a concentration in Gadsden County, but also in Leon and Madison in Florida and Decatur and Grady in Georgia. Kincaid reports the major single production costs as by far labor and farm supervision, followed by shade cloth and maintenance, then fertilizers. Cigar manufacturing was important during that period in Florida, with factories from Quincy in the north to Key West in the south, but with most in Tampa. Kincaid also refers to wrapper produced elsewhere, principally Connecticut Valley, Cuba, and Indonesia. In 1959, according to USDA figures, imports were principally from Cuba (seven hundred thousand pounds in comparison with imports from Indonesia (the year after nationalization of foreign companies there) of only fifty thousand pounds. See also W. B. Tisdale, "Tobacco Growing in Florida," *Florida Agricultural Experimental Station Bulletin* 198 (1928): 379–428.

29. *Connecticut and Tobacco*, 43–46.

30. Anderson, "Growing Tobacco," 1. States came to be known for their different tobaccos: Ohio and Pennsylvania, filler; Wisconsin, filler and wrapper; Connecticut Valley, binder and wrapper, especially Sumatra, deemed the finest wrapper with the exception of Cuba's, which was

produced in small quantity and first exported in 1900. Tobacco was grown from imported or Florida-grown seed, in beds preferably heated by artificial means and heavily fertilized. Both Cuban and Sumatran tobaccos were grown in the Northwest and West and, mainly, Cuban on the Florida peninsula. Sumatra harvesting was from June to September, whereas Cuban, especially under irrigation further south in Florida, had two main crops: spring and autumn. See Milton Whitney, "Methods of Curing Tobacco," *USDA Farmers' Bulletin* 6, 2nd rev. ed. (Washington, D.C.: Government Printing Office, 1902).

31. From the 1890s, the Connecticut Tobacco Valley Experiment Company in Poquonock carried out fertilizer experiments in tandem with experiments in curing tobacco. In the early 1920s, the Experimental Tobacco Station, directed by Anderson, was the only one in New England and one of only four or five in the United States.

32. The Dodd Research Center holds CVTGA records and printed materials for 1920–1949, as well as runs of the trade journals *Tobacco* (1920–1949) and *Tobacco Leaf* (1930–1944) and photocopies of *Connecticut Valley Tobacco Grower*, the official publication of CVTGA (1923–1927).

33. Merrill Crawford, "Tobacco Valley," *Connecticut Circle*, November 1940, 24. This marked Tobacco Valley Centenary, with photos and text.

34. Ibid., 29.

35. Examples of the many local press articles from the time are "Farmers Vote for Federal Price Support," "Referendum Vote Approves Quotas," "Nu Way Tobacco Co. Starts Production of Processed Cigar Binder," "Outdoor Acreage Reduced by 12.5%," and "Connecticut-Massachusetts Tobacco Cooperative." All from CSL NCF.

36. Synthetic fibers were also tested from time to time, but the preference remained for cotton. See "Shade-Grown Tobacco Lends Color to Valley" *Hartford Courant*, May 26, 1968, CSL NCF. In Brazil, black petroleum-based synthetic nets would be used.

37. See Russ Harvard, "Economics Shrinking State Tobacco Fields," *Hartford Courant*, February 7, 1972; Harold Street, "Consolidated Won't Buy Annual Broadleaf Crop," *Hartford Courant*, December 20, 1960; "Production of Valley Broadleaf Dropping This Year to New Low," *Hartford Courant*, March 1, 1961 — all CSL NCF.

38. Child labor is discussed in Jay, "Historical Perspective." For a press report, see John J. Egan, "Tobacco Child Labor under Fire by Labor Commissioner," *Hartford Times*, December 31, 1946, CSL NCF.

39. *Windsor Storyteller: A Chronicle of 20th Century Life in Windsor* (Windsor, CT: Windsor Historical Society, 1999).

40. A good discussion of this can be found in S. K. Close, "The Ties That Bind: Southwest Georgians, Black College Students, and Migration to Hartford," *Journal of South Georgia History* 15 (2000): 19–27. See also Marcia Hinckley, "'We just went on with it': The Black Experience in Windsor, Connecticut, 1790–1950," master's thesis, Trinity College, Connecticut, 1991. There was much local press coverage, as in "Florida Teenagers Work on Tobacco Farms," *Hartford Courant*, July 21, 1957, CSL NCF.

41. Fay Clarke Johnson provides a moving account in *Soldiers of the Soil* (New York: Vantage Press, 1995).

42. Chapter 2 in Ruth Glasser, *"Aquí me quedo": Puerto Ricans in Connecticut* (Middletown: Connecticut Humanities Council, 1997) is titled "Tobacco Valley" and provides an incisive overview. The rich collections in the Library of the Center for Puerto Rican Studies, Hunter College, City University of New York, hold records of the Farm Labor Program, 1948–1993, including correspondence of the Hartford Office of the Puerto Rican Migrant Labour Division and the Shade Tobacco Growers Association (STGA). Trinity College Hartford Project has in its holdings two excellent videos: *Connecticut River Valley* (narrator Lowell Thomas) and *Puerto Rican Passages* (narrator José Feliciano).

66 : Jean Stubbs

43. Among the press articles, see Johanna Ball, "Tobacco Grower to Switch Crops," *Hartford Courant*, November 17, 1978, CSL NCF.

44. "U.S. Cigar Sales Left in Ashes," *Hartford Courant*, June 14, 1979, CSL NCF.

45. Kristina Goodnough, "Summer Jobs Wither in Tobacco Cutback," *Hartford Courant*, December 8, 1981, CSL NCF.

46. Martin Kearns, "Tobacco Demand Lessens: Pressure Put on County Growers by Profit Drop," *Hartford Courant*, December 14, 1981, CSL NCF.

47. Samuel G. Freedman, "Connecticut's Tobacco: Gone with the Wind?" *New York Times*, July 6, 1982, CSL NCF.

48. Lee Grabar, "State Tobacco Industry Not Expected to Suffer," *New Haven Register*, January 12, 1964, CSL NCF.

49. Insurance and heath were big business in Connecticut, so this was big news. See Kevin Sack, "Cuomo Weighs Move to Drop Tobacco Stocks," *New York Times*, June 9, 1990; Robert S. Capers, "Yale–New Haven Hospital to Sell Its Tobacco Stocks," *Hartford Courant*, August 15, 1991; Robert S. Capers, "Synagogue Sells Off Tobacco Investments," *Hartford Courant*, January 1, 1992 — all CSL NCF.

50. Dirk Vaughan, "Wrapped Up: Some of the Best Cigars Use Connecticut's Tobacco Wrapper Leaves," *Cigar Aficionado*, Winter 1992, http://www.cigaraficionado.com/Cigar/CAArchives/CA_Show_Article/0,2322,854,00.html.

51. See Saptari, "Politics of Land, Labour and Leaf"; T. S. Raffles *History of Java* (Kuala Lumpur: Oxford University Press, 1978).

52. Soegijanto Padmo, *The Cultivation of Vorstenlands Tobacco and Besuki Tobacco in Besuki Residency and Its Impact on the Peasant Economy and Society, 1860–1960* (Yogyakarta: Additya Media, 1994). See also S. Nawiyanto, "Growing 'Golden Leaf': Tobacco Production in Besuki Residency, 1860–1970," *Historia* 4, no. 2 (2009): 144–58.

53. S. Nawiyanto, *The Rising Sun in a Javanese Rice Granary: Change and the Impact of Japanese Occupation on the Agricultural Economy of Besuki Residency, 1942–1945* (Yogyakarta: Galangpress, 2005). See also S. Nayiwanto, "The Economy of Besuki in the 1930s Depression," in *Weathering the Storm: The Economies of Southeast Asia in the 1930s Depression*, ed. I. Brown and P. Boomgard (Singapore: Institute of Southeast Asian Studies, 2000).

54. The Dutch disputed Indonesian nationalization in a landmark case over Indonesian tobacco, better known as the Bremen Tobacco Case, of August 21, 1959, in the Bremen Court of Appeal. The court ruled the expropriation and/or nationalization of Dutch companies legal and gave the green light to Indonesia's decision to trade on the Bremen market in place of Amsterdam. See *The Bremen Tobacco Case* 60 (special issue), Department of Information, Republic of Indonesia (1960).

55. Suckling, "Tobacco Mecca." For a study of Jember, see A. C. Mackie, "The Changing Political Economy of an Export Crop: The Case of Jember's Tobacco Industry," *Bulletin of Indonesian Economic Studies* 21 (1985): 113–38.

56. At the time, Central African wrapper supplies had declined in quality and quantity during the 1980s because of internal problems in the tobacco-producing nations of Cameroon and the Central African Republic, as well as poor relations between the African growers and their French backers.

57. Saptari, "Politics of Land, Labour, and Leaf," refers to the reports of the burning of tobacco barns in the principalities and the Javanese protest of *pepe*, sitting down en masse, over company occupation of communal lands. Among the studies of conflict in Java, see M. L. Lyons, *Bases of Conflict in Rural Java* (Berkeley, CA: Center for South and Southeast Asia Studies, 1970). See also Jan Breman, *Good Times and Bad Times in Rural Java: A Study of Socio-Economic Dynamics towards the End of the Twentieth Century* (Leiden: KITLV Press, 2002).

58. James Suckling, "A Connecticut Leaf in Cuba," *Cigar Aficionado*, Autumn 1995, http://www.cigaraficionado.com/Cigar/CA_Archives/CA_Show_Article/0,2322,687,00.html.

59. David Savona, "Made in the Shade: For a Century, Connecticut Farmers Have Grown Some of the World's Finest Cigar Wrapper Tobacco," *Cigar Aficionado*, November–December 1999, http://www.cigaraficionado.com/Cigar/CA_Archives/CA_Issue_Index?issueId=35.

60. Conceptualizing the global history approach to commodity chains, migration, and labor is beyond the scope of this article, but for a succinct discussion, see Marcel van der Linden, *Transnational Labour History: Explorations* (Aldershot, U.K.: Ashgate, 2003). Such an approach shapes, for example, the Commodities of Empire British Academy Research Project (the Open University's Ferguson Centre and the University of London's Institute for the Study of the Americas) in the United Kingdom, the Anti-Commodities Project at Wageningen University, the International Institute of Social History (Amsterdam) in the Netherlands, and *Journal of Global History*.

61. The company's U.S. premium brands include Macanudo, once produced in Jamaica, and Partagas, Punch, Hoyo de Monterey, La Gloria Cubana, and Cohiba — all Cuban — made in the Dominican Republic or Honduras.

62. The focus of this article has been on cigars, which constitute but one small sector of the global tobacco industry, dominated as it is by cigarettes and, in several parts of the world, by chewing tobacco. The 2010 dispute between the United States and Indonesia erupted over the United States' blocking of Indonesia's very popular local *kretek*, or clove, cigarettes. See "WTO to Rule on U.S. Clove Cigarette Ban," Reuters, July 20, 2010, http://uk.reuters.com/article/idUKLDE66J1A52010 0720. At the same time, in the context of U.S. President Barack Obama's July 2010 visit to Indonesia, scientists there were calling for reopening the debate on the medicinal properties of tobacco. See "Indonesia, President Obama and Tobacco," *Jakarta Post*, July 27, 2010, http://www.thejakartapost.com/news/2010/03/19/indonesia-president-obama-and-tobacco.html. Therein lies another story in the making.

SARA VEGA

Soy Cuba, de cierta manera

RESUMEN

El triunfo revolucionario en 1959 y la inmediata creación del Instituto Cubano del Arte e Industria Cinematográficos (ICAIC) posibilitaron la aparición de un cine cubano diferente al producido hasta entonces y, al mismo tiempo, la exhibición de filmes de otras latitudes casi desconocidas por el público. Esta profunda transformación cultural trajo consigo una nueva manera de promocionar el cine mediante un movimiento de diseño gráfico en la cartelística que rápidamente marcó pautas en la esfera de las artes visuales en el país. Los carteles recién creados fueron conocidos de inmediato como los carteles del ICAIC, y llamaron la atención por utilizar una amplia gama cromática, por su impresión en serigrafía y por sus imaginativas propuestas conceptuales y formales. En muy corto tiempo modificaron la fisonomía de nuestras ciudades, edificios públicos y casas.

ABSTRACT

The triumph of the Cuban Revolution in 1959 and the subsequent creation of the Cuban Institute for Cinematographic Arts and Industry (ICAIC) made possible the creation of a new type of Cuban cinema that broke with past traditions while also facilitating the exhibition of foreign films previously unknown to the Cuban public. This profound cultural transformation also changed the way Cuban cinema was promoted and a new graphic movement of poster design (*cartelística*) led to a turning point for the field of visual arts in Cuba. The posters were immediately recognized as the posters of ICAIC and grabbed attention through their use of a broad chromatic spectrum, engravings and screen printing techniques and for their imaginative conceptual proposals and formats. In a short period of time, the posters changed the look of Cuban cities and their buildings and houses.

> Y nació, por ello, el arte del afiche cinematográfico cubano que, más que afiche, más que cartel, más que anuncio, es una siempre renovada muestra de artes sugerentes, funcionales si se quiere, ofrecida al transeúnte.
>
> Alejo Carpentier

Resaltar la importancia alcanzada por la gráfica política y cultural posterior al triunfo revolucionario resulta, sin lugar a dudas, un lugar común. Durante los años sesenta y setenta, una nueva visualidad se impuso en la cultura cubana y, específicamente, en la ciudad. Portadores de increíbles imágenes, los carteles aparecieron por todas partes y en los más diversos formatos, y casi de golpe

68

concitaron al público a decodificar otro tipo de mensajes, que lo convertían en un receptor más avisado y con un mayor y mejor sentido de lo estético.

Con anterioridad al triunfo revolucionario ocurrido en Cuba en 1959, el carácter artesanal y esporádico de la producción cinematográfica no propició el surgimiento y desarrollo de una gráfica de valor en la cartelística cubana. Los carteles que acompañaron la exhibición tanto nacional como foránea obedecieron a los cánones de la época, fuertemente influidos en un primer momento por los filmes europeos y posteriormente por los norteamericanos.

Entre los elementos utilizados con más frecuencia por los diseñadores del período están la imagen de los rostros protagónicos de los actores del filme en primer plano, la exaltación del tropicalismo —colocación de bohíos, palmas reales, carretas—, la música, el baile, el erotismo y el paisaje como conceptos mal entendidos de la cultura cubana lo que visto en la actualidad resulta banal y maniqueo.

En general, la impresión de carteles cinematográficos se realizó en serigrafía, —técnica introducida en la isla en la década de 1910—, y que se mantuvo como opción para la reproducción múltiple durante mucho tiempo. Fue utilizada para campañas políticas y anuncios públicos de bailes, espectáculos u otras actividades, pues este método artesanal permitía una inversión ínfima teniendo en cuenta las escasas cantidades de ejemplares que se imprimían en cada tirada.

El cine nacional fue despreciado y subvalorado ante la abrumadora exhibición de películas extranjeras y la indiferencia de las instituciones autorizadas en el país; entonces, ¿cómo pretender interés en la realización de carteles? Quizás esta limitante impidió, a pesar de recurrir a similares concepciones de diseño, que los carteles de filmes cubanos alcanzaran el atractivo de los carteles norteamericanos o mexicanos de la época. Exigirle al cartel cubano realizado con anterioridad a 1959 valores más allá de los relacionados con los índices de taquilla o intentar colocarlo a la altura del resto de las artes visuales en el país, es analizarlo fuera de su contexto histórico. La concepción del cartel prerrevolucionario respondió a imperativos que no fueron precisamente artísticos.

Independientemente del escaso valor otorgado a esta variante promocional, la inexistencia del concepto patrimonial —que resulta relativamente nuevo— hizo que se perdieran gran cantidad de carteles realizados durante la primera mitad del pasado siglo. Impresos en papel de pésima calidad, estaban destinados a una vida efímera. El paso del tiempo se encargó de su pérdida y destrucción. Sin embargo, algunos resistieron y hoy podemos contar con material para reconstruir, en alguna medida, la iconografía de un período de la historia cinematográfica de Cuba.

El primero de enero de 1959, Cuba fue estremecida por la revolución, cisma que abarcó todos los órdenes y cambió de golpe las coordenadas políticas, sociales, económicas y estéticas. La nueva política cultural en el caso del cine, pretendió llevar a cabo una descolonización de las pantallas y favoreció el desarrollo de otra sensibilidad. El gusto del espectador cubano, hasta ese momento estaba condicionado por los cánones del cine norteamericano, cinematografía más exhibida en la isla. A partir de la apertura del espectro de exhibición de filmes de otras latitudes, el público tuvo acceso a otras propuestas cinematográficas que sin duda, trajeron consigo una paulatina transformación del gusto y la apreciación de propuestas muy diferentes a las conocidas hasta ese momento.

El cartel en general desempeñó un papel fundamental para la promoción de todo lo nuevo que aparecía como consecuencia de la revolución. Se produjo un gran volumen de carteles políticos, se realizaron carteles para campañas de ahorro y educacionales, para movilizaciones masivas y por supuesto, para promocionar filmes, espectáculos y eventos culturales.

Esta nueva gráfica, nacida al calor de una necesidad de cambios llegó a alcanzar, en muy corto tiempo, valores que nada tenían que ver con los modelos desarrollados con anterioridad en el país.

La realidad de la isla había cambiado sustancialmente y, por supuesto, las nuevas campañas: económicas, educacionales, de salud, de medio ambiente y culturales, en sentido general, exigieron nuevas imágenes visuales.

Se realizaron miles de carteles políticos pero también los carteles culturales alcanzaron cifras inimaginables. Entre las instituciones que desarrollaron, mediante sus carteles, una gráfica que pudiera entenderse como revolucionaria, se encontraban el Instituto Cubano del Arte e Industria Cinematográficos (ICAIC), la Casa de las Américas y el Consejo Nacional de Cultura (CNC).

En muy corto tiempo, los carteles fueron también la expresión de una ruptura con los cánones publicitarios asumidos en la isla como consecuencia de la influencia norteamericana, que había alcanzado un desarrollo acelerado durante la década del cincuenta. La gráfica se cargó de un significado diferente, cumplió con otros requerimientos y asimiló influencias de las escuelas del cartel polaco, checo y japonés. Las necesidades provocadas por un proceso tan complejo, que traía consigo el deber de explicar exhortar, convencer y provocar cambios en todo el país, convirtió al diseño gráfico en una herramienta vital para conseguir de manera acelerada los propósitos de la revolución.

El 24 de marzo de 1959 se fundó el ICAIC. Se establecieron nuevos presupuestos en el diseño cultural, organizativo y técnico para el desarrollo de una nueva cinematografía cubana, a la vez que la producción fue asumida económicamente de manera diferente a como se hacía hasta entonces.

A partir de 1960, el ICAIC protagonizó las más profundas transformaciones en la cultura cubana. Se dieron importantes pasos para la creación de una cinematografía verdaderamente nacional, absolutamente diferente de la producida hasta entonces. Los filmes del ICAIC expusieron con lucidez temas inéditos con una estética diferente, contraria al mimetismo y la superficialidad de la cinematografía anterior.

Junto con el nacimiento del nuevo cine cubano, y como necesidad ineludible para promocionar estos nuevos filmes en 1960 se marcó el inicio de una tradición en la historia del cartel, que comenzaba a apuntar importantes experimentaciones formales y la absoluta libertad para la búsqueda de nuevos caminos en la comunicación visual.

Uno de los elementos más importantes que definen a la gráfica del momento fue el abandono de los patrones comerciales. La publicidad se vació de contenido en una sociedad a la que no interesaba auspiciar ventas.

Muchos artistas y publicistas provenientes de muchas de las agencias que fueron nacionalizadas, comenzaron a colaborar con la institución: Umberto Peña, Fernando Pérez O'Reilly, José Lucci, Raúl Martínez, René Portocarrero, Servando Cabrera Moreno, Rafael Morante, Holbeín López y Raúl Oliva, asumieron los códigos del diseño gráfico y realizaron carteles cinematográficos.

Saúl Yelín, director de Relaciones Internacionales, desde 1963 tomó bajo su cargo una nueva política de promoción cinematográfica y fue, sin dudas, el gestor de una nueva gráfica para la promoción de un gran volumen de filmes de todas las cinematografías que comenzaron a ser exhibidos. Yelín supo desde el inicio escoger el cartel que mejor representara a cada uno de los filmes y diseñó con efectividad una política promocional nueva en el país.

Promotor por excelencia de los carteles de cine, su labor hizo posible un cambio sustancial en la visualidad y propició la aparición de una auténtica expresión gráfica en la cinematografía. Su sensibilidad y acierto hicieron que los carteles cinematográficos comenzaran a ser conocidos nacional e internacionalmente como los carteles del ICAIC.

Pero la transformación de los carteles de cine no ocurrió de golpe. A pesar de los nuevos presupuestos, en muchos de los primeros carteles realizados entre los años 1960 y 1963 todavía aparecían rasgos de la gráfica anterior: predominio de lo figurativo, utilización de la pintura sin tomar en cuenta códigos del diseño para carteles, y colores y tonos discretos. Muchos diseñadores que quedaron atrapados en el conservadurismo fueron relegados por los más jóvenes, quienes se aventuraron en la experimentación formal y conceptual. Los nombres de Eduardo Muñoz Bachs, René Azcuy, Alfredo Rostgaard, Antonio Fernández Reboiro y más tarde Ñiko permanecieron en el interés del público y la crítica. Y surgieron otros nuevos. El rechazo a todo lo realizado con anterioridad y, en ocasiones, la escasez de recursos, especialmente a partir de 1964, fueron un reto para la imaginación y la creación.

Los diseñadores acudían a cualquier recurso que tuviesen a su alcance para expresarse. Utilizaron el *collage*, recortaron textos de revistas para sugerir a los serígrafos el lugar, tamaño y estilo que tendría la tipografía para el título y los créditos del filme. Muchos aprovecharon sus experiencias en la publicidad y las transformaron en función de los nuevos mensajes culturales. Dibujaban o componían a partir de fotografías, papeles de colores, viñetas e imágenes impresas que pegaban en la cartulina para esbozar sus ideas.

Desde los inicios del proceso revolucionario se nacionalizaron agencias publicitarias y talleres de impresión. Las grandes imprentas se destinaron a la propaganda política, mientras que los pequeños talleres de serigrafía —dedicados con anterioridad a campañas electorales, ya sin sentido— se emplearon para las tiradas en serigrafía de la gráfica cultural.

Los serígrafos del taller del ICAIC, por su parte, hacían posible la impresión de las obras y enfrentaron y resolvieron carencias de todo tipo (tintas, papel, cartulina, caladores), a la vez que descubrieron caminos para conciliar pinturas, bases, alcoholes y otros artículos de diferentes procedencias. Desde el calado hasta la preparación de las tintas para hallar los tonos precisos y finalmente la impresión de cada uno de los colores, todo se desarrollaba de manera absolutamente artesanal.

En 1969, para la celebración de su décimo aniversario en el ICAIC se organizaron muestras de cine, exposiciones de fotografías, trofeos y equipos de cine. Paralelamente, el Ministerio de Comunicaciones puso en circulación una serie de sellos de correo con diseños de carteles realizados para la Cinemateca de Cuba, filmes documentales y de ficción y para los cine-móviles. Con sólo diez años de existencia, los carteles del ICAIC ya eran tan importantes como el nuevo cine cubano.

A comienzos de la década del setenta los diseñadores polacos Wiktor Gorka, Waldemar Swerzy y Bonislaw Zelek, invitados por el taller de divulgación de la Comisión de Orientación Revolucionaria (COR), visitaron Cuba. Dictaron conferencias sobre el diseño polaco, intercambiaron impresiones con los diseñadores cubanos y valoraron los carteles producidos en Cuba durante una década. Luego llegaron muchos pintores y diseñadores extranjeros como el polaco Tadeuz Judkowski, el gran artista español Antonio Saura y el italiano José Lucci colaboraron con el ICAIC realizando carteles. La confrontación con estos profesionales trajo consigo la evaluación racional de un trabajo que hasta ese momento se venía realizando de manera casi intuitiva.

En muy corto tiempo el número de carteles creció. El incremento y la diversidad en la exhibición cinematográfica impusieron la realización de afiches no sólo para filmes exhibidos en los circuitos comerciales, sino también para semanas de cine cubano en el extranjero y muestras de cine internacional exhibidas en el país. Como una variante en la nueva promoción de trabajo los diseñadores, según los intereses de la cinemateca, también diseñaron programas, folletos y carteles para ciclos, homenajes, retrospectivas, eventos y clásicos de la cinematografía universal. Los carteles tanto para ciclos como el de *Marilyn Monroe* o para filmes clásicos de la cinemateca como *La quimera del oro, Avaricia, El acorazado Potemkin* y *El gabinete del doctor Caligari,* entre otros forman parte de las obras que conforman el imaginario colectivo de una época de esplendor del cartel y de la Cinemateca de Cuba.

Los carteles del ICAIC propiciaron el *boom* de la cartelística cubana a nivel internacional con excelentes diseños, la utilización sin restricciones de tintas e innumerables tiradas para alcanzar la riquísima gama cromática que los definió. La técnica del *silkscreen* aportó una textura muy especial a los nuevos carteles, al conjugar valiosos diseños y una depurada realización artesanal. Consiguieron un gran impacto visual, y fueron conservados por su significación artística y su gran plasticidad, muchas veces comparable a una obra de arte en el sentido convencional del término. Se consideró de buen gusto utilizarlos como decoración en hogares, oficinas y calles.

Fue tal la admiración despertada, que la ensayista Susan Sontag caracterizó la producción de afiches posterior a 1959 de la siguiente manera:

[L]os cubanos realizan carteles para promover la cultura en una sociedad que no busca tratar la cultura como un conjunto de mercancías, acontecimientos y objetos diseñados, conscientemente o no, para su explotación comercial. Así, el propio proyecto de la promoción cultural se convierte en paradójico, si no gratuito. Y, verdaderamente, muchos de estos carteles no satisfacen realmente ninguna necesidad práctica [...] son objetos de lujo, algo realizado en última instancia por amor al arte. Con mucha más frecuencia, un cartel realizado en el ICAIC por Tony Reboiro o Eduardo Bachs constituye el advenimiento de una nueva obra de arte, en vez de un anuncio cultural en el sentido familiar del término. (Sontag 1970, 14)

En la grafica realizada para la promoción cinematográfica es notable la experimentación en la búsqueda de soluciones novedosas y eficaces. A partir de elementos abstractos, simbólicos — que requerían de mucha imaginación — , alteraron los códigos de la comunicación visual, se abrieron a cualquier influencia e iniciaron búsquedas sin trabas de ninguna índole. Asumieron elementos del *pop art*, el *op art*, el arte cinético y todo lo que les resultara válido para exponer el mensaje.

Entonces, los carteles cubanos cumplieron con el concepto de efectividad expuesto por Susan Sontag (1970, 14), "El cartel efectivo [...] lleva siempre en sí la dualidad que enmarca propiamente el arte: la tensión entre el deseo de decir (claridad, exactitud literal) y el deseo del silencio (mensaje trunco, economía de medios, condensación, evocación, misterio, exageración)".

Ocurrió un fenómeno difícil de entender. Un público, en su mayoría carente aún de referencias culturales, alienado y acostumbrado a asimilar la información a partir de esquemas impuestos aceptó en muy breve tiempo los nuevos carteles y disfrutó de sus nuevas propuestas.

Aunque en los comienzos los carteles tuvieron diversos formatos muy pronto se imprimieron con medida estándar más funcional: setenta y seis por cincuenta y uno centímetros. Pasaron a formar parte de la ambientación de los cines a partir de su colocación en estructuras modulares que permitió su renovación sin alterar la ambientación general de las salas cinematográficas.

Rebasaron los emplazamientos comunes —fachadas y vestíbulos de cines— y tomaron las calles ubicados en estructuras metálicas cubiertas por una cúpula, llamadas popularmente paragüitas. Esto permitió que los transeúntes pudieran observar de golpe y desde cualquier ángulo ocho carteles que promocionaban los filmes que serían exhibidos en los próximos días. También fueron expuestos en vallas que, al igual que el cartel, se dirigían a toda clase de público. Nuevas formas y colores que tenían el único objetivo de promocionar la cultura concitaron el asombro de todos.

El espacio público se convirtió en el escenario ideal para la expresión y discusión de temas políticos, económicos y culturales. A partir de una ruptura con el viejo lenguaje visual los carteles, las vallas y los murales hicieron posible que el interés y la reflexión se tornaran esenciales.

A diferencia de otros, los carteles de cine nunca se basaron en el condicionamiento ideológico ni en principios comerciales, sino que tuvieron el propósito de coadyuvar a la educación visual del espectador en función de valores culturales.

A nivel mundial, la década del sesenta fue pródiga en cambios políticos y artísticos. Era una época de crisis, deslumbramientos y pretensiones de cambiar el mundo, romper con el *establishment*, negar el conservadurismo. En Francia se desencadenó el Mayo Parisino, mientras que en Checoslovaquia la primavera no era sólo una estación sino un violento enfrentamiento. En la Plaza de Tlatelolco, México, fueron masacrados jóvenes estudiantes que abogaban por cambios revolucionarios y en Estados Unidos aparecieron el *black power* y la llamada contracultura, mientras la generación *hippie* norteamericana opuso la paz y el amor a la guerra, cantó en Woodstock, quemó banderas así como boletas de reclutamiento militar y se negó a participar en la guerra de Vietnam. En una cañada de Bolivia moría Ernesto Che Guevara.

Los años sesenta resultaron trascendentes para el cine cubano: el ICAIC produjo algunos de los más valiosos filmes de su historia, nació la escuela cubana del documental y se fomentó el dibujo animado con características nacionales. Entre las obras más destacadas se incluyen: *La primera carga al machete, Lucía, Memorias del subdesarrollo, Coffea Arábiga y Now*, por citar sólo algunas. El nuevo cine se definió, y fue reconocido internacionalmente; otra estética, nuevas tendencias y nuevos realizadores reflexionaron sobre aspectos esenciales de nuestra identidad y de los cambios en todo el sistema de valores. Fueron años trascendentes también para todo el universo visual de la gráfica, devenida entonces un instrumento eficaz en la propaganda revolucionaria.

Los carteles del ICAIC acompañaron y sustentaron el esplendor de esa década, contribuyeron a la transformación paulatina de un espectador en un ser apto para valoraciones críticas, poseedor de una mirada más inteligente del mundo.

Desde el mismo momento del triunfo revolucionario, el país enfrentó una severa crisis económica originada por el bloqueo norteamericano. Más tarde, durante el año 1968, se produjo una ofensiva revolucionaria que redujo a cero toda iniciativa privada en lo económico, por lo que este sector quedó totalmente en manos del estado. Se tomaron severas medidas para llevar a cabo una vasta centralización económica, social y política. En 1971 se celebró el Primer Congreso de Educación y Cultura. La función del arte y la cultura fue replanteada en todos sus niveles en 1975 se celebró el Primer Congreso del Partido Comunista de Cuba y se instrumentó finalmente la institucionalización del país.

El rumbo y la política del ICAIC se mantuvieron sin alteraciones, a pesar de la crisis que afectó en cierta medida la producción de cine nacional y la exhibición de filmes extranjeros. La realización de carteles sobrevivió: se sucedieron exposiciones y premios en eventos nacionales e internacionales. Superada la impronta de los sesenta, los diseñadores continuaron con nuevas búsquedas conceptuales y definieron estilos personales hasta alcanzar, en la década de los setenta, su afirmación y madurez. Puede decirse que lograron un mayor dominio del oficio, una técnica más depurada y su sello definitivo.

Los carteles en este período se tornaron más intelectuales a partir de la inserción de nuevos símbolos que enriquecieron los códigos reconocidos. Floreció un cierto tipo de experimentación: la decodificación se hizo más compleja. Sin embargo, aunque los carteles imponían retos mayores en su interpretación, continuaron siendo admirados por un público entrenado.

El número de carteles ascendía. La mayoría tenía gran frescura y alto nivel artístico, consecuencias de la consolidación de la impronta de los años sesenta para el cartel cinematográfico cubano.

En estos años se incorporan al ICAIC otros diseñadores como Damián González, Julio Eloy Mesa o Jorge Dimas, quienes también realizaron diseños funcionales y de gran belleza.

A finales de la década, con motivo del vigésimo aniversario del ICAIC y como homenaje a Saúl Yelín, fallecido en 1977, se celebró en el Museo Nacional de Bellas Artes la exposición *1000 carteles cubanos de cine*. Por primera vez, el museo abría un importante espacio a la gráfica cinematográfica. Un inmenso volumen de carteles firmados por Eduardo Muñoz Bachs, Antonio Fernández Reboiro, Alfredo Rostgaard, Rafael Morante, Julio Eloy Mesa o Antonio Pérez (Ñiko) conseguía impactar al público. Una amplia selección de carteles de cine demostró la trascendencia alcanzada en tan poco tiempo por el diseño gráfico. Se abrió un debate en el que participaron importantes críticos y personalidades de la plástica y la cultura —Rosario Novoa, Manuel López Oliva, Alfredo Guevara, Mariano Rodríguez, Graziella Pogolotti, Roberto

Segre, Alejandro G. Alonso, Fernando Salinas, entre otros —, quienes ana-
lizaron la condición del cartel como vehículo de difusión y portador de valores
estéticos, su función educadora del gusto y la capacidad de percepción del
público nacional y extranjero. La exposición demostró una vez más la trascendencia alcanzada en tan poco tiempo por los carteles del ICAIC. En el catálogo
de la exposición, la destacada ensayista cubana Graziella Pogolotti apuntó:

> Un balance de los veinte años transcurridos evidencia que el cartel cinematográfico del
> ICAIC ha adquirido la jerarquía propia de un hecho cultural nacido con la Revolución.
> Ensancha la historia de nuestra plástica, contribuye a la educación visual del nuevo
> público, marca con su sello original nuestras calles y ha penetrado en los interiores de
> nuestras viviendas y a las de otros países adonde ha llegado el cartel. Junto al talento de
> los creadores, es justo reconocer el acierto de los dirigentes de la cinematografía cubana
> que supieron promover esta importante línea de desarrollo.

Desafortunadamente, todo ese amplio movimiento cultural en Cuba, alcanzado durante los primeros años sesenta y elevado a clímax en gran parte de
los setenta, comenzó a sufrir signos de debilitamiento y decadencia durante los
ochenta cuando comenzaron a desaparecer las causas y los variados elementos
que lo hicieron posible.

La muerte de Saúl Yelín en 1977, la disminución de la exhibición de cine internacional, entre otros factores, atentaron contra las exigencias artísticas y el
rigor en la creación de los carteles. Se quebró así la continuidad lograda en
veinte años. Algunos de los diseñadores gráficos más notables y de larga experiencia se marcharon a trabajar a otras instituciones e incluso emigraron del país.

A fines de la década de los ochenta disminuyó la realización de carteles
para filmes extranjeros hasta casi desaparecer: se diseñaba sólo para filmes
cubanos de ficción. Salvo excepciones la mayoría no alcanzó el impacto gráfico
ni la eficacia comunicativa de los períodos anteriores. Casi todo había cambiado para entonces. En la primera mitad de los años noventa, las carencias
materiales en el país se agudizaron a niveles altísimos y lograron repercutir en
la visualidad cubana. Las afectaciones abarcaron todos los sectores de la vida
por lo que resultó notable la disminución de la producción cinematográfica
nacional en primer lugar y, por consiguiente, la de sus carteles.

Durante la primera mitad de los años noventa, las carencias materiales en
el país se agudizaron como consecuencia del derrumbe del campo socialista.
Los escasos carteles producidos adolecieron de un recurso que hasta entonces
resultaba distintivo: el color, y se perdió la coherencia y continuidad en la
promoción cinematográfica. La visualidad cubana se resentía ante la ausencia
de imágenes que en otros tiempos resultaban habituales para su renovación.

La economía cubana afrontó la más profunda crisis de su historia. Las
afectaciones abarcaron todos los sectores; la cultura, por supuesto, no escapó a

FIGURE 1. Poster for *Cines moviles en la escuela rural* (Mobile cinemas and the rural school) created by Eduardo Muñoz Bachs. Used with permission of Fabián Muñoz.

la recesión. Es notable la disminución en la producción cinematográfica y, por consiguiente, la de sus carteles. Las restricciones económicas hicieron imposible la compra de copias de cine extranjero.

En la gráfica continuaron percibiéndose los signos de la crisis, tanto en la cantidad como en la calidad de los diseños. Disminuyó el ya reducido grupo de diseñadores en activo. Algunos mostraron cierta osadía formal y conceptual, con la pretensión de recuperar los tiempos en que el cartel formaba parte de la cultura y los valores de la cinematografía cubana.

Al parecer, la suerte estaba echada. Sin embargo, algunos jóvenes profesionales que cursaron estudios en el Instituto Superior de Diseño (ISDI), o surgían como sus primeros egresados, sintieron la necesidad de participar en el llamado a realizar carteles cinematográficos e intentaron remontar la crisis con sus obras, que si bien no alcanzaban a aquellas del período de esplendor, resultaron la evidencia y la esperanza de una posible renovación. En 1991, en un intento de revitalizar el diseño gráfico Alfredo Guevara convocó a jóvenes profesionales con referencias culturales contemporáneas. Realizaron carteles, vallas, plegables, invitaciones y catálogos vinculados por lo general al Festival Internacional del Nuevo Cine Latinoamericano.

Se incorporaron las técnicas de computación y el *offset* como modos de democratizar el diseño y se introdujeron concepciones artísticas más complejas, dejando a un lado la serigrafía, sello distintivo de la gráfica del ICAIC. Estos diseños incursionaron en la búsqueda de nuevos presupuestos aunque, en ocasiones, se abusó de las bondades de las nuevas tecnologías y supeditaron el talento a las posibilidades de los *software*. El atiborramiento de elementos visuales y la desacertada utilización de recursos como el *degradée*, la superposición y los difuminados, tanto en la imagen como en el color, impidieron alcanzar la fuerza de la gráfica anterior y confundieron las fronteras autorales.

Algunos de estos jóvenes asumirían, con nuevas propuestas, el tránsito entre el legado de la gráfica de décadas anteriores y una nueva expresión que comenzaba a manifestarse: Eduardo Marín, Vladimir de León Llaguno, Manuel Marcel y Ernesto Ferrand, resultaron esa punta de lanza que incursionó con creatividad en el diseño de carteles para cine.

En 1999, conscientes de la existencia ya de un talento evidente surgido en el Instituto Superior de Diseño se convocó, por la Cinemateca de Cuba y con el auspicio del Festival Internacional del Nuevo Cine Latinoamericano, un concurso para jóvenes diseñadores.

Ese proyecto experimental tuvo como objetivo la demostración palpable de una nueva generación de profesionales de la gráfica mediante la convocatoria a realizar diseños de carteles a partir de una selección de filmes cubanos de todos los tiempos. Dichos carteles se expondrían conjuntamente con los realizados en su momento para el estreno del filme por los conocidos diseñadores del ICAIC, e incluso por algunos casi desconocidos que desempeñaron su labor con anterioridad a 1960. El concurso propuso una experiencia comparativa que aportó nuevas herramientas y valoraciones, tanto en el diseño como en la interpretación de los filmes.

Los carteles de los jóvenes pusieron de manifiesto una visión diferente de los filmes a partir de propuestas artísticas y técnicas diversas concebidas para acercarse a la producción fílmica cubana de casi un siglo.

Por otra parte, se advirtió la perfección típica del trabajo realizado sobre aplicaciones computarizadas como Corel Draw y Photoshop, entre otros medios técnicos, y la capacidad para diseñar tomando en cuenta una técnica de impresión absolutamente artesanal como la serigrafía.

La exposición resultante del concurso, *Ayer y hoy: Carteles de cine cubano*, se llevó a cabo en la Galería Chaplin de la Cinemateca de Cuba y atrajo la atención de profesores, críticos y profesionales del medio cultural cubano. El público se sorprendió con estas nuevas imágenes y descubrió nuevos talentos en la cartelística que, en algunos casos, lograron superar la admiración, hasta entonces indiscutible, de viejos carteles como *Siete muertes a plazo fijo*, *Memorias del subdesarrollo*, *El arte del tabaco*, *Clandestinos* y *La muerte de un burócrata*... o salían airosos en la comparación, con carteles clásicos realizados con anterioridad para el estreno de los filmes: *Lucía*, *Por primera vez*, *Fresa y chocolate*, *Ciclón*.

En la muestra se percibió la influencia de los anteriores carteles del ICAIC. Los jóvenes extendieron los presupuestos estéticos que revolucionaron las artes visuales cubanas y continuaron una trayectoria que, en su momento, se colocó a la vanguardia de la gráfica cinematográfica en América Latina.

La muestra devino inevitablemente una comparación entre aquellos carteles realizados en décadas anteriores y los nuevos, en los que el tiempo transcurrido aportó otras herramientas, pero también nuevas valoraciones tanto en el diseño como en la interpretación de los filmes. Luego, en el 2002, la aparición de la Muestra Nacional de Nuevos Realizadores auspiciada por el ICAIC propició nuevamente un espacio para continuar explorando el talento y las posibilidades de los jóvenes diseñadores. A Pedro Juan Abreu se le encargó la identidad visual que definiría a la muestra a partir de entonces: su labor resultó adecuada al espíritu de la misma al conseguir una imagen coherente de alto impacto gráfico que evidenciaba el contenido y las características de este evento de cine alternativo y encontrar, además, resonancia e identificación con el público asistente. Esta labor fue continuada por Raúl Valdés (*Raupa*) a partir de la sexta edición, 2007, sobre la base de otra estética aunque manteniendo los presupuestos anteriores.

También la Muestra de Nuevos Realizadores, desde el año 2003, convoca anualmente a los estudiantes del ISDI para realizar carteles en pequeño formato que promocionen —durante el corto período de la muestra— filmes alternativos realizados también por jóvenes cineastas. Aunque estos trabajos no son

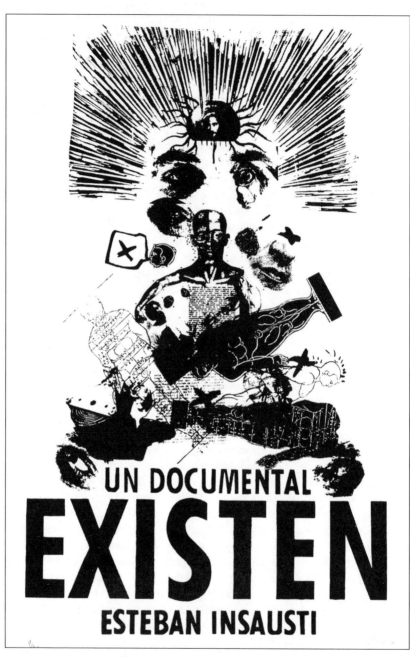

FIGURE 2. Poster for *Existen* (They exist), film by Esteban Insausti. Courtesy of the artist, Samuel Riera.

impresos en serigrafía, por razones económicas, han resultado eficaces desde el punto de vista comunicacional, cultural y creativo, a pesar de que algunos acusan problemas en la composición o no resuelven adecuadamente tipografía y puntaje. Estas obras de pequeño formato, trasmiten un sentido de síntesis y contemporaneidad, y coinciden con los presupuestos del cine realizado por jóvenes al margen de la industria.

En febrero de 2005, a propósito de la celebración del aniversario 45 de la Cinemateca de Cuba, y con el auspicio de la Muestra Nacional de Nuevos Realizadores, se realizó la exposición *La Cinemateca en el cartel*, en la que se mostraron carteles del viejo cine cubano — *Bella la salvaje*, *Cancionero cubano*, *El derecho de nacer* — , carteles realizados para aniversarios y ciclos de filmes de la cinemateca — *Cinemateca de Cuba: 10 años de programación*; *Garbo, Dietrich, Valentino*; *Marilyn Monroe in Memoriam* — y nuevos carteles seleccionados a partir de otro concurso convocado especialmente para esa ocasión. Algunos jóvenes cuyos carteles fueron escogidos ya habían participado con obras en diferentes ediciones de la Muestra Nacional de Nuevos Realizadores como Idania del Río, Félix Chi, Raúl Valdés, Maday García, Pablo Montes de Oca, Claudio Sotolongo y Nelson Ponce quien había tenido su primer acercamiento al ICAIC con su participación en la exposición *Ayer y hoy: Carteles cubanos de cine*. Ellos favorecieron — llamémoslo así — una mirada más contemporánea a la Cinemateca de Cuba, pues en varios carteles se aprecia el uso de nuevos elementos figurativos y abstractos para acercarse a la esencia de esta institución con delicado humor y una más clara integración entre imagen y tipografía.

En el 2007, también auspiciada por la sexta Muestra de Nuevos Realizadores, se realizó la exposición *Carteles de relevo* para mostrar las mejores obras realizadas por jóvenes desde 1989 hasta esa fecha, con lo que se demostró una vez más la existencia de un grupo de diseñadores — casi todos egresados del ISDI — decididos a asumir la realización de carteles en serigrafía para filmes de ficción, documentales, aniversarios y homenajes. Fabián Muñoz, Pedro Juan Abreu, Ernesto Ferrand, Eduardo Marín, Vladimir Llaguno, Manuel Marcel, y Erick Grass, Osmany Torres, Ingrid Behety, Carlos José Núñez, Nelson Ponce, Raydel Viqueira, Fernando Bencomo, Irelio Alonso, Lorenzo Santos, Pavel Giroud, Anet Melo, Pepe Menéndez, Laura Llópiz, Eduardo Moltó, Yoana Yelín, Pablo Montes de Oca, Idania del Río, Felix Chi, Claudio Sotolongo, Maday García y Raúl Valdés fueron los diseñadores participantes de esa exposición de cincuenta y dos obras que ya marcaba rumbos casi definitivos en el relevo de la cartelística cinematográfica cubana.

Algunos de estos diseñadores como Osmany Torres y Nelson Ponce ya habían realizado carteles para el ICAIC. Otros que se iniciaron presentando carteles en pequeño formato para las diferentes ediciones de la muestra nacional de nuevos realizadores ya son convocados, incluso en exclusiva, para diseñar carteles para filmes, semanas, muestras, ciclos de la cinemateca y homenajes, tal es caso de Idania del Río, Maday García, Pablo Montes de Oca, Claudio Sotolongo y Raúl Valdés, entre otros.

Recientemente se han vinculado otros diseñadores, también egresados del ISDI, como Michelle Holands y Giselle Monzón o el caso del dúo *Liseloy* conformado por los diseñadores Liset Vidal de la Cruz y Eloy Hernández Dubrosky.

A esto se suma una intensa línea de trabajo de la Vicepresidencia de Patrimonio del ICAIC, a cargo de Pablo Pacheco López, con vistas a dar continuidad a lo que durante décadas fue uno de los más emblemáticos signos y símbolos de la visualidad cubana.

En un corto período de tiempo, se ha producido una importante cantidad de carteles para filmes de ficción, documentales, animados, homenajes, exposiciones, ciclos de conferencias y ciclos de la Cinemateca de Cuba y todo parece indicar que el camino está allanado para la recuperación de tan valioso legado.

Esta nueva producción ha salido a la calle, por el momento, de una forma modesta — aún no puede hablarse de una impronta visual a nivel citadino. Sin embargo, los carteles de *Madrigal*, de Erick Grass; *La noche de los inocentes*, de Osmany Torres; *Te espero en la eternidad, El premio flaco* y *Semana de cine brasileño*, de Nelson Ponce; *Camino al Edén, Personal Belongings, Nunca será fácil la herejía* y *Ciclo de conferencias cine Cubano y Revolución*, de Michelle Hollands; *Donde habita el corazón, Los vivos y los muertos, Homenaje a Nelson Rodríguez* y *Salvador de Cojímar*, de Giselle Monzón; *Una pelea cubana contra los demonios... y el mar, La primera carga al machete. 40 aniversario* y *Poética gráfica insular* de Claudio Sotolongo, entre otros, han aparecido en fachadas de cines y en murales y paredes de centros docentes.

Durante más de cuarenta años el taller de serigrafía del ICAIC ha reproducido la gráfica cinematográfica y ha contribuido al alto nivel que la ha hecho trascender y ser reclamada como obra de valor. La impresión de los nuevos carteles impuso a los operarios del taller desafíos que habían desaparecido. El ritmo de trabajo ha vuelto a intensificarse y en corto tiempo se han realizado decenas de carteles, algunos de gran complejidad. Aun en medio de la crisis y de la ruptura en la continuidad de la producción, la carencia de instrumentos, medios de trabajo y disminución del personal, los resultados alcanzados en la impresión de estos nuevos carteles son óptimos y demuestran el profesionalismo de los serígrafos.

Estas obras emulan, consciente o inconscientemente, la gráfica realizada para cine en su período de esplendor, y si bien no todos alcanzan aún el impacto gráfico y la eficacia comunicativa de aquella etapa, al menos estos jóvenes diseñadores tienen la oportunidad de realizarse con mayor frecuencia en el ejercicio del diseño y encontrar el camino que posibilite una nueva imagen.

Un elemento los hace deudores de la gráfica anterior: la técnica de impresión, que les obliga a utilizar colores planos y perseguir cierta simplicidad debido a las limitaciones del calado. A diferencia de los creadores anteriores, estos diseñan en una computadora que les ofrece, por un lado, múltiples posibilidades al usar programas de punta, pero al mismo tiempo se descartan sobreimpresiones o difuminados, y enfrentan al reto de la impresión serigráfica.

En la actualidad, a pesar de que los jóvenes diseñadores trabajan generalmente con la libertad y las ventajas que ofrece la técnica de impresión *offset*, asumen el reto, con excelentes resultados, de concebir sus obras para ser impresas en *silkscreen*, con la condición de utilizar una reducida gama cromática, con sus implicaciones de diseños sencillos y obvias restricciones: colores planos, imposibilidad de utilizar difuminados y sobreimpresiones. Mientras acceden a medios sofisticados de diseño, la serigrafía como técnica se mantiene rudimentaria y artesanal.

Sin dudas, el cartel cubano de cine vuelve a estar de moda. Numerosos turistas, estudiosos o coleccionistas se interesan por la historia de la gráfica cinematográfica de la isla y, conozcan o no sus orígenes, centran su interés en los internacionalmente conocidos carteles del ICAIC.

Ha transcurrido casi medio siglo desde el comienzo de la historia de los carteles del ICAIC. La misma ha atravesado por períodos de búsquedas y experimentación hasta alcanzar niveles altos, y períodos de crisis y decadencia de los que hasta los más esperanzados dudaban salir.

Sin embargo, comienza a ponerse de manifiesto una paulatina recuperación en la producción de filmes de ficción, documental y animación además de que se ha puesto de manifiesto una voluntad de asumir con rigor el estilo de trabajo que posibilitó la trascendencia de la gráfica y que de seguro permitirá, a corto o mediano plazo, el renacer y el fortalecimiento de la cartelística cinematográfica. Quizás ahora, los nuevos carteles del ICAIC aparecerán de nuevo en las calles de las ciudades y darán continuidad y trascendencia a una revolución visual iniciada en los años sesenta. En estos momentos los diseñadores conscientes de esa historia y de su importancia patrimonial —y de la nostalgia por una época en la que fueron ejemplos de una nueva visualidad— se enfrascan en la concepción d nuevas propuestas gráficas esenciales para la cultura cubana.

REFERENCIAS

López Oliva, Manuel. "Carteles cubanos de cine, impresos de veinte años". *Cine Cubano* 95: 95–107.
Peña, Humberto. "Cine en serigrafía". *Cine Cubano* 133(1991): 60–61.
Pogolotti, Graziella. Palabras de presentación sobre *1000 carteles cubanos de cine*. La Habana: 1979.
Sontag, Susan. "Introductory Essay". In *The Art of the Revolution*. London: Pall Mall Press, 1970.

84 : SARA VEGA

BIBLIOGRAFÍA SELECCIONADA

Bermúdez, Jorge R. *La imagen constante: El cartel cubano del siglo XX.* La Habana: Editorial Letras Cubanas, 2000.

Bermúdez, Jorge R. "La otra pared: El cartel cubano de los 90". *Arte Cubano* 1 (2000): 64–67.

Carpentier, Alejo. "Una siempre renovada muestra de artes sugerentes". *Cine Cubano* 54–55: 90–91.

González, Augusto, y Luciano Castillo. "El cartel cubano de cine en toma panorámica". *Cine Cubano* 125: 20–30.

González Acosta, Alejandro. "Un hombre locuaz." *Cine Cubano* 103: 33–37.

Hernández Cava, Felipe. *Carteles cubanos de cine.* Huesca: Festival de Cine de Huesca, Diputación Provincial de Hueca, 1997.

Juan, Adelaida de. *Pintura cubana: Temas y variaciones.* La Habana: Ediciones UNEAC, 1978.

Pérez, Miguel A., ed. *La publicidad actual: Teoría y práctica.* La Habana: Asamblea Nacional de Poder Popular, 1957.

Pogolotti, Marcelo. *La república al través de sus escritores.* La Habana: Editorial Letras Cubanas, 2002.

Rivadulla Eladio. *La serigrafía artística en Cuba.* La Habana: Ediciones UNIÓN, 1996.

Rodríguez Alemán, Mario. "Affiches de cine y otros temas". *La Tarde*, 29 de julio de 1964.

Rodríguez González, Marina. *El cartel cubano: Conversando con Rostgaard.* La Habana: Editora Política, 1999.

Stermer, Dugald, y Susan Sontag. *The Art of the Revolution.* London: Pall Mall Press, 1970.

Trujillo, Marisol. "Cuatro pintores en torno al cartel". *Cine Cubano* 95: 87–94

Vega, Jesús. *El cartel cubano de cine.* La Habana: Editorial Letras Cubanas, 1996.

Vega, Sara, y Alicia García. *La otra imagen del cine cubano.* La Habana: Cinemateca de Cuba, ICAIC, 1997.

JULIE M. FEINSILVER

Fifty Years of Cuba's Medical Diplomacy: From Idealism to Pragmatism

ABSTRACT

Medical diplomacy, the collaboration between countries to simultaneously produce health benefits and improve relations, has been a cornerstone of Cuban foreign policy since the outset of the revolution fifty years ago. It has helped Cuba garner symbolic capital (goodwill, influence, and prestige) well beyond what would have been possible for a small, developing country, and it has contributed to making Cuba a player on the world stage. In recent years, medical diplomacy has been instrumental in providing considerable material capital (aid, credit, and trade), as the oil-for-doctors deals with Venezuela demonstrates. This has helped keep the revolution afloat in trying economic times. What began as the implementation of the one of the core values of the revolution, namely health as a basic human right for all peoples, has continued as both an idealistic and a pragmatic pursuit. This article examines the factors that enabled Cuba to conduct medical diplomacy over the past fifty years, the rationale behind the conduct of this type of soft power politics, the results of that effort, and the mix of idealism and pragmatism that has characterized the experience. Moreover, it presents a typology of medical diplomacy that Cuba has used over the past fifty years.

RESUMEN

La diplomacia médica, la colaboración entre países para que simultáneamente se produzcan beneficios en la salud y mejoren las relaciones, ha sido la esencia de la política exterior de la revolución desde sus inicios hace cincuenta años. Esto ha ayudado a que Cuba gane capital simbólico (buena voluntad, influencia y prestigio) más allá de lo posible para un pequeño país, en vías de desarrollo, y además ha contribuido a que Cuba sea un factor en el ámbito mundial. En los años recientes, la diplomacia médica ha sido instrumental en la adquisición de capital material considerable (ayuda, créditos y comercio), como lo demuestra el arreglo con Venezuela de doctores por petróleo. Esto ha ayudado a que la revolución sobreviva en momentos económicos muy difíciles. Lo que empezó como la ejecución de uno de los valores esenciales de la revolución, es decir, la salud como un derecho humano básico para todas las personas, ha continuado siendo objetivo tanto en términos idealistas como pragmáticos. El presente artículo analiza los factores que le han permitido a Cuba ejercer la diplomacia médica en los cincuenta años que han transcurrido, la lógica racional que subyace en la conducción de este tipo de política de poder inteligente, los resultados de este esfuerzo y la mezcla de idealismo y pragmatismo que han caracterizado esta experiencia. Además, se presenta una tipología de la diplomacia pública utilizada por Cuba en los pasados cincuenta años.

85

Prologue

Twenty years ago, I examined thirty years of Cuban medical diplomacy based on research that I had conducted over the previous decade.[1] In reviewing the past fifty years of Cuban medical diplomacy for this article, I revisited my earlier writings of 1989; my 1993 book, *Healing the Masses: Cuban Health Politics at Home and Abroad*; a series of articles I have written over the past four years; and new data.[2] At the conceptual level, the more things changed, the more they have stayed the same.

Clearly, there have been several key changes affecting Cuba over the past two decades. Since 1989, we have witnessed the collapse of the Soviet Union and the web of trade and aid relationships Cuba had with the countries in the old Soviet sphere of influence. The resulting economic crisis for Cuba made the decade of the 1990s, to a large extent, a lost decade. Then, just in the nick of time, Hugo Chávez came to power in Venezuela in 1998, ushering in a new era of preferential trade and aid agreements that provides economic largesse for Cuba. The global financial and economic crisis that began in late 2007 and three devastating hurricanes in 2008 have again thrown Cuba's economy into a tailspin. What stayed the same is the subject of this article: Cuba's commitment to and conduct of medical diplomacy.

Introduction

Medical diplomacy, the collaboration between countries to simultaneously produce health benefits and improve relations, has been a cornerstone of Cuban foreign policy since the outset of the revolution fifty years ago. It has helped Cuba garner symbolic capital — goodwill, influence, and prestige — well beyond what would have been possible for a small, developing country, and it has contributed to making Cuba a player on the world stage. In recent years, medical diplomacy has been instrumental in providing considerable material capital — aid, credit, and trade — to keep the revolution afloat. This analysis examines why and how Cuba has conducted medical diplomacy over the past fifty years, the results of that effort, and the mix of idealism and pragmatism that has characterized this experience. A revolution can be measured by its actions to implement its ideals, something the Cubans have done successfully through medical diplomacy.

The Nature of Cuban Medical Diplomacy

Enabling Factors

From the initial days of the revolutionary government, Cuba's leaders espoused free universal health care as a basic human right and responsibility of the state.

They soon took this ideological commitment to the extreme and contended that the health of the population was a metaphor for the health of the body politic. This assertion led to the establishment of a national health system that, over time and through trial and error, has evolved into a model lauded by international health experts, including the World Health Organization (WHO). The Cuban health system has produced key health indicators, such as infant mortality rate and life expectancy at birth, comparable to those of the United States, even though there is a vast difference in the resources available to Cuba to achieve them.

At the same time, Cuban health ideology always has had an international dimension. It has considered South-South cooperation to be Cuba's duty as a means of repaying its debt to humanity for support it received from others during the revolution. Therefore, the provision of medical aid to other developing countries has been a key element of Cuba's international relations despite the immediate postrevolutionary flight of nearly half of the island's doctors and the domestic hardship this aid may have caused.

The medical brain drain contributed to the government's decision to reform the health sector, revamp medical education, and vastly increase the number of doctors trained. These factors combined made possible the large-scale commitment to medical diplomacy and lent credibility to Cuba's aid offers. They also demonstrated Cuba's success on the ground in reducing mortality and morbidity rates, which are primary goals of all health-care systems. By the mid-1980s, Cuba was producing large numbers of doctors beyond its own health-care-system needs specifically for its internationalist program. The latest available data from late 2008 indicate that Cuba has one doctor for every 151 inhabitants, a ratio unparalleled anywhere.[3]

Cuba's Initial Foray into Medical Diplomacy

Despite Cuba's own economic difficulties and the exodus of half of its doctors, Cuba began conducting medical diplomacy in 1960 by sending a medical team to Chile to provide disaster relief aid after a major earthquake. Three years later, and with the U.S. embargo in place, Cuba began its first long-term medical diplomacy initiative by sending a group of fifty-six doctors and other health workers to provide aid in Algeria on a fourteen-month assignment. Since then, Cuba has provided medical assistance to more than one hundred countries throughout the world both for short-term emergencies and on a long-term basis. Moreover, Cuba has provided free medical education for tens of thousands of foreign students in an effort to contribute to the sustainability of its medical assistance.

Perhaps as a portent of things to come, even during the 1970s and 1980s, Cuba implemented a disproportionately larger civilian aid program — particularly medical diplomacy — than its more developed trade partners: the Soviet

Union, the Eastern European countries, and China. Cuban civilian aid workers constituted 19.4 percent of the total provided by these countries, although Cuba accounted for only 2.5 percent of the population. This quickly generated considerable symbolic capital for Cuba, which translated into political backing in the UN General Assembly, as well as material benefits in the case of Angola, Iraq, and other countries that could afford to pay fees for professional services rendered, although the charges were considerably less than market rates.[4]

Typology of Cuba's Medical Diplomacy

The following typology of Cuba's medical diplomacy initiatives facilitates understanding at a glance the depth and breadth of Havana's use of this type of soft power as a major instrument of foreign policy. Cuba's aid can be divided into two major categories: short-term and long-term initiatives, although some short-term initiatives may have long-term effects. Moreover, some subcategories are not mutually exclusive as the particular initiative may be conducted on either a short-term or long-term basis.[5]

Short-term initiatives can then subdivided into nine categories:

1. Disaster relief
2. Epidemic control and epidemiological monitoring
3. On-the-job training for health-care professionals to improve their skills
4. Direct provision of medical care in Cuba
5. Health system organizational, administrative, and planning advisory services
6. Donation of medicines, medical supplies, and equipment
7. Vaccination and health education campaigns
8. Program design for human resource development and for the provision of specific medical services
9. Exchange of research findings and knowledge transfer through the sponsorship of international conferences and the publication of medical journals

Cuba's long-term medical diplomacy initiatives can be categorized in seven areas:

1. Direct provision of primary health care in the beneficiary country, particularly in areas where local doctors will not work
2. Staffing of secondary and tertiary care hospitals in beneficiary countries
3. Establishment of health-care facilities (e.g., clinics, diagnostic laboratories, hospitals) in beneficiary countries
4. Establishment of comprehensive health programs in beneficiary countries
5. Establishment and/or staffing of medical schools in beneficiary countries and/or in-country community clinic–based medical education combined with distance learning under Cuban supervision in country

6. Provision of full scholarships to study in Cuba for medical school and allied health professional students
7. Scientific exchanges

Already by the mid-1970s, Cuba had used all but two of the foregoing instruments. Not developed until much later, the two are establishment of comprehensive health programs in country, an approach first developed in 1998, and in-country community clinic–based medical education combined with distance learning, the Virtual Health University established in 2006. A few examples of some of these initiatives over the past fifty years demonstrate that, although Cuba is a small, developing country, it has been able to conduct a world-class foreign policy from which President Barack Obama recently said the United States could learn.[6]

Disaster Relief

Cuba has been quick to mobilize well-trained disaster relief teams for many of the major disasters in the world. Among its recent activities were specially trained disaster relief medical brigades — sixty doctors — immediately dispatched to Haiti after the January 2010 earthquake to supplement the existing four-hundred-strong medical brigade and more than five hundred Haitian graduates of Cuban medical schools who worked with them. Because the Cuban doctors were already working in all ten departments in Haiti and teams of Cuban doctors had worked in country since 1998, they were the first foreigners to respond to the great earthquake. After three weeks, they had assisted over 50,000 people; conducted 3,000 surgeries, 1,500 of which were complex operations; delivered 280 babies; vaccinated 20,000 people against tetanus; established 9 rehabilitation wards; and began providing mental health care, particularly for children and youths.[7]

After Hurricane Georges devastated Haiti in 1998, Cuba also was the first country to send medical aid to Haiti. After immediate disaster-relief work, Cuba began providing free medical care to the Haitian people on a long-term basis, implementing their model Comprehensive Health Program, and providing full scholarships to Haitian medical students for study in Cuba. In response to Tropical Storm Jeanne in 2004, Cuba sent an additional team of sixty-four doctors and twelve tons of medical supplies to Haiti. Between 1998 and 2010, 6,094 Cuban medical professionals have worked in Haiti, conducting more than 14 million patient visits, 225,000 surgeries, 100,000 birth deliveries, and saving more than 230,000 lives. In addition, by 2010, with Venezuelan support, Cuba had established five of ten planned comprehensive diagnostic centers, which provide not only a range of diagnostic services but also emergency care. Cuba had also trained 570 Haitian doctors on full scholarships. Finally, since

2004, slightly more than forty-seven thousand Haitians have undergone free eye surgery as part of Operation Miracle.[8]

Other recent disaster areas to which Cuba deployed its specialized medical brigades are China after the May 2008 earthquake, Indonesia after the May 2007 earthquake, Bolivia after the February 2008 floods, and Peru after the December 2007 earthquake. Cuban medical missions provided assistance as well in post-2004-tsunami Indonesia and post-2005-earthquake Pakistan. In both cases, the Cuban medical teams initially provided disaster relief but then stayed on after other disaster relief teams had left to provide preventive and curative care. Data for the medical mission to Pakistan indicate that, right after the earthquake, Cuba sent a team of highly experienced disaster-relief specialists comprising 2,564 doctors (57 percent of the team), nurses, and medical technicians.[9] Part of the team worked in refugee camps and Pakistani hospitals. Working in thirty field hospitals located across the earthquake-stricken zone, the team brought everything it would need to establish, equip, and run those hospitals. The cost to Cuba was not insignificant. Two of the hospitals alone cost US$500,000 each. In May 2006, Cuba augmented its aid with fifty-four emergency electrical generators.

Over the years, Cuba also has provided disaster relief aid to Armenia, Iran, Turkey, Russia, Ukraine, Belorussia, and most Latin American and Caribbean countries that have suffered either natural or man-made disasters. For example, over almost two decades, Cuba has treated free of charge almost 20,000 children — more than 16,000 Ukrainians, almost 3,000 Russians, and 671 Belorussians — mainly for post-Chernobyl radiation-related illnesses.[10] This type of medical diplomacy in the affected country's time of need has garnered considerable bilateral and multilateral symbolic capital for Havana, particularly when the aid is sent to countries considered more developed than Cuba.

Direct Provision of Medical Care: Selected Examples

The Cuba-Venezuela-Bolivia Connection: Comprehensive Health Programs It is indeed ironic that, in 1959, Fidel Castro unsuccessfully sought financial support and oil from Venezuelan president Rómulo Betancourt. It would take forty years and many economic difficulties before another Venezuelan president, Hugo Chávez, would provide the preferential trade, credit, aid, and investment that the Cuban economy desperately needed. This partnership is part of the Alternativa Bolivariana para los Pueblos de Nuestra América (ALBA) to unite and integrate Latin America in a social justice–oriented trade and aid block under Venezuela's lead. Despite Fidel's three-decade-long obsession with making Cuba into a world medical power, ALBA also has created an opportunity to expand the reach of Cuba's medical diplomacy well beyond anything previously imaginable.[11]

Cuba's current medical cooperation program with Venezuela is by far the largest it has ever attempted. These oil-for-doctors trade agreements allow for the preferential pricing of Cuba's exportation of professional services vis-à-vis a steady supply of Venezuelan oil, joint investments in strategically important sectors for both countries, and the provision of credit. In exchange, Cuba not only provides medical services to unserved and underserved communities in Venezuela — the initial agreement for massive medical services exports in 2005 was for thirty thousand medical professionals, six hundred comprehensive health clinics, six hundred rehabilitation and physical therapy centers, thirty-five high-technology diagnostic centers, one hundred thousand ophthalmologic surgeries, and so on — but also provides similar medical services in Bolivia on a smaller scale at Venezuela's expense.[12]

A later agreement included the expansion of the Venezuela-financed Cuban ophthalmologic surgery program — Operation Miracle — to perform six hundred thousand eyesight-saving and restoration operations in Latin America and the Caribbean over a ten-year period. That number was surpassed already in late 2007, when the one-millionth patient was operated on. As of February 2010, 1.8 million patients had benefited from the program.[13] To achieve these numbers, Cuba established sixty-one small eye-surgery clinics in Venezuela, Bolivia, Ecuador, Guatemala, Haiti, Honduras, Panama, Nicaragua, Paraguay, Uruguay, Peru, St. Lucia, St. Vincent, Suriname, and Argentina; and Cuba extended the program to Africa, establishing clinics in Angola and Mali, to handle some of the demand from those and neighboring countries and to reduce the strain on facilities at home.[14]

The second-largest medical cooperation program is with Bolivia, where in June 2006, 1,100 Cuban doctors were providing free health care, particularly in rural areas, in 188 municipalities. By July 2008, Cuban health personnel worked in 215 of Bolivia's 327 municipalities, including remote rural villages. It was reported that over the two-year period of medical diplomacy in Bolivia, Cuban doctors had saved 14,000 lives; had conducted more than 15 million medical exams; and had performed eye surgery on approximately 266,000 Bolivians and their neighbors from Argentina, Brazil, Paraguay, and Peru, the latter as part of Operation Miracle.[15] Ironically, through the Operation Miracle program in Bolivia, Cuba saved the eyesight of Mario Terán, the Bolivian man who killed Che Guevara.

Other Latin American and Caribbean Examples   Cuban medical teams had worked in Guyana and Nicaragua in the 1970s, but by 2005, they were implementing the Comprehensive Health Program in Belize, Bolivia, Dominica, Guatemala, Haiti, Honduras, Nicaragua, and Paraguay. They also had established two comprehensive diagnostic centers, one on the island of Dominica and one on Antigua and Barbuda. Both Jamaica and Suriname's health systems are being bolstered by the presence of Cuban medical personnel, and the latter is implementing the Comprehensive Health Program.[16] Throughout the years,

Cuba also has provided free medical care in its hospitals for individuals from all over Latin America and not just for the Latin American left.

Medical Diplomacy beyond the Western Hemisphere Cuba dispatched large civilian aid programs in Africa to complement its military support to Angola and the Horn of Africa in the 1970s and early 1980s. With the withdrawal of troops and the later geopolitical and economic changes of the late 1980s and the 1990s, Cuba's program remained but was scaled back.[17] Having suffered a postapartheid brain drain — white flight — South Africa began importing Cuban doctors in 1996. Already in 1998, 400 Cuban doctors practiced medicine in townships and rural areas, and in 2008, their number had increased slightly to 435. Cuban doctors began working in the Gambia in 1996, and since then and through 2009, 1,034 doctors, nurses, and medical technicians have served there.[18] By 2004, there were about 1,200 Cuban doctors working in other African countries, such as Angola, Botswana, Cape Verde, Côte d'Ivoire, Equatorial Guinea, Gambia, Ghana, Guinea, Guinea-Bissau, Mozambique, Namibia, Seychelles, Zambia, Zimbabwe, and areas in the Sahara. By December 2005, Cuba was implementing its Comprehensive Health Program in Botswana, Burkina Faso, Burundi, Chad, Equatorial Guinea, Eritrea, Gabon, Gambia, Ghana, Guinea-Bissau, Guinea-Conakry, Mali, Namibia, Niger, Rwanda, Sierra Leone, Swaziland, and Zimbabwe.

On the African continent, South Africa is the financier of some Cuban medical missions in third countries. This South African–Cuban alliance has been much more limited in scope than the Venezuelan-Cuban deal. An agreement to extend Cuban medical aid into the rest of the African continent and a trilateral agreement to deploy more than one hundred Cuban doctors in Mali with US$1 million of South African financing were concluded in 2004. In January 2010, another South-South cooperation agreement was concluded for South African financing, also totaling $1 million, to support thirty-one Cuban medical specialists who already had been working in Rwanda for a year and had treated 461,000 patients.[19]

Cuban medical teams also have worked and are working in such far-flung places as Timor-Leste (East Timor) in Southeast Asia and the Pacific island countries of Nauru, Vanuatu, Kiribati, Tuvalu, and the Solomon Islands, none of which might be considered in Cuba's strategic areas of interest. However, with one nation, one vote in the UN General Assembly, even these small islands are important where voting is concerned. The medical cooperation program in Timor-Leste began in December 2003 with the objective of creating a sustainable health-care system by establishing the Cuban-model Comprehensive Health Program. In 2008, 177 medical professionals were providing a variety of services in Cuba's Comprehensive Health Program there.[20]

Although the actual numbers of Cuban doctors working in the Pacific islands is small, their impact is great. For example, when Cuba sent eleven doctors to the island of Nauru in September 2004, it provided 78 percent of all doctors in Nauru, an increase of 367 percent.[21] Two Cuban doctors were work-ing in the Solomon Islands in 2008, and the remaining seven arrived in early 2009.[22] Three Cuban doctors currently work in Tuvalu, the first of whom arrived in October 2008. As of February 2009, they had attended 3,496 patients and saved fifty-three lives.[23] Vanuatu and Cuba signed an agreement in 2008 for six Cuban doctors to work in provincial hospitals. Vanuatu's Director of Public Health Len Tarivonda indicated that his country would pay for return airfare and provide accommodations and a small local allowance, whereas the Cuban government paid the doctors' salaries. At that rate, he said: "Cuban doctors cost less than those from Australia and New Zealand."[24]

Medical Education

To contribute to the sustainability of other countries' health programs, Cuba has long provided full scholarships for foreign students to study medicine, nursing, dentistry, and medical technicians' courses in Cuba and has provided on-the-job training abroad. Likewise, Cuba has assisted other countries in establishing and staffing their own medical schools. However, it was not until 1999, the year after Hurricanes Mitch and Georges struck Central America and Haiti, that Cuba created the Escuela Latinoamericana de Medicina (ELAM) to provide personnel for the rehabilitation of those countries' health systems. Enrollment, however, was not limited to the affected countries. The six-year medical school program is provided free for low-income students who commit to practice medicine in underserved communities in their home countries on graduation. As part of the Cuba-Venezuela cooperation accords, Cuba agreed to train forty thousand doctors and five thousand health-care workers in Vene-zuela and provide full medical scholarships to Cuban medical schools for ten thousand Venezuelan medical and nursing students. In addition, Cuba offered Bolivia five thousand more full scholarships to educate doctors and specialists as well as other health personnel at the ELAM in Havana. In 2006, there were some five hundred young Bolivians studying at the school — about 22 percent of the total foreign scholarship student body — and another two thousand had started the premed course there.

During the ELAM'S first graduation in August 2005, Hugo Chávez an-nounced that Venezuela would establish a second Latin American Medical School so that, jointly with Cuba, the two countries would be able to provide free medical training to at least one hundred thousand physicians for develop-ing countries over the next ten years. This led Cuba to implement the tutorial method of training medical personnel, whereby as of mid-2005, twelve thou-sand Cuban doctors serving in the Barrio Adentro program in Venezuela be-came tutors for some ten thousand Venezuelan medical students. In March

2009, approximately twenty-six thousand Venezuelan medical students were studying in the first four years of medical training as part of this new program to train comprehensive community doctors (*médicos integrales comunitarios*). This educational modality has been extended to six other countries in Asia, Africa, and Latin America, and another fourteen thousand students from thirty-six countries are studying under this modality in Cuba itself. Furthermore, in the 2008–2009 academic year, more than 24,000 foreign medical students were studying medicine at the ELAM (more than 7,900) and other Cuban institutions (more than 14,000).[25]

In 2008, Cuba offered full medical school scholarships for 800 East Timorese students to begin work on the sustainability of their health system, of which 697 were studying in medical schools in Cuba and another 105 were studying under Cuban medical professors in East Timor.[26] In 2009, in one medical faculty alone in the town of Sandino in western Cuba, there were a number of students from various South Pacific Islands and Timor-Leste studying medicine with full Cuban government scholarships: 199 from Timor-Leste, 50 from the Solomon Islands, 20 from Kiribati, 10 from Tuvalu, 7 from Nauru, and 17 from Vanuatu.[27] Also in 2009, more than three hundred nursing students from the English-speaking Caribbean, and two from China, participated in the Cuba–Caribbean Community (CARICOM) training program for the provision of services to HIV/AIDS patients.[28] During the 2009–2010 academic year, Cuba was training 51,648 medical students either in Cuba or in their own countries under the tutelage of Cuban professors. Of that number, 8,170 are enrolled in ELAM, 12,017 in the new program to train doctors (polyclinic based), 29,171 are being trained by Cuban medical brigades abroad, 1,118 are matriculated under other projects, and 1,172 are studying medical technician careers.[29]

The humanitarian benefits of this effort are enormous but so are the symbolic ones — prestige, influence, and goodwill — created. Moreover, the political benefits could be reaped for years to come as students trained by Cuba, with Venezuelan support, become health officials and opinion leaders in their own countries. Today, some of the 50,000 foreign scholarship students who trained in Cuban universities since 1961 (11,811 as doctors) are now in positions of authority and increasing responsibility.[30]

The Costs and Risks of Medical Diplomacy

The costs for beneficiary countries are relatively low. In most cases, the Cuban government pays doctors' salaries and the host country pays for airfare, room and board, and stipends of approximately $150–$375 per month depending on the country. This is far less than the costs of recruitment in the international marketplace, although it can still be a strain for cash-strapped economies. Perhaps more significant are the nonmonetary costs and risks involved. Cuban doctors serve the poor in areas in which no local doctor would work, make house calls a routine part of their medical practice, live in the neighborhood, and are available free of charge 24/7. This is changing the nature of doctor-patient relations and patients' expectations in the host countries. As a result, the presence of Cuban doctors has forced the reexamination of societal values and, in some cases, the structure and functioning of the health systems and the medical profession within the countries to which they were sent and where they continue to practice.

In countries such as Bolivia and Venezuela, although Cuban doctors generally are employed in areas where there are no local doctors, this different way of doing business has resulted in strikes and other protest actions by the local medical associations, as they are threatened by these changes and by what they perceive to be competition for their jobs. In the English-speaking Caribbean and in some Latin American countries, most particularly in Trinidad and Tobago, local medical associations have protested the different registration or accreditation standards applied to them and those applied or not applied to the Cuban doctors. Moreover, in Trinidad and Tobago, unlike other places where Cuban doctors serve, they pose a very real threat to local physicians' jobs because they were brought in by the government to fill vacancies left by both striking doctors and an overall insufficient number of local physicians to meet the country's health needs.[31]

The costs for Cuba, however, are more complicated partly because of the government's long-term investment in the education of medical personnel. Although Cuba pays the doctors' salaries, the pay scale is low by relative and absolute standards. In Cuba, doctors earn the equivalent in Cuban pesos of about US$25 per month. When they are abroad, that amount ascends to around US$185 per month. Since the Venezuelan agreement began, a significant amount of the costs for Cuba are, in fact, covered by Venezuela both for medical services and education for and in Venezuela and that provided to third countries. Previously, Cuba had fully funded these. However, money is fungible, and any aid Cuba receives could be channeled to this area.

A recent added cost has been the state's investment in the education and development of professionals who defect from medical diplomacy programs in third countries. Material conditions of life in Cuba are very difficult, and salaries are a fraction of those that can be earned abroad. These, as well as other factors, have enticed an estimated nine hundred to two thousand medical professionals, not all doctors, to defect to the United States with a little stimulus from Uncle Sam.[32] In August 2006, the U.S. government announced the Cuban Medical Professional Parole Program, which grants Cuban doctors serving abroad fast-track asylum processing and almost-guaranteed entry into the United States. Although this program has encouraged more defections and even has provided a reason for some Cuban doctors to go abroad in the first place, some have found that they are held in limbo in Colombia or other points of arrival without the promised fast-track visa approval and with little or no money.[33] Others have made their way to the United States only to find that they cannot practice their profession because they must first pass the same four exams taken by U.S. medical graduates, but with the handicap of doing so in a foreign language in which they did not study medicine. And the focus of their medical education, primary care, and access to the latest technology differs from that of the United States. Cuban doctors also are older when they come to the United States and, thus, may have family responsibilities that could preclude their taking preparatory courses and studying for the exams instead of working in whatever jobs they might find.[34]

A further risk for Cuba is increased dissatisfaction on the part of its own population as medical staff goes abroad, leaving some local health facilities and programs with insufficient staff despite the impressive ratio of doctors to population. As a result, a population accustomed to having a doctor on every block is finding that waiting times are now longer; medicines and supplies are scarcer; and where doctors are overworked, the quality of care declines.[35] Recognizing this problem in April 2008, Raúl Castro announced a reorganization of the Family Doctor Program at home to create greater efficiency by rationalizing the number and dispersion of family doctor offices but increasing the hours of operation for those outside of Havana until sufficient staff would become available. A year later, he announced further rationalization and cost containment with definite declines in both health care and education spending. Given the government's own proclamations that the health of the individual is a metaphor for the health of the body politic and that health indicators are a measure of government efficacy,[36] this situation could contribute to a delegitimization of the regime if insufficient attention is paid to the domestic health system.

Benefits of Medical Diplomacy

The value of Cuban medical diplomacy for the beneficiaries is clear. Over the past fifty years, Cuba's conduct of medical diplomacy has improved the health of the less privileged in developing countries while improving relations with their governments. Since 1961, Cuba has conducted medical diplomacy with 107 countries, deploying 134,849 medical professionals abroad, the large majority of whom were doctors.[37] In April 2008, more than thirty thousand Cuban medical personnel were collaborating in seventy-four countries around the globe.[38] Data as of October 2009 indicate that more than thirty-seven thousand Cuban medical professionals were deployed in ninety-eight countries and four overseas territories.[39] Overall, Cuban data show that, as of February 2009, Cuba's medical personnel abroad have saved more than 1.97 million lives, treated more than 130 million patients (of whom more than 39 million were seen on "house calls" at the patients' homes, schools, jobs, and so on), performed more than 2.97 million surgeries, and vaccinated with complete dosages more than 9.8 million people.[40] Added to this are the previously mentioned 1.8 million sight-restoring and preserving eye surgeries conducted under Operation Miracle. Consequently, Cuban medical aid has affected the lives of millions of people in developing countries each year.

To make this effort more sustainable, over the years, more than twelve thousand developing-country medical personnel have received free education and training in Cuba, and many more have benefited from education by Cuban specialists engaged in on-the-job training courses and/or medical schools in their own countries. In the largest enrollment ever, more than fifty thousand developing-country scholarship students — and a small number of less-privileged Americans — were studying either in Cuban medical schools or under Cuban professors in their home countries during the 2009–2010 academic year. Furthermore, Cuba has not missed a single opportunity to offer and supply disaster-relief assistance irrespective of whether Cuba had good relations with that government. In fact, when Cuba established ELAM to help hurricane-ravaged Central American and Caribbean countries strengthen their health systems, none of the beneficiary governments was particularly friendly toward Cuba. In a more astonishing example, Cuba offered to send more than one thousand doctors trained in disaster relief as well as medical supplies to the United States in the immediate aftermath of Hurricane Katrina. Although the Bush administration chose not to accept the offer, the symbolism of this offer of help by a small, developing country that has suffered fifty years of U.S. hostilities, including an economic embargo, is remarkable.[41]

Since Cuba first sent a medical brigade to Chile in 1960, it has used medical diplomacy both to improve the health and win the hearts and minds of aid recipients and to improve relations with their governments.[42] Medical diplomacy has been a critical means of gaining symbolic capital — prestige, influence, and goodwill — which can translate into diplomatic support and material capital, such as trade or aid. It has been a way to project Cuba's image abroad as increasingly more developed and technologically sophisticated. More important, the practice of medical diplomacy also projects an image of Cuba as righteous, just, and morally superior because it is sending doctors rather than soldiers to far-flung places around the world. This latter comparison is important in Cuba's symbolic struggle as David versus the Goliath of the United States.

Cuba's success in this endeavor has been recognized by the WHO and other UN bodies, as well as by numerous governments, 107 of which have been direct beneficiaries of Cuba's medical largesse. It also has contributed to support for Cuba and rebuke of the United States in the UN General Assembly, where for the past eighteen consecutive years members voted overwhelmingly in favor of lifting the U.S. embargo of Cuba. In fact, only Israel and Palau have supported the U.S. position, and the Marshall Islands and Micronesia abstained.[43] With equal voting rights for all members of the UN General Assembly, Cuba's medical diplomacy with such a large number of member states is a rational endeavor, however humanitarian the impetus may be.

Furthermore, the success of Cuba's medical diplomacy was made evident once again at the Summit of the Americas in Trinidad in April 2009. The Latin American heads of state frequently mentioned it in their discussions with President Obama. Cuba's medical diplomacy underpins their support for lifting the U.S. trade embargo on Cuba and normalizing relations, including the reinstatement of Cuba into the Organization of American States (OAS), agreed to in the June 2009 OAS meeting in Honduras, although Raúl Castro indicated that Cuba was disinterested. In turn, Obama mentioned this fact in his own remarks, even indicating that the United States could learn from Cuba. He has been widely quoted as later saying, "We have to use our diplomatic and our development aid in more intelligent ways so that people can see the very practical, concrete improvements in the lives of ordinary persons as a consequence of U.S. foreign policy."[44]

Economic benefits have been very significant since the rise of Chávez in Venezuela. Trade with and aid from Venezuela in a large-scale oil-for-doctors exchange have bolstered Cuba's ability to conduct medical diplomacy and, importantly, have helped keep its economy afloat. Earnings from medical services, including the export of doctors, equaled 28 percent of total export receipts and net capital payments in 2006. This amounted to US$2.312 billion, a figure greater than that for both nickel and cobalt exports and tourism.[45] In fact, the export of medical services is thought to be the brightest spot on Cuba's economic horizon.[46] Data for 2008 demonstrates that Cuba earned about US$5.6 billion for the provision of all services to Venezuela, most of which were medical, although the figure includes teachers and other professionals. The total value of the Venezuelan trade, aid, investments, and subsidies to Cuba for 2008 was US$9.4 billion.[47]

Medical diplomacy also paves the way for Cuba's export of a range of medical products. In this context, for example, Cuban exports of medicines to ALBA countries increased by 22 percent from 2008 to 2009.[48] It is quite likely that other countries receiving Cuban doctors will also purchase Cuban vaccines, medicines, medical supplies, and equipment. Cuba's biotech industry holds 1,200 international patents and earned US$350 million in product sales in 2008.[49] Potential for growth in the export of vaccines is good, particularly in joint ventures with other countries, such as Cuba has already with Brazil and China, and with big pharmaceutical companies, like GlaxoSmithKline.[50]

Symbolic capital garnered from both the success of the domestic health system and medical diplomacy made possible Cuba's establishment of a medical tourism industry. Although begun as a small program in 1980, medical tourism became important by 1990, with the collapse of the Soviet Union and after Cuba had vastly increased its production of doctors for medical diplomacy programs. The number of patients participating in medical tourism in Cuba for the first eight years of the program was equal to 55 percent of medical tourists in 1990 alone. Revenue from health tourism in 1990 was US$2 million.[51] This program received renewed impetus during the mid-1990s as the government sought to increase its foreign exchange earnings through a variety of methods, including limited foreign investment. By 1997, revenue had increased to US$20 million, 98.5 percent of which was plowed back into the domestic health system.[52]

On the domestic front, medical diplomacy has provided an escape valve for disgruntled medical professionals who earn much less at home than less skilled workers in the tourism sector. Their earning potential is much greater abroad, both in the confines of the medical diplomacy program and even more so beyond it. This constant lure of defection has led the Ministry of Public Health to establish a coefficient for possible defections — 2–3 percent of the total number of international medical collaborators — as part of precise human-resources-planning exercises.[53] Moreover, medical diplomacy has given Cuban doctors and other medical personnel an opportunity to bring home from their deployment station consumer goods unavailable in Cuba. In this way, it is has helped defuse the tension between the moral incentives of socialist ideology and the material needs of Cuba's decidedly hardworking and no-less-dedicated medical personnel.[54]

Conclusion

Medical diplomacy has been a cornerstone of Cuban foreign policy since the outset of the revolution fifty years ago. It has been an integral part of almost all bilateral relations agreements that Cuba has made with other developing countries. As a result, Cuba has positively affected the lives of millions of people per year through the provision of medical aid, as well as tens of thousands of foreign students who receive full scholarships to study medicine either in Cuba or in their own countries under Cuban professors. At the same time, Cuba's conduct of medical diplomacy with countries whose governments had not been sympathetic to the revolution, such as Pakistan, Guatemala, Honduras, and El Salvador, to name only a few, has led to improved relations with those countries.

Medical diplomacy has helped Cuba garner symbolic capital (goodwill, influence, and prestige) well beyond what would have been possible for a small, developing country, and it has contributed to making Cuba a player on the world stage. In recent years, medical diplomacy has been instrumental in providing considerable material capital (aid, credit, and trade), as the oil-for-doctors deals with Venezuela demonstrates. This has helped keep the revolution afloat in trying economic times.

What began as the implementation of one of the core values of the revolution, namely health as a basic human right for all peoples, has continued as both an idealistic and a pragmatic pursuit. As early as 1978, Fidel Castro argued that there were insufficient doctors to meet demand in the developing world, despite the requesting countries' ability to pay hard currency for their services.[55] Because Cuba charged less than other countries, with the exception at that time of China, it appeared that it would win contracts on a competitive basis. In fact, during the following decade (1980s), Cuba's medical contracts and grant aid increased. In most cases, aid led to trade, if not to considerable income. With the debt crises and the International Monetary Fund's structural adjustment programs of the 1980s, grant aid predominated. In 1990, Cuban medical aid began to dwindle as neither the host countries nor Cuba could afford the costs, the former because of structural adjustment–mandated cuts in social expenditures and the latter because of the collapse of its preferential trade relationships following the demise of the Soviet Union. As Cuba's ability to provide bilateral medical aid diminished, its provision of medical aid through multilateral sources (contracts) increased.[56] Cuba's medical diplomacy continued, albeit on a smaller scale during the 1990s, until the rise of Hugo Chávez in Venezuela.

With medical services leading economic growth in the twenty-first century, it seems unlikely that even the more pragmatic Raúl Castro will change direction now. In contrast, dependency on one major benefactor and/or trade partner can be perilous, as the Cubans have seen more than once. If Chávez either loses power or drastically reduces foreign aid in an effort to cope with Venezuela's own deteriorating economic conditions and political opposition, Cuba could experience an economic collapse similar to that of the Special Period in the early 1990s. In fact, the global financial and economic crisis has compounded existing problems. In an effort to avert that type of collapse, Raúl Castro has been trying to further diversify Cuba's commercial partners.[57] In July 2009, Cuba received a new US$150 million credit line from Russia to facilitate technical assistance from that country, and companies from both countries signed various agreements, including four related to oil exploration.[58] Furthermore, Raúl Castro made clear in his August 1, 2009, speech before the National Assembly of People's Power, that Cuba could not spend more than it made.[59] He asserted that it was imperative to prioritize activities and expenditures to achieve results, overall greater efficiency, and to rationalize state subsidies to the population.

Despite a little help from its Venezuelan friend, the Cuban government has had to embark on austerity measures that hark back to the worst of times right after the collapse of the former Soviet Union.[60] With two budget cuts already this year, restrictions on electricity distribution, and a 20 percent decrease in imports,[61] it is likely that the Cuban government will attempt to increase its medical exports to countries that can afford to pay for them. In fact, in August 2009, Raúl Castro indicated that Cuba would need to increase the production of services that earn hard currency.[62] Pragmatism clearly dictates this course of action even if it also is imbued with strong revolutionary idealism about humanitarian assistance.

Economic and political benefits of medical diplomacy aside, Fidel, both when he was president and today as an elder statesman and blogger, most sincerely cares about health for all, not just for Cubans. His long-term constant involvement in the evolution both of the domestic health system and of medical diplomacy has been clear through both his public pronouncements and actions, and the observations and commentary of his subordinates and external observers.[63] Today, this concern for health is part of the social agenda of ALBA, through which, for example, additional Cuban medical aid to Haiti post-2010 earthquake is being conducted.

Unable to offer financial support, Cuba provides what it excels at and what is easily available, its medical human resources. International recognition for Cuba's health expertise has made medical diplomacy an important foreign policy tool that other, richer countries would do well to emulate. After all, what country could refuse humanitarian aid that for all intents and purposes appears to be truly altruistic?

NOTES

1. Julie M. Feinsilver, "Cuba as a World Medical Power: The Politics of Symbolism," *Latin American Research Review* 24, no. 2 (1989): 1–34; Julie M. Feinsilver, "Cuban Medical Diplomacy: Realpolitik and Symbolic Politics," paper presented at meeting of the Latin American Studies Association, Halifax, Nova Scotia, November 1–4, 1989.

2. Julie M. Feinsilver, "Cuba's Health Politics at Home and Abroad," in *Morbid Symptoms: Health under Capitalism, Socialist Register 2010*, ed. Leo Panitch and Colin Leys (London: Merlin Press, 2009), 216–39; Julie M. Feinsilver, "Cuban Medical Diplomacy," in *A Changing Cuba in a Changing World*, comp. Mauricio A. Font (New York: Bildner Center, City University of New York, 2009), 273–85, available at http://web.gc.cuny.edu/dept/bildn/publications/ChangingCuba.shtml; Julie M. Feinsilver, "Médicos por petróleo: La diplomacia médica cubana reciba una pequeña ayuda de sus amigos," *Nueva Sociedad* (Buenos Aires), 216 (July–August 2008): 107–22 (English version: "Oil-for-Doctors: Cuba's Medical Diplomacy Gets a Little Help from a Venezuelan Friend," available at http://www.nuso.org/revista.php?n=216; Feinsilver, "Medical Diplomacy"; Julie M. Feinsilver, "La diplomacia médica cubana: Cuando la izquierda lo ha hecho bien," *Foreign Affairs en Español* 6, no. 4 (2006): 81–94 (English version: "Cuban Medical Diplomacy: When the Left Has Got It Right," available at http://www.coha.org/2006/10/30/cuban-medical-diplomacy-when-the-left-has-got-it-right/; Julie M. Feinsilver, *Healing the Masses: Cuban Health Politics at Home and Abroad* (Berkeley: University of California Press, 1993), 9–25, 156–95, 196–211. Although the statistical data in the book are dated, the overall analysis of the whole book has, as Dr. Peter Bourne — executive producer of *Salud! The Film* — indicated in a personal communication of November 13, 2006, "withstood the test of time."

102 : Julie M. Feinsilver

3. Oficina Nacional de Estadísticas, República de Cuba, *Anuario estadístico de Cuba 2008: Edición 2009*, http://www.one.cu/aec2008/esp/20080618_tabla_cuadro.htm.

4. Feinsilver, *Healing the Masses*, 159–60.

5. Ibid., 157.

6. Mike Blanchfield, "Harper Hails Unplugging of Ideological Megaphones at Hemispheric Summit," Canwest News Service, April 19, 2009, available at http://www.canada.com/business/Harper+hails+unplugging+ideological+megaphones+hemispheric+summit/1512580/story.html.

7. "Cuban Doctors in Haiti Boost Integral Assistance," *Prensa Latina*, February 2, 2010, http://www.solvision.co.cu/english/index.php?option=com_content&view=article&id=862:cuba-doctors-in-haiti-boost-integral-assistance-&catid=7:health&Itemid=128; "Cuba considera ayuda a Haiti prioritaria," *Granma*, January 13, 2010, http://www.granma.cubaweb.cu/2010/01/13/nacional/artic28.html.

8. Embassy of Cuba in Nueva Zelandia, Pacific Press Release, "Cuba Stands by the Haitian People," January 22, 2010, http://pacific.scoop.co.nz/2010/01/cuba-stands-by-the-haitian-people/.

9. Ibid.

10. "Cuba Has Treated over 20,000 Children from Chernobyl Disaster," *Havana Journal*, April 2, 2009, http://havanajournal.com/forums/viewthread/1145/.

11. Feinsilver, "Cuando la izquierda lo ha hecho bien," 84; Feinsilver, "Médicos por petróleo," 111.

12. Ibid.

13. "The Open Eyes of Latin America," *Granma*, February 3, 2010, http://translate.google.com/translate?langpair=eslen&u=http%3A%2F%2Fwww.radioangulo.cu%2Fenglish%2Findex.php%3Foption%3Dcom_content%26task%3Dview%26id%3D5909%26Itemid%3D28.

14. "Nuevo impulso a Operación Milagro en Argentina," *Radio Sucro*, December 3, 2009.

15. "Report on Cuban Healthcare Professionals in Bolivia," *Periódico*, July 16, 2008, http://www.periodico26.cu/english/health/jun_sep2008/doctors-bolivia071608.html.

16. Cuba Coopera Web site; "Cubans to Help Boost Local Health Sector," *Jamaica Observer*, May 10, 2008, http://www.jamaicaobserver.com/news/html/20080510T000000-0500_135451_OBS_CUBANS_TO_HELP_BOOST_LOCAL_HEALTH_SECTOR.asp.

17. Feinsilver, *Healing the Masses*, 156–95.

18. "Gambia: 1034 Cuban Medical Personnel Work in the Country," *Banjul Daily Observer*, December 7, 2009, http://allafrica.com/stories/200912080823.html.

19. "MoH gets $1m to Facilitate Cuban Medical Volunteers," *Rwanda New Times*, January 22, 2010, http://www.newtimes.co.rw.

20. Cuba Coopera Web site, March 11, 2008.

21. "Cuban Doctors Help Alleviate Nauru Health Problems," ABC News Online, September 7, 2004, http://www.abc.net.au/news/newsitems/200409/s1194185.htm.

22. "Cuban Doctors Arrival a Blessing, Says Solomons Health Dept.," Radio New Zealand International, June 10, 2008, http://www.rnzi.com/pages/news.php?op=read&id=40275; "Solomon Islands Welcome Cuba Doctors," Radio New Zealand International, March 25, 2009, http://www.rnzi.com/pages/news.php?op=read&id=40275.

23. "Cuban Doctors Inaugurated New Health Services in Tuvalu a Small Pacific Island," *Cuba Headlines*, June 14, 2009, http://www.cubaheadlines.com/2009/06/14/17664/cuban_doctors_have_inaugurated_a_series_new_health_services_tuvalu_a_small_island_nation_pacific.html.

24. "Vanuatu to Get Six Doctors from Cuba," Radio New Zealand International, August 10, 2008, http://www.rnzi.com/pages/news.php?op=read&id=41373.

25. http://www.cubacoop.com/cubacoop/FRH_NPF.html.

26. Tim Anderson, *The Doctors of Tomorrow: The Timor L'este-Cuba Health Cooperation* (documentary film), University of Sydney (2008).

27. Tim Anderson, *The Pacific School of Medicine* (documentary film), University of Sydney (2009), part 1 available at http://www.youtube.com/watch?v=AhMAncnEDQQ; part 2 available at http://www.youtube.com/watch?v=j-AoKYCDmlo&feature=related.

28. http://www.cubacoop.com/cubacoop/FRH_NPF.html.

29. Personal communication with Dr. Francisco Rojas Ochoa, distinguished professor and editor, *Revista Cubana de Salud Pública*, February 3, 2010.

30. *Prensa Latina*, April 11, 2008; data on medical graduates from 1963 to 2008 from personal communication on February 3, 2010, from Dr. Francisco Rojas Ochoa, Distinguished Professor and editor of *Revista Cubana de Salud Pública*.

31. Lara Pickford-Gordon, "Cuban Doctors and TT's Medical Development," *Trinidad and Tobago's Newsday*, August 9, 2009, http://www.newsday.co.tt.

32. Anti-Castro Cuban-American Representative Lincoln Diaz-Balart's (R-FL) chief of staff, Ana Carbonell, told Mirta Ojito of the *New York Times* that about two thousand Cuban medical professionals, not all doctors, had settled in the United States since the 2006 program began. However, I have not been able to corroborate these numbers despite attempts through various government agencies and officials. See Mirta Ojito, "Doctors in Cuba Start Over in the US," *New York Times*, August 4, 2009, http://www.nytimes.com/2009/08/04/health/04cuba.html?pagewa nted=1.The Cuban Ministry of Public Health planners calculate a defection rate of between 2 percent and 3 percent when planning their human resource needs. From interview with Dr. Félix Rigoli, Pan-American Health Organization (PAHO), April 30, 2009.

33. Mike Ceasar, "Cuban Doctors Abroad Helped to Defect by New U.S. Visa Policy," *World Politics Review*, August 1, 2007.

34. Ojito, "Doctors in Cuba."

35. For some excellent discussions of the material problems facing Cuban doctors and their patients in post-Soviet Cuba based on anthropological field work, see Pierre Sean Brotherton, "Macroeconomic Change and the Biopolitics of Health in Cuba's Special Period," *Journal of Latin American Anthropology* 10, no. 2 (2005): 339–69; Elise Andaya, "The Gift of Health: Socialist Medical Practice and Shifting Material and Moral Economies in Post-Soviet Cuba," *Medical Anthropology Quarterly* 23, no. 4 (2009): 357–74.

36. Ministerio de Salud Pública, República de Cuba, *Salud para todos: 25 años de experiencia cubana* (Havana: Ministerio de Salud Pública, 1983), 35, qtd. in Feinsilver, *Healing the Masses*, 1, 217.

37. http://www.cubacoop.com. Data as of October 12, 2009; Rojas Ochoa personal communication.

38. *Prensa Latina*, April 11, 2008.

39. http://www.cubacoop.com.

40. http://www.cubacoop.com/cubacoop/Cooperacion_ResultadosG.

41. Feinsilver, "La diplomacia médica cubana."

42. In a recent article, Fidel Castro refuted the idea that Cuba has used medical diplomacy to gain influence. Nonetheless, the evidence suggests that it has done so, even though this might not have originally been the primary reason for doing so. It is an intelligent use of Cuba's comparative advantage, its medical human resources. See "Reflexiones del compañero Fidel: La cumbre secreta," *Diario Granma*, April 21, 2009, http://www.granma.cubaweb.cu/secciones/ref-fidel/art125 .html.

43. For example, "U.N. Votes Against U.S. Embargo on Cuba for 18th Year," Reuters, October 28, 2009, http://www.reuters.com/article/idUSTRE59R4LQ20091028/.

44. Laura Carlsen, "Words and Deeds in Trinidad," *Foreign Policy in Focus*, April 22, 2009, http: //www.fpif.org/articles/words_and_deeds_in_trinidad; Blanchfield, "Harper Hails Unplugging."

45. Embassy of India (Havana), "Annual Commercial and Economic Report—2006," No .Hav/Comm/2007, April 13, 2007.

46. Carmelo Mesa-Lago and Archibald Ritter, remarks at the City University of New York Bildner Center Conference, "A Changing Cuba in a Changing World," March 13–15, 2008.

47. Carmelo Mesa-Lago, "The Cuban Economy in 2008–2009: Internal and External Challenges, State of the Reforms and Perspectives," Adiestramiento Político Administrativo, San José, Costa Rica, February 3–4, 2009 (this work is forthcoming as a chapter in a book edited by Paolo Spadoni).

48. "Más medicamentos cubanos para el ALBA Salud," *Radio Sucro*, January 6, 2010, http://www.radiosucro.cu/Salud.php?id=4786.

49. Patricia Grogg, "Welfare of Cuban People Is Bottomline of Cuba's Pharmaceutical Industry," December 1, 2009, http://www.newjerseynewsroom.com/international/welfare-of-the-people-is-bottomline-for-cubas-pharmaceutical-industry/page-2; "Cuban Exports: Sugar, Cigars . . . and Cancer Drugs?" *Healthcare Economist*, March 26, 2009.

50. "Cutting-Edge Biotech in Old World Cuba," *Christian Science Monitor*, April 17, 2003, http://www.latinamericanstudies.org/cuba/biotech.htm.

51. Feinsilver, *Healing the Masses,* 190.

52. P. Sean Brotherton, " 'We Have to Think Like Capitalists but Continue Being Socialists': Medicalized Subjectivities, Emergent Capital, and Socialist Entrepreneurs in Post-Soviet Cuba," *American Ethnologist* 35, no. 2 (2008): 259–74.

53. Interview with anonymous source no. 25, April 30, 2009.

54. On the "economy of favors" or "the moral economy of ideal socialist medical practice . . . based on reciprocal social exchange," see Andaya, "Gift of Health," 357.

55. *Bohemia,* September 15, 1978, 39, cited in Feinsilver, *Healing the Masses*, 193, 264n201.

56. Feinsilver, *Healing the Masses*, 193–94.

57. Mesa-Lago, "Cuban Economy in 2008–2009."

58. "Cuba y Federación Rusa estrechan colaboración económica," *Granma Internacional*, July 29, 2009, http://www.granma.cu/espanol/2009/julio/mier29/colaboracion.html.

59. Speech by Army General Raul Castro Ruz, President of the Councils of State and Ministers, at the Fifth Regular Session of the Seventh Legislature of the National Assembly of Popular Power in the International Conference Center, August 1, 2010, "Year 52 of the Revolution," http://prensacubana.e-datalink.net/speech-by-army-general-raul-castro-ruz-president-of-the-co uncils-of-state-and-ministers-at-the-fifth-regular-session-of-the-seventh-legislature-of-the-nation al-assembly-of-popular-power-in-the-inter/.

60. Carmelo Mesa-Lagos, "La paradoja económica cubana," *El País,* July 12, 2009, http://www.elpais.com/articulo/semana/paradoja/economica/cubana/elpepueconeg/20090712elpnegls e_10/Tes.

61. "Cuba Runs Out of Lavatory Paper," *London Telegraph*, August 9, 2009, http://www.tele graph.co.uk/news/newstopics/howaboutthat/6001005/Cuba-runs-out-of-lavatory-paper.html; "Cuba Sounds Summer Emergency Alarm, Plans Blackouts," May 26, 2009, http://www.azcentral .com/news/articles/2009/05/26/20090526cuba-blackouts0526-ON.html.

62. Raúl Castro stated that Cuba will increase production of services that generate foreign exchange. See Castro Ruz, "Year 52 of the Revolution."

63. Feinsilver, *Healing the Masses*; Peter G. Bourne, *Fidel: A Biography of Fidel Castro* (New York: Dodd, Mead, 1986), 284.

MARTA NÚÑEZ-SARMIENTO

Cubans Abroad: A Gendered Case Study on International Migrations

ABSTRACT

Cubans who have migrated since the 1990s after living for two decades or more in their country of origin left with an embedded gender ideology that they acquired in a society where gender relations were undergoing radical transformations. As a result, Cuban feminization of migrations has its peculiarities. In this context, there are three issues to consider: explaining how gender relations attained in Cuba, as part of the overall attitudes gained since childhood, influenced Cuban migrants who have left the island permanently since 1990, introduced uniqueness in their migration processes, and made up a different feminization of migration; identifying the features of Cuban social structure that shaped the gender ideology of Cuban migrants; and producing new knowledge about Cuban international migration processes by using a gender perspective and by analyzing the gender relations prevailing in the years before the crisis of the 1990s, as well as since the beginning of the twenty-first century. The first part of this article focuses on gender distinctiveness of recent Cuban migrants, and the second summarizes some traits of the Cuban social structure — mainly referred to female employment — that could explain the gender training of the migrants.

RESUMEN

Las cubanas y los cubanos que emigraron en los años noventa tras vivir por dos décadas o más en Cuba llevaron consigo una ideología de género adquirida en una sociedad que transformó radicalmente las relaciones de género. Como resultado la feminización de las migraciones internacionales en Cuba tiene sus peculiaridades. El artículo tiene tres propósitos: aproximarse a las especificidades de las personas que se marcharon de Cuba a partir de los años noventa, para identificar las singularidades de su ideología de género; encontrar los orígenes de esas actitudes en las estructuras sociales prevalecientes en Cuba a lo largo de su infancia, adolescencia y adultez temprana, así como en la ideología de género prevaleciente en Cuba, y, por último, producir nuevos conocimientos sobre los procesos migratorios externos cubanos usando la perspectiva de género y analizando las relaciones de género prevalecientes en Cuba en los años anteriores a la crisis de los noventa y desde el inicio de este siglo. La primera parte del artículo se dedica a las características genéricas de los migrantes cubanos recientes, mientras que la segunda parte resume algunas tendencias de las estructuras sociales cubanas — sobre todo aquellas referidas al empleo femenino — que podrían explicar el entrenamiento de género de estos migrantes.

105

Cubans who have migrated since the 1990s after living for two decades or more in their country of origin left with an embedded gender ideology that they acquired in a society where gender relations were undergoing radical transformations. As a result, Cuban feminization of migrations has its peculiarities. In this context, there are three issues to consider: explaining how gender relations attained in Cuba, as part of the overall attitudes gained since childhood, influenced Cuban migrants who have left the island permanently since 1990, introduced uniqueness in their migration processes, and made up a different feminization of migration; identifying the features of Cuban social structure that shaped the gender ideology of the Cuban migrants; and producing new knowledge about Cuban international migration processes by using a gender perspective and by analyzing the gender relations prevailing in the years before the crisis of the 1990s, as well as since the beginning of the twenty-first century.

The worldwide trend of feminization of international migrations is present in the Cuban case.[1] Women migrants slightly exceed the total number of males: from 1960 to 2008, they represented 50.89 percent of the 1,332,432 persons who left Cuba.[2] However, these women and men differ in their gender attitudes according to the years when they left Cuba and to the gender "training" acquired in their native country.

The fifty-five migrants interviewed for this case study were born in the 1970s and left Cuba in their early adulthood — between 1997 and 2008. Therefore, Cuban social structures had influenced them for more than two decades. The findings in this article were based on a case study with thirty-five Cuban women and twenty men who have migrated from Havana, Cuba, since 1998, and who left with a university degree or with a completed technical education. The majority of the interviewees were between twenty-six and thirty-six years of age upon leaving Cuba, and only three of them were fifty-five years or older. All of them left Cuba legally. As I decided to personally interview individuals in my study but did not have funds to travel to the main countries in which Cubans were living, and because the U.S. Treasury Department was imposing extreme restrictions on visits to the United States by Cuban scholars, I interviewed Cuban migrants while visiting relatives in Havana from 2003 to 2008. Therefore, their countries of residence were selected randomly. Among the interviewees, there was a relatively high presence of Cubans in the Dominican Republic; thus, I talked to Cuban migrants during my stays in the Dominican Republic as a visiting professor. The rest lived in the United States, Spain, Italy, and Germany. I also consulted Cuban experts on gender and migration, analyzed literature dealing with these topics, and kept a diary with my observations beginning from 2003. I also analyzed statistical sociodemographic data.

Focus on the last decade of the twentieth century in Cuba is important, as it was a period of severe crisis that imposed a turning point in Cuban development strategies because it stopped the upward social mobility that the whole population had experienced from 1959 to 1989. These were the worst years of the Cuban transition to a socialist order — based on international and national experiences — because society experienced a fall in living standards from which it still has not fully recovered. In the first thirty years of the revolution, the gains experienced at the individual and social levels encouraged Cubans' aspirations. The crisis of the 1990s made many Cubans consider that they could not fulfill their life projects in their home country and decide to emigrate to carry them out in other countries. When they left, they took within them peculiarities in their gender ideology gained in Cuba.

Gender Characteristics of Cuban Migrants

Feminization of Migration

The UN Fund for Population (UNFPA) reported in its *State of the World Population 2006* dedicated to women and international migrations: "Over the last 40 years almost as many women have migrated as men. . . . By the year 2005, there were slightly more female than male immigrants in all regions of the world except Africa and Asia."[3] In Cuba, this tendency has been conditioned by the deep changes in social structures over the past fifty years, by the programs to promote gender equality, and by the migration policies effective in Cuba and in the destination countries, basically the United States. At present, most Cuban migrants live in the United States. The UNFPA report adds that, "Among developed regions, North America is exceptional in that female immigrants have outnumbered male immigrants since 1930."[4] This quality of the feminization of migrations to the United States and Canada is also present among Caribbean countries. The UNFPA states that "starting with the decade of 1950, every decade the quantities of Caribbean migrant women to North America have exceeded that of men, and women are well represented in the categories of qualified workers."[5] According to the U.S. Census Bureau, in 2000, 50.8 percent of Cubans residing in the United States and born in Cuba were women.[6]

Therefore, the flow of Cuban women migrants toward North America, basically to the United States, is similar to the migration currents from other Caribbean countries. The UNFPA acknowledged that Latin American and Caribbean women have also increased their migration flows to other regions of the world. As of 2005, Cubans were living in 148 countries.[7]

Still, Cuban feminization flows to the United States differ from those coming from Latin America and the Caribbean, at least because of the preferential and selective migration policies that Washington applies to Cuban citizens.[8] Susan Eckstein wrote that, in the United States during the Cold War era, "Cubans became the most privileged immigrant group," with the United States subsidizing many of them and offering them certain benefits to ease their adaption process.[9]

There are also variations in gender attitudes between Cuban women who left the country in the 1960s and 1970s and those who migrated after 1990. Although my present case study does not render the necessary basis to prove this assertion, I hypothesize that the former did not experience the profound changes in gender relations through which Cubans lived after the early 1970s and that became pre-emigration assets for the Cubans who have left since the 1990s. These transformations benefited women and men in terms of better levels of education, advanced professional job skills, comprehensive health habits, family-planning know-how, sexual education patterns, and equal rights, among other new gender expertise. Changes in gender ideology started with the struggles for female emancipation in the early 1960s and explain why women have changed their gender ideologies much more than men have.

Throughout these transformations, decision making has become one of the new gender attributes that Cuban women acquired in more comprehensive ways than they had before 1959 — Cuban working women's high educational standards grant them the ability to organize or "program" both their job and their work during the second shift (i.e., at home) at the same time. Cuban women in my sample used this decision-making capacity in the ways in which they left the country. Two-thirds of migrant women whom I interviewed departed from Cuba alone, the majority without a partner accompanying and/or waiting for them in their countries of destination. Three left with prearranged fictitious marriages so as to enter their new countries of residence. The rest traveled with their husbands, followed them to the selected destinations, or left before them. The Cuban sociologists Gretel Marrero and Elpidia Moreno found the same trend in their studies.[10] Men in my research behaved similarly. Women and men included in this investigation stated that they emigrated because they were anxious to fulfill their life projects in other countries. They answered that they selected this alternative because they were sufficiently "independent" and "prepared" to do so: they had a university degree, had worked for two or more years in their professions under conditions of low salaries, and had friends or relatives living abroad who had promised to give them a hand. Several added that Cuba had twenty or more years to revive its economy, and they were unwilling to wait that long to fulfill their life projects. These schemes included having a job with a good salary; founding a family; buying a house, apartment, or car; helping their relatives in Cuba; and traveling regularly to Cuba and other countries. Experts in gender and migration consulted for this research explained that this is a dream common to all migrants that only some can realize.

In my study, professionally qualified migrants represent at least two generations that were trained in Cuba to behave with self-determination regardless of their gender. They studied for at least seventeen years at educational institutions

— from preprimary to university graduation. Two more years could be added if they attended nurseries in their early childhood. Since the seventh grade, they spent at least one month every year working in the fields, attended boarding high schools, and continued living in university dormitories if they lived far from these tertiary-level institutions. Therefore, they shared as much daily experience with members of their cohorts as they did with parents and relatives. Many of their parents studied abroad in the Soviet Union and Eastern European countries and/or worked in cooperation missions in other countries; hence, present migrants constructed a close paradigm of what it means to live abroad.

Employment and the Second Shift

Migrants in my study graduated from Cuban universities during the 1990s and the first years of the twenty-first century. Except for one woman and one man, the rest were employed at jobs linked to their professions for at least two years before leaving the country. In their countries of destination, only one-third of the women and less than half of the men were employed in jobs according to their professions. Almost all have more than one job to cover their budgets, and some have to rush daily from one job to another during rush-hour traffic. Nearly everyone said that they preferred to develop their professions but were satisfied with their present job situation because they earned enough to cover their expenses. Nearly everyone stated that they had little opportunity to upgrade their job training. Gretel Marrero confirmed this behavior in her study. She quoted Sussie Jollie and Hazel Reeves, saying that, worldwide, the majority of migrant women perform nonqualified jobs, such as domestic workers, caretakers, and in manufacturing — mainly in the textile and food industries. They added that gender-segregated job markets discriminate against migrant women such that they are exploited in terms of salaries and risks. Men tend to work in regulated and more visible jobs than women.[11]

Cuban experts I consulted in my study stated that it was far more difficult for women than men to find jobs according to their professional training in the countries where they emigrated. Cuban women were very disappointed by this, but they said that they had to adapt to the situation in their new countries of residence. They pointed to several discrimination traits: less pay for women than men, little or no paid leave, extremely intense job schedules, and two mentioned cases of sexual harassment by coworkers. It is easier for men to find jobs in general and as professionals, as employers are often prejudiced against pregnancy and childbearing. Experts met few men and almost no women who held leading positions at their new jobs. It is far more difficult to work as professionals in countries where languages other than Spanish are spoken. Women and men alike considered themselves well trained to perform not only their professions but also any "appropriate," "decent," "convenient" job that produced income. This capacity could derive from their prolonged educational training in Cuba that disciplined them to fixed schedules from early morning to late afternoon. It could also stem from working paradigms — of both men and women — that they observed in their parents.

In my previous studies concerning the influence of women's employment on gender ideology in Cuba, I predicted that working mothers' children would be educated to admit that female employment was something natural and — in the case of sons — would be prepared to accept women as coworkers and managers and to marry working women. Cuban migrants took this training to the new places where they are living, and thanks to it, they understood that both members of the couple should be employed. This preparation promoted a new view on the second shift, as husbands and wives — or partners — engaged in domestic chores alike, much more than did their parents. It is a sort of delayed blooming of men's abilities to participate in the private sphere, which they did not observe in Cuba, though they had the training to do so. Cuban migrants who lived in countries where domestic workers were paid very little hired them to perform the second-shift tasks, including taking care of children.

Remittances

The fifty-five emigrants in my study aided family members in Cuba by sending them money and/or goods — footwear, clothing, food, and medicines — with no fixed regularity. Few channeled money through banks or financial institutions; they more often sent it through individuals traveling to Cuba. The amounts varied, as did the regularity of forwarding it. Women and men in my study sent remittances separately, according to their personal incomes. Only two of the fifty-five persons interviewed combined their funds in remitting money to family members. But they generally brought their incomes together when they bought presents for common friends.

According to these findings, it is difficult to infer a gendered pattern of forwarding remittances and administering them in Cuba. It is usually said that mainly women recipients manage the funds in Cuba, but this did not come out of the interviews.[12] Interviewees believed that the money that they sent was used to buy food, clothing, footwear, electrical appliances, and cell phones, mainly in the government stores or at agricultural markets. Money went also to repair and enlarge houses. Nobody mentioned that relatives and friends at home saved the remittances for the future. One woman said, "Cubans live on a day-by-day basis with little perspective on future outcomes." And as others observed, there is no need to send money to pay rents or mortgages, to enroll children in schools or at universities, or to pay for health care. "Nobody buys cars or houses," said many, so money goes to everyday needs. Although studies on remittances in Cuba mention buying houses,[13] nobody in my research group mentioned this possibility.

A World Bank study has concluded the following:

[T]he share of female migrants has a significant negative effect on remittance flows . . . caused by two forces. . . . First, a higher level of female migration indicates that more people are migrating as families and are less likely to have relatives behind; second, female migrants' labor market participation levels and incomes are likely to be lower in the destination countries, which mean there is less disposable income to be sent back as remittances.[14]

Neither of these two forces seem to limit interviewees in my study from remitting to Cuba. First, even though the women and men reunited with their original partners, formed new marital unions, or simply stayed alone, they kept ties with members of their extended families in Cuba. I did not ask for amounts sent, so I cannot confirm whether they were sending more or less than they did when they arrived in their new countries of residence. They simply stated that they help relatives and friends back home. Most of their parents and grandparents stayed in Cuba, and the émigrés also supplied money to pay those who aided their family members. Interviewees kept tight bonds with their grandparents, as many were raised by them while their mothers worked for a salary. Second, even if the women were not employed in jobs according to their original professional status, they kept helping their relatives back home. One said, "As long as the situation in Cuba is depressed I have to help those who raised me." Niimi and Ozden also concluded that "increase in the overall education level of migrants reduces remittances sent" because "more educated migrants are likely to come from wealthier families, which are less dependant on remittances"; "educated migrants can bring their families with them more easily, which also decreases the demand for remittances"; and "educated migrants are likely to settle permanently and invest in the destination's country assets."[15]

The fifty-five persons interviewed achieved university-level education in Cuba, but this does not mean that they come from wealthier families. Universal and free access to education had been practiced in Cuba for almost four decades when they graduated from university. Therefore, highly educated émigrés did not necessarily come from better-off families. When they left, women and men in my study had relatively good living standards compared to Cuban standards. Their families were not wealthier than the rest but were distinctly better off. Yet they considered that they could not accomplish in Cuba their material and spiritual (i.e., relating to the spirit or soul) aspirations. Although I did not directly ask interviewees about the reasons that made them migrate, their needs must have played a very important role in their decision. This would be a paradoxical output of the social mobility promoted by the revolution: potential migrants want more than the educational, job, and living standards that social policies in Cuba allow for and look to materialize their aspirations elsewhere. This is same middle-class aspiration for upward status in the United States and other countries.

Once they started channeling money and goods back home, they started introducing differences between their relatives and the other families who do not obtain remittances. What makes a difference among Cuban families is who receives remittances and who does not. The economic readjustments introduced on the island in the first half of the 1990s to overcome the crisis included allowing the free flow of hard currency inside the country. Mayra Espina wrote, "Remittances as a differentiating factor alien to work performance in Cuba during the years of the reforms is not sufficiently documented, but its stratifying impact is empirically evident."[16] Remittances grew from 1993 to the present, and their "differentiated effect widens because they are not a simple additional income but an extraordinary and definite one, since they lead to notoriously higher levels of consumption compared to the devaluated national currency and because they are not distributed homogenously in the Cuban population but according to family links with migrants."[17] Espina cites a study by the Cuban geographer Luisa Iñíguez, who found that "35 percent of the families included in a sample of the City of Havana received remittances, and this proportion increased up to 63 percent in the highest income strata, while it fell to 5 percent in the lowest strata."[18] A Brookings Institution report found that, "because most of those who have left the country are Caucasian, far fewer Afro-Cubans enjoy access to foreign remittances."[19]

The "educated" migrants do not tend to bring the rest of their family members from Cuba permanently but keep helping them economically to make their lives "more comfortable" and "easier" and to improve their original homes in Cuba. They do not want these relatives to lose access to health care, social security, and their island dwellings. Some even invite their parents to visit them for several months for a double purpose: to give them a break from the difficult conditions in Cuba and for parents to assist the migrants bringing up their children.

Marital Trends

Marital trends among Cuban migrants are of central importance in this study. I asked the research group if they married foreigners as a way to emigrate; if they emigrated alone, without a partner, to construct new life projects; or if they reunited with their partner and/or children in the destination country. I compared their behaviors with marriage rates in Cuba.

Marriage rates in Cuba have decreased and, at present, are at their lowest levels in five decades. In 1995, Cuban marriage rates were 6.4 per 1,000; in 2006, that fell to 5.0.[20] Between 1990 and 2006, the median marriage age went up: for women, it increased by eight years, from twenty-four to thirty-two, whereas for men it increased by nine years, from twenty-seven to thirty-six years.[21] The trend in cohabitation in Cuba is to live in consensual or common-law unions rather than legal marriages. Although most interviewees left Cuba without a marital relation, by the time they were interviewed, fifty of the fifty-five lived as couples, including lesbians and gays. They reproduced the same tendency followed in Cuba. Also, the interviewees tended to live with Cuban partners, even those who at some point had established a stable relationship with a foreigner. This situation has to do more with identity than with demography, and it is something that must be dealt with in comparative studies and with the help of anthropology, history, and psychology. It also has to do with the gender relations prevailing in the new country of residence

Male émigrés living in the Dominican Republic acknowledged that the women there were extremely dependent on men, that they only wanted to get married to stop working and become housewives supported by their husbands, and that they valued men by their money and properties; they had "no conversation topics" and were "not resourceful in bed." They preferred Cuban women with their extreme independence — although "sometimes they are too independent" — their willingness to work, and their professional abilities to do so. "Cubans in general can talk about everything, and I longed for this," added an engineer. On the other side, Cuban female migrants found native men in the Dominican Republic extremely *machista*, even violent. A woman lawyer said, "They want to keep their wives at home to raise children, keep everything tidy and let them play around with lovers."

Men and women living in Miami believed that it was easier to find Cuban partners either among members of that community or among Cubans visiting the city. It is much more difficult to find Cuban partners in U.S. cities outside South Florida. Cuban men and women interviewed in Canada arrived with their Cuban partners because Canadian migration regulations favor families. They considered it difficult to match with a Canadian in their home country, and they added that it was easier to arrive in Canada with a Canadian partner who they met in Cuba. Gays and lesbians living with Cuban partners related that they can live as couples, but they must be extremely careful so that their neighbors do not learn of their sexual preference. Indeed, lesbian couples are much more accepted in Havana than gay couples.

The interviewees used their marital status to adapt to their new country of residence. Some married citizens of the country to which they wanted to emigrate or legalized their marriage status with their common-law Cuban partner to comply with migration rules at the destination country. Three women divorced legally but stayed with their husbands to be considered single mothers so that their newborn children received services from social welfare. I am not able to calculate with precision the ages at which women and men in my sample married for the first time. However, they related having more than one conjugal union before and after emigrating, which coincides with multiple-marriage trends among Cubans. This behavior does not always suit the rules or values of the destination country. One man commented that, in the city where he lived with his wife and her son, "I do not stress that previous to our present marital union my wife and I were divorced and I never mention that we are not legally married. We could be negatively judged and my stepson could be made fun of at his school."

Fertility

Cuba is at the end of the first stage of its demographic transition.[22] The country simultaneously shows characteristics of an underdeveloped country and those of a developed one. Furthermore, the demographic transition is homogenously coming to an end in all regions of Cuba. In 2006, there was a decrease in population growth: −0.4 births for every thousand inhabitants, the lowest rate in Latin America. Other demographic indicators include a fertility rate of 1.39 children per woman, 0.67 daughters per woman, an infant mortality rate of 5.3 per thousand born alive, and 75.3 percent live in urban settings. In 2003, life expectancy for both sexes was 76.15 years. The sociologist and Cuban specialist Juan Carlos Alfonso stresses that fertility contraction during the past three decades has been the main cause of the aging of the population.[23] During those years, Cuba's fertility rate was lower than population replacement because, on average, there was less than one daughter born to each woman in her reproductive years. During the 1960s and 1970s, there were 250,000 births each year; in 2005, there were slightly more than 120,000, although there were 1 million more women in their fertile years. Alfonso considered that birth rates were low after 1978 because of a complex set of variables, among which were female employment, universal access to family planning since 1964, legal abortion since 1962 (at times used as a contraceptive), lack of housing, one-third of Cuban families being headed by women, and women emigrating during their reproductive years. Alfonso has long been advocating the need to approach demographic studies with a gender perspective.[24] This research project does so.

More than half of the fifty-five migrants had no children when they were interviewed — fourteen of the twenty-five men and sixteen of the thirty women. The latter emigrated in their fertile years. They did not give birth in Cuba because they decided to emigrate first; only when they had all necessary conditions would they plan to have children. Women and men defined these conditions as having a stable partner, both partners having a job, owning a house or an apartment and at least one car, and being able to pay for one of their mothers' plane ticket so she could share in taking care of the young child for a few months or even years. All the mothers looked forward to the children born in the destination country holding dual citizenship: the country of birth and Cuba. This would "anchor" the child and their parents to their new country of residence and, at the same time, allow them to regularly visit Cuba.

All of the interviewees — women and men alike — believed that they benefited from the family-planning programs in Cuba in that there is a "culture" of using contraception from an early age. Women consulted with doctors at poly-clinics (i.e., local clinics that are the intermediate step between family doctors and hospitals) or hospitals and jointly decided which contraceptive methods were best for them. They usually check their intrauterine devices (IUDs) while visiting Cuba and even carry back with them additional IUDs and/or Cuban contraceptive pills. They acknowledged that, as a rule in couples, women are responsible for using contraceptives. When asked whether their husbands used condoms during intercourse, they answered no and added that, before they engaged with a stable partner, they asked men to wear condoms for fear of AIDS. Men answered the same way: they let their wives use contraceptive methods and they use condoms only in sexual relations outside their marital unions to prevent HIV. Women migrants in my sample did not contribute to fertility rates in Cuba, for they left the country in their fertile years. They also reduced Cuba's population of potential future mothers because they took their daughters with them.

Another of the needed conditions to give birth to a child in the country of residence is being able to pay for education. The interviewees introduced this provision at the same level as the rest. They wanted their children to attend "good" schools, preferably private, in countries where they considered that public schooling was poor. They were willing to assign funds from their bud-gets for their children's education even if they had less to eat. "It is a need that I inherited from my parents. They told me that it is something that you carry all your life with you." All migrants in my study benefitted from universal and free education in Cuba and were able to surpass their parents' educational levels.

Gender Roles in Keeping Cuban Traditions

I asked interviewees to name the Cuban ways of life that they practice in their countries of residence and to explain the distinctive roles of women and men in carrying them out. In the first place, they mentioned the relevance of education for their children — whether or not they had children at the time of the interview — and for themselves. One of the conditions for having children was being able to secure a good education for them from preschool to university. Interviewees were also concerned about the need to upgrade their present professional knowledge, such as in training programs to apply for job licenses, by revalidat-ing their university diplomas, studying language, and enrolling in master's-degree programs. But it is highly difficult for them to comply with all the requisites demanded in terms of money and language skills. Attaining a good education for their children has always been a goal for Cubans. It became true for all citizens since 1961 with the literacy campaign and the nationalization of private schools. Half the women and men in my sample are second-generation professionals; at least one of their parents graduated from tertiary education after 1959. It is therefore understandable that men and women prioritize education as a Cuban tradition that they are willing to maintain.

They also talked about keeping family links with those relatives who stayed in Cuba and with those who emigrated. They stressed their need to be updated on family matters and to share in caring for the elderly. Those who have access to electronic means of communication at both ends find it easier to keep in touch. Flowing from these desires, they referred to using their native tongue at least at home if they are living in countries where Spanish is not an official language. This turns out to be very difficult, at least for their children, if they are living where there are no Spanish-speaking communities. They in no particular order referred to cooking Cuban food or eating at Cuban restaurants, listening and dancing to Cuban music, watching films and television shows produced on the island, decorating their homes with Cuban elements, and celebrating traditional feasts in a Cuban style (e.g., birthday parties; *quinceaños* celebrations; Mother's and Father's Days; Christmas; New Year's Eve; and the feast days of St. Lazarus, the Virgin of the Caridad del Cobre, and St. Barbara).

Men and women in this study distinguished at least three scenarios for keeping Cuban traditions and for being updated on what is happening in the island. First, women are the ones who reproduced Cuban traditions in the families abroad when they head them or are engaged in a stable marital relationship. However, I found men in the group who promoted these traditions even more than their Cuban spouses did. I also met Cuban women married to foreigners who reproduced the ethics of care practiced in Cuba; that is, the wife took care of her husband's mother. Second, interviewees mentioned the relevance of keeping in touch with Cuban friends to exchange on Cuban topics whether they lived in the same countries or different ones. Once more, the importance of electronic communications came up, as many interviewees used such media to keep in touch, even daily. The third scenario is the Internet. They accessed electronic media produced in Cuba or in those cities where Cuban émigrés reside; they downloaded Cuban films and music; and they visited blogs related to Cuban issues. I asked them whether they reproduced gender patterns common in Cuba in their daily lives and whether they thought about introducing them in their children's upbringing. Although men and women acknowledged behaving in *machista* ways consciously and unconsciously, they considered themselves less male oriented than their parents' generation. In relation to their children, those who live in countries with a *machista* culture confessed that it was very hard because at home they taught their children some of the gender codes brought from Cuba, and then they were trained in others completely different at the schools and among their classmates.

Cuban Development Strategies and Gender Relations

Cubans experienced increasing social mobility for first three decades after 1959 as a result of the Cuban conception of development that implied that economic transformations should provide material well-being to all and contribute to changing the ideological and cultural patterns of inequality and discrimination. Women were among the poorest Cubans and benefited from the very beginning by strategies implemented to change social relationships that conditioned poverty.[25] The economy was organized in such a way that the state used the growth of the gross domestic product (GDP) to stimulate those social policies that promoted universal and free access to education, health, social security, nutrition, social welfare, culture, and sports, areas that the Cuban sociologist Mayra Espina has defined as "spaces of equality."[26] In Cuba, the state is the main provider of these spaces, or venues, whereas private providers have a very low profile. Such venues initially fractured the cycle of inequalities in society and at home, including discrimination against women. Women benefited much more than men because these venues were feminized almost immediately (i.e., women incorporated themselves quickly in these previously "male" spaces), and in the past women had less access to them than men did.

Another feature of the development strategies benefiting women was that there was no need to wait to accomplish economic growth as a precondition to advance women in society. Therefore, actions were taken from the beginning to implement policies specifically geared at women's equality; these included economic and legal regulations, social policies, and procedures mainly of an ideological nature to counter gender discrimination. A purely economic notion would have postponed these decisions, thereby reducing the importance of women's participation and delaying women's possibilities to become agents of change.

The policies of full employment regarded differentiated treatment for women; as women were more disadvantaged than men, the policies aimed to end this situation by allowing women's salaries to contribute to their independence as income earners. Nonetheless, early in the 1970s, the Second Congress of the Federation of Cuban Women acknowledged that the instability of the female labor force was due to, above all, the pressure of household chores, the nonexistence in many labor centers of specific work conditions for women, and the lack of economic incentives.[27] Among the most successful actions to confront the latter problem in the 1970s was the encouragement to qualify and retrain female workers to increase the number of women who became professionals and technicians. However, the burden of work at home continued to be a great difficulty. Work conditions fit for women were set up slowly and according to the ideas of the men who designed them, not to the real needs of women.

This demand was progressively satisfied when women started to have access to senior leading positions at their jobs toward the mid-1980s.

The feminization of education has had such an influence that, since 1978, working women had higher educational levels than working men.[28] The 1961 literacy campaign, the nationalization of the education system from the primary level to the university in the same year, and campaigns for working adults to attain sixth and ninth grades in 1963 allowed women to rise above their low education status. As women who took up jobs continued their education, they qualified to be promoted for more complex and better-paid occupations. Preschool child care began in 1961, when the first public day-care centers with schools to train staff were established. Universal and free access to education guaranteed children the right to enroll from primary school to university. Children in primary schools (on the *doble turno* system) were provided with free lunch, and teachers' aides looked after them during the afternoon sessions. Furthermore, students at all levels of education were provided with boarding-houses if they required them. Thus, working women relied on the fact that their children regularly attended school during the week and were assured that they did not have to save part of their salaries for their children's education. This allowed them to remain and advance in their jobs.

Before 1959, Cuba lacked a state-controlled social security system. During the 1960s and the 1970s, legislation was passed to make social security and social welfare universal, thus benefiting working women and single mothers. Working women had guaranteed retirement, sick benefits, and pensions upon the death of their spouse. The husbands' pensions also contributed to the family budget. The Maternity Law included in the Labor Code in 1974 regulated maternity leave. Single mothers received small pensions that contributed to raising their children until they began to work. This legislation stipulated that fathers must pay child support to their children if divorced or separated from their spouses or partners, and although this definition was poorly implemented, mothers could legally claim the benefit. Policies of full employment in the public service guaranteed equal pay for equal work.

These processes coincided with the massive incorporation of women into the workforce.[29] Women became salaried workers under the same legal conditions as men, though in practice statistical data showed that they earned less than men. Actually, women held jobs with lower salaries; they were absent more because they had to take care of the children, the sick, and the elderly; and they had higher morbidity rates than men. By the end of the 1980s, circumstances seemed to foretell that in the near future, Cuban woman could access leadership positions in the workplace. In the first instance, women workers had high levels of education, which allowed them to perform complex jobs. Second, they were working in all sectors of the economy, even in those traditionally considered nonfemale sectors. Third, women were engaged in all occupational categories, including leadership positions and accounted for more than half of professionals and technical workers. Finally, and paradoxically, although women struggled to divide their work time between their jobs and a second shift at home, doing so trained them in decision making.

An outstanding trait of Cuban development strategies from 1959 to 1989 was how Cuba envisaged using social policy to solve the problems of poverty by promoting new social projects that led to innovative and rational patterns of consumption for all.[30] This notion led to a distribution and consumption system based on an egalitarian and homogenized conception capable of satisfying a set of the population's basic needs. However, this conception did not consider two indispensable monetary requirements to comply with the Marxist axiom "from each according to his/her capacity, to each according to his/her work." First, it did not consider that people have different needs and tend to satisfy them in different ways. Second, while distributing goods homogenously, it treated the more disadvantaged sectors of the population in similar ways as the rest of society, disregarding that they required different approaches. Nonetheless, this had a positive effect on women.

As women embodied the most disadvantaged sectors of the population, the homogenized distribution of goods benefited them because they accessed consumer goods that they had not had access to before. In a familial context, this meant improvement in nutrition, toiletries, clothing, and footwear, and even regarding the heretofore-insufficient domestic appliances used by them and their families. Following the patriarchal tradition, women were the homemakers who managed the commodities distributed in an egalitarian manner through the state's centralized decision making, thus creating new patterns of consumption. Whether as sole salary earners who headed their homes and supplied the main revenues for them, as providers additional to the man as the head of the home, or as housewives who did not participate in paid work, they dealt on a daily basis with the results of social policies regarding consumption. This created decision-making capacities in them, especially in working women who had a second shift at home. This training process took place in a social context that promoted women in the public and private life of the country. Women also participated as agents of change in transforming consumption as part of the struggle against poverty. These changes show the importance of understanding the functions of Cuban women in the struggle against poverty and inequality and toward their empowerment.[31]

During the first three decades of the Cuban Revolution, women led and encouraged changes in gender relationships. They worked harder than men to surmount sexist inequalities because they started dismantling the cultural patterns of patriarchal ideology existing in both society and themselves. They did not stop there because they also built new, nonsexist ideological patterns. In this endeavor, they advanced more than men did. Contrary to what has happened in other countries — including the United States — where women have been "revolutionized" (i.e., have changed their patriarchal attitudes under the influence of various women's movements but global structures in those same countries have not changed accordingly) but society has stagnated regarding gender relationships, in Cuba, society changed; and women changed because they participated in the social transformation from the very beginning.[32]

On the threshold of the 1990s, the upward social mobility that Cubans evidenced during the first thirty years of the revolution stopped for at least three reasons: the younger generation could not experience the dramatic increase in living standards their parents had experienced; development strategies of the early 1970s and the 1980s proved ineffective in many aspects and were being rectified; and finally, Cuba entered an overall crisis due to the disappearance of its main trading partners — the Soviet Union and the Eastern European socialist countries — the strengthening of the U.S. blockade, and the inability to finish its process of rectification.[33] Women suffered the most from this downturn, mainly working women burdened by the second shift. In 1994, Cuba started to "come out" of the crisis, and by 2004, GDP reached 99 percent of that of 1989 in terms of 1997 constant prices.[34] In 2007, the economy grew 7.5 percent, showing its gradual consolidation based on a 42.5 percent increase in GDP since 2004.[35]

During the economic readjustment process, the legal and political framework that promoted women's incorporation and permanence in the labor force stayed and adjusted to the new characteristics of the Cuban situation. Women remained in the labor force during the years of crisis and readjustment, and their participation in labor categories did not deteriorate. The proportion of women among workers had reached 39 percent in 1989, just before the economic crisis began.[36] Until that moment, women's participation had grown steadily, but starting with the crisis, this process stopped and even led to a small decrease.[37] The proportion of technicians among women workers increased in the years coming out of the crisis — 39 percent in 1996 and 45 percent in 2008 — whereas among all working men, the rate grew only from 13 percent to 18 percent.[38] Women's predominance among technical workers is sustained by the fact that, since 1978, they have higher educational levels than working men considered as a whole.[39] But women still have the lowest representation regarding senior administrative positions: of all working women, 6 percent were senior administrators in 1996 and 2008. Men's participation in this category grew slightly: 8 percent of all working men in 1996 and 9 percent in 2008. Participation by gender among senior administrators showed stable rates in 1996 and 2008: 71 percent and 70 percent for men and 29 percent and 30 percent for women, respectively. The latter are present in nontraditionally women-occupied sectors — steel manufacture, the sugar industry, science, telecommunications, and computers — and in traditional ones. Although nominal salaries started increasing in 2005, they have not overcome their deterioration because consumer prices are still high. This leads to disadvantages among citizens, mainly those dependent on social security and social care pensions.

Part of the labor force that on the threshold of the crisis accounted for 95 percent of the public sector reoriented toward the private, joint venture, and cooperative sectors, and to those state enterprises that paid workers in hard currency. At present, 75 percent of all workers are part of the public sector. Those Cubans whose salaries are paid in Cuban pesos and the population dependent on social security pensions and social care were, thus, most affected in their incomes when the crisis started. On the basis of the scarce information available on incomes by gender, as well as several case studies dealing with this topic, women have been more affected than men in the process of decreased real salary values and pensions. They represent only one-tenth of self-employed citizens in the private sector (11.9 percent), one-third of personnel in joint ventures (35.4 percent), and the majority of the beneficiaries of social care.[40]

Over the past 20 years, an increasing number of Cubans have had access to hard currency: people receiving remittances from family members; the self-employed who charge for their work in hard currency (men constitute 88 percent of this category); workers in tourism and joint ventures, as well as in state enterprises, where hard currency is the medium of exchange; and small landowners, who are among the most affluent citizens and can convert their peso incomes to hard currency (men are the absolute majority here). According to official calculations, and despite the fact that no data are available on gender distribution, 50 percent of all citizens in 1997 had access to hard currency, which had increased to 62 percent by 2001.[41] Overall, remittances are the basic source for individual incomes in hard currency; and case studies point out that women account for the majority in terms of managing these incomes. It is worth studying from a gender perspective this process of receiving and administering remittances.

The crisis and reform processes of the 1990s paralyzed the trend of extending social equality among all Cubans and of eliminating the conditions that generated social disadvantages. An extremely complex situation appeared that demanded rethinking those actions that the state had implemented since the beginning of the decade. Although it maintained social policies, the state allowed incomes and consumption to deteriorate heavily.[42] Mayra Espina has argued that the diminishing of real salary values weakened the financing of families. In addition, when some goods that were part of the subsidized family basket started being sold in hard currency, broad sectors of the population had limited access to them. Although this situation especially affected women and men who received public-sector salaries, it had greater impact on female-led households; in 2002, such households represented 32 percent of all families.[43] Women had to devise strategies to confront limited consumption while performing the second shift. For instance, to make ends meet, women workers started taking on other paid employment to supplement their regular salaries; multiple employment was not practiced before the crisis.

Weakening incomes from social security and social care affected families with pensioners. Pensioners' contributions to the family budget shrank precisely when pensioners needed additional care that their incomes could not cover. This was a new situation from the first years of women's incorporation in the workforce until the crisis of the 1990s. The mothers of women workers were usually housewives and took care of their grandchildren. As they aged, their daughters began to take care of them — without abandoning their jobs — and had to create strategies to meet their additional duties, known in Cuba as the ethics of care. Coincidentally, this new situation affected women more than men. Women workers had to ask for unpaid work leaves or simply had to abandon their jobs to look after elderly family members on their side or their husband's side of the family.

Poverty levels rose. In 1985, the poor represented 6 percent of the population; ten years later, they constituted 15 percent; and at present, 20 percent of the urban population falls into this category.[44] It is difficult to describe poverty levels by gender, as no national statistics measure population groups according to income. Recent case studies indicate that differences in income range from 1 to 24 in the extreme. This index is very different from the one calculated in 1978 that showed differences in income from 1 to 4.[45] The last decade of the twentieth century in Cuba was a turning point in the development strategies that were initiated during the first thirty years of the revolution to improve the population's quality of life and to change gender relations. The readjustment policies to surpass the crisis introduced inequalities that all members of society strongly felt. One of the outcomes was an increase in emigration flows.

Conclusion

The economic, political, ideological, and social aspects of the Cuba's social structures that have characterized its socialist experiment influenced the lives of all Cubans. They have affected the lives of those who decided to emigrate and the lives of those who decided to stay. Therefore, social sciences researchers must understand the individual motivations that led the former to leave the country, linked to the understanding of the social structures that influenced all society. Cuban social structures of the past fifty years are part of a socialist experiment, brought about by the 1959 revolution, which has not been completed primarily because of the U.S. hostility toward Cuba and also internal mistakes committed in this enormous transformation process. On the threshold of the crisis of the 1990s derived from the disintegration of the Soviet Union, Cuba's main foreign economic counterpart, the island had to interrupt its rectification process when the U.S. government intensified its blockade of the island. Cubans were plunged into the crisis and have not yet been able to come out of it, and they have suffered nineteen years of enormous material shortages, a duration that is comparable to a generation that is now entering adulthood.

In the past twenty years, the differences between Cuban migrants and those from Caribbean and Latin American countries must be found in Cuban economic, social, political, and ideological structures. Three of the distinctions to be considered among Cuban migrants in the past twenty years in relation to the ones coming from Latin American and Caribbean countries are that many of them are highly qualified women and men, with an advanced gender ideology and an ability to act independently. Cuban migrants who have left Cuba since the 1990s did so not only for economic reasons — trying to find better living standards than those they had in Cuba — but also because of the skyrocketing social mobility experienced in Cuba in the 1960s, 1970s, and 1980s that included material and spiritual conditions and was halted by the crisis of the 1990s. They desired to continue moving upward in their ways of life, and considering that they could not accomplish this goal in the short or medium term in Cuba, they decided to fulfill these dreams individually in other countries. A gender perspective will contribute to unraveling these unanswered questions.

NOTAS

1. See Marta Núñez Sarmiento, "Género y migraciones externas en Cuba entre 1985 y 2005: Resultados preliminares," *Novedades de Población* 3, no. 6 (2007): 45–70.

2. Calculated by the author on the basis of Oficina Nacional de Estadísticas (ONE), *Anuario demográfico de Cuba 2008* (Havana: República de Cuba), chart 4.2, http://www.one.cu/publica ciones/cepde/anuario_2008/10_anuario_migraciones.pdf.

3. UN Population Fund, *State of the World Population 2006: A Passage to Hope — Women and International Migration* (New York: UN Population Fund, 2006), 23.

4. Ibid.

5. Ibid.

6. CD 25th International Population Conference (Tours, France, 2005), http://www.census .gov/population/cen2000/stp159/stp159-cuba.pdf.

7. Antonio Aja, "Cuba: País de emigración a inicios del siglo XXI," *Anuario CEMI* (2006): 152.

8. Susan Eckstein, *The Immigrant Divide* (New York: Routledge, 2009): 12–13; Ileana Sorolla, "The Cubans in the U.S. and Their Special Status: 50 Years After" (paper presented at the conference "Measure of a Revolution," Queen's University, Kingston, Ontario, May 7–9, 2009).

9. Eckstein, *Immigrant Divide*, 12.

10. Gretel Marrero Peniche, "Migraciones internacionales en Cuba y su conexión con la migración externa en el mundo" (Havana: University of Havana, 2008), 114–15; Elpidia Moreno, "Las relaciones de género en la feminización de las migraciones internacionales en Cuba" (master's thesis, Center for Study of International Migrations, University of Havana, 2009).

11. Sussie Jollie and Hazel Reeves, *Gender and Migration: General Report* (Sussex, U.K.:

124 : MARTA NÚÑEZ-SARMIENTO

Institute of Development Studies, University of Sussex, 2005), qtd. in Marrero Peniche, "Migraciones internacionales," 93–94.

12. I could not find information that would allow me to compare the answers of my respondents with gender patterns of remittances in Cuba, worldwide, or according to regions.

13. See Eckstein, *Immigrant Divide*, 353–90; Lorena Barbería, "Remesas a Cuba: Una evaluación de las medidas políticas gubernamentales de Cuba y Estados Unidos," in *La economía cubana a principios del siglo XXI*, ed. J. Dominguez, O. Everleny, and L. Barbeia (Cambridge, MA: David Rockefeller Center for Latin American Studies, Harvard University, and El Colegio de México, 2007), 391–450.

14. Yoko Niimi and Caglar Ozden, "Migration and Remittances in Latin America: Patterns and Determinants," in *Remittances and Development: Lessons from Latin America*, ed. Pablo Fajnzylber and J. Humberto Lopez (Washington, D.C.: World Bank, 2008), 78.

15. Ibid., 77–78.

16. Mayra Espina Prieto, *Políticas de atención a la pobreza y la desigualdad: Examinando el rol del estado en la experiencia cubana* (Havana: Consejo Latinoamericano de Ciencias Sociales [CLACSO] and Comparative Research Program on Poverty [CROP], 2008), 174.

17. Ibid.

18. Luisa Iñiguez et al., *La exploración de las desigualdades espacio-familias en la Ciudad de La Habana* (Havana: Centro de Estudios de Salud y Bienestar Humano, 2001), qtd. in Espina Prieto, *Políticas de atención*, 174.

19. Brookings Institution, *U.S. Policy toward Cuba in Transition* (Miami: University of Miami, 2008).

20. Sonia Catasús, "La nupcialidad en Cuba: Características y evolución en el contexto de la conclusión de su transición demográfica," http//:ivssp2005.princeton.edu/sessionviewer.aspx.submission=50855; ONE, *Anuario demográfico 2006* (Havana: República de Cuba, 2007).

21. Ibid.

22. Catasús, "La nupcialidad en Cuba"; ONE, *Anuario demográfico 2006*, 16, 46, 18, 119.

23. Orfilio Peláez, "Disminución acelerada de la natalidad y envejecimiento poblacional" (interview with Juan Carlos Alfonso Fraga, director of the Centro de Estudios de Población y Desarrollo [CEPDE], ONE), *Granma*, October 30, 2006.

24. See Centro de Estudios de Población y Desarrollo (CEPDE), ONE, and UN Development Programme (UNDP), *Información para estudios en población y desarrollo con enfoque de género 200, La Habana*; see also quotes by Juan Carlos Alfonso in Marta Núñez-Sarmiento, "Gender Studies in Cuba: Methodological Approaches, 1974–2007," in *Global Gender Research: Transnational Perspectives*, ed. C. Bose and M. Kim (London: Routledge, 2009), 202, 204.

25. See Marta Núñez-Sarmiento, "Cuban Alternatives to Market Driven Economies: A Gendered Case Study on Women's Employment" (paper presented at the UNDP colloquium "Assessing and Rebuilding Progress through Women's Knowledge," Rabat, Morocco, October 2008).

26. Mayra Prieto Espina, "Efectos sociales del reajuste económico: Igualdad, desigualdad y procesos de complejización en la sociedad cubana," in Dominguez et al., *La economía cubana*, 247; Espina Prieto, *Políticas de atención*, 144–45.

27. *Memoria II Congreso Nacional de la Federación de Mujeres Cubanas* (Havana: Editorial Orbe and Instituto del Libro, 1975), 118, 119.

28. In 1978, of all working women, 5 percent had concluded higher education and 3.5 percent of working men had university degrees; 23 percent of all working women had finished twelve grades, compared to 13 percent of all working men. In 1986, 12 percent of working women were university graduates; in that same year, 7 percent of working men had university degrees. Of all working women, 35 percent had concluded twelve grades, in comparison with 27 percent of

working men. Calculations made by the author from ONE, *Anuario estadístico 1988* (Havana: ONE, 1988), chart 4.16.

29. Women in the workforce increased steadily between 1959 (13 percent) and 1970 (19 percent). Between 1970 and 1989 the increase was greater than previously: 19 percent in 1970 and 38.7 percent in 1989. Absolute numbers also grew; see Marta Núñez Sarmiento, "La mujer cubana y el empleo en la Revolución," in *Equipo internacional de investigaciones comparadas sobre la mujer* (Havana: Editora de la Mujer, 1988), 20; Marta Núñez Sarmiento, "Cuban Strategies for Women's Employment in the 1990's: A Case Study of Professional Women," *Socialism and Democracy* 15, no. 1 (2001): 43–44.

30. Espina Prieto, "Efectos sociales del reajuste económico," 245.

31. D. Elson, S. Chacko, and D. Jain, "Interrogating and Rebuilding Progress through Feminist Knowledge" (notes for the UNDP project Assessing and Rebuilding Progress through Women's Knowledge, 2008), 6.

32. See Arlie Hochschild, with Anne Machung, *The Second Shift* (New York: Avon Books, 1989), 12.

33. The "Rectification of Mistakes and Negative Trends" process began at the end of 1984. It sought not to change development strategies but to mend its failures, caused mainly by mimicking Soviet models. Based on Cuban experiences and conditions, the process aimed to upgrade the socialist model by learning from the experiences of socialist and nonsocialist societies worldwide.

34. Omar Everleny Pérez, "La situación actual de la economía cubana y sus retos futuros," in Dominguez et al., *La economía cubana*, 71.

35. José Luis Rodríguez, "Report on 2007 Economic Results by the Minister of Economy and Planning to the National Assembly of the Popular Power," *Granma*, December 29, 2007, 6.

36. ONE, *Anuario estadístico de Cuba 1996* (Havana: ONE, 1996).

37. Between 1996 and 2008, women's participation in the total labor force stayed at 38 percent; in the same period, men's participation remained at 62 percent. See ONE and CEPDE, *Perfil estadístico de la mujer cubana en el umbral del siglo XXI* (Havana: ONE-CEPDE, 1999), 144; ONE, *Anuario estadístico de Cuba 2008*, chart 7.9, http://www.one.cu/aec2008/esp/08_7_9.htm.

38. In 1996, women represented 64 percent of all technicians, whereas men accounted for 36 percent. In 2008, women's numbers diminished in this category but they kept their 60 percent majority. Men increased their participation to 40 percent. Taken from ONE and CEPDE, *Perfil estadístico*; ONE, *Anuario estadístico 2008*, chart 7.9.

39. For all female workers, the rate of blue-collar workers diminished from 22 percent (1996) to 16 percent (2008). The rate of blue-collar workers among male workers also decreased from 51 percent (1996) to 49 percent (2008).

40. Instituto de Investigaciones y Estudios del Trabajo, *La presencia femenina en el mercado de trabajo, en las diferentes categorías ocupacionales y sectores de la economía, la segregación horizontal y vertical, los salarios e ingresos en general* (Havana: Instituto de Investigaciones y Estudios del Trabajo, 2007).

41. Pérez, "La situación actual," 79.

42. Espina Prieto, "Efectos sociales del reajuste económico," 251–52.

43. ONE, *Censo de población y viviendas de la República de Cuba, 2002* (Havana: ONE, 2002).

44. Espina Prieto, "Efectos sociales del reajuste económico," 255.

45. Ibid., 254.

MERVYN J. BAIN

Havana and Moscow, 1959–2009: The Enduring Relationship?

ABSTRACT

Havana's relationship with Moscow that developed in the late 1950s and early 1960s quickly became vital for the Cuban Revolution, but it originated as a result of timing, at the height of the Cold War. However, other reasons and pressures rapidly appeared that affected the relationship for the following thirty years. Some of these began to be questioned in the late 1980s as a result of the reform processes instigated in Cuba and the Soviet Union, but many simply vanished in the aftermath of the implosion of the Soviet Union, which put an end to Cuban-Soviet relations. The relationship unquestionably suffered a dramatic political and economic downturn, but not all the pressures evaporated, and even from 1992 to 1995, more than diplomatic relations continued to function, most noticeably oil for sugar swaps. As the 1990s progressed, new pressures began to appear, and remarkably, some from the Cold War era, including the geostrategic importance of the island for the Kremlin, began to resurface. The result has been an improvement in relations from 1995 that has remained important in the twenty-first century for both countries, which illustrates the enduring qualities of the relationship.

RESUMEN

Las relaciones desarrolladas entre la Habana y Moscú a finales de la década de los años 50 e inicios de los 60 devinieron en vitales para la Revolución Cubana, pero su origen fue el resultado de un período de tiempo particular: la Guerra Fría. Sin embargo, otras razones y fuerzas surgieron y impactaron las relaciones en los siguientes treinta años. Algunas empezaron a ser cuestionadas a finales de la década de los 80, a raíz de procesos de reformas que tuvieron lugar en ambos países, pero otras simplemente desaparecieron como resultado de la implosión de la otrora Unión Soviética, lo cual tuvo como resultado el fin de las relaciones soviéticas-cubanas. Como resultado, sin duda las relaciones sufrieron una dramática declinación tanto en lo político como en lo económico. Sin embargo, no todo se evaporó; incluso entre 1992 y 1995, más allá de las continuas relaciones diplomáticas se mantuvieron intercambios, probablemente siendo el más notable el intercambio de petróleo por azúcar. En la medida que los años 90 fueron avanzando, nuevas fuerzas empezaron a emerger, incluso algunas provenientes de la época de la Guerra Fría, incluida la importancia geoestratégica de la isla para el Kremlin. El resultado ha sido una mejoría de las relaciones a partir de 1995, y en el siglo XXI se mantienen con una importancia singular para ambos países, lo cual ilustra la cualidad de la permanencia de la relación.

At their inception following the Cuban Revolution of 1959, Cuban-Soviet relations appeared somewhat unusual because of both the geographical distance between the two countries and the lack of a shared heritage. However, the relationship quickly became vital for the new Cuban regime; but throughout its long duration, the Cuban-Russian relationship has endured several turbulent episodes, not least the implosion of the Soviet Union in December 1991. Notwithstanding this development, in the twenty-first century, the relationship remains significant for both countries, something that Dmitry Medvedev's visit to Havana and Raúl Castro's visit to Moscow in late 2008 and early 2009 demonstrate. A wide variety of reasons and pressures explain the relationship's fifty-year history. The timing of the victory of the Cuban Revolution at the height of the Cold War was important, but quickly other pressures appeared that would also impinge on the relationship for the following thirty years. Reform processes instigated in both countries began to question many of these issues in the late 1980s, with a number of issues simply vanishing with the end of the Cuban-Soviet Russian relationship. However, others did not; and as the 1990s progressed, not only did new issues evolve but also, remarkably, others that had disappeared remerged, though at reduced levels, to again have an impact on the relationship. Now that the Cuban Revolution has celebrated its fiftieth anniversary and relations between Havana and Moscow are half a century old, the relationship does have an enduring quality.

The Cold War Setting

Cuban-U.S. relations from the time of Cuban independence to the victory of the Cuban Revolution were vital for the relationship that would develop between Havana and Moscow after 1959. Washington had dominated the island both politically and economically, and although it was unclear what type of revolution had taken place in Cuba, there was certainty that the new Cuban regime wished its relationship with the United States to be dramatically altered. The importance of nationalism to the revolution and the fact that Ernesto "Che" Guevara had witnessed the overthrow of the progressive government of Jacobo Árbenz in Guatemala in 1954 by American-backed exiles diminished the likelihood of cordial Cuban-U.S. relations still further. Fidel Castro would later comment: "We would not in any event have ended up as close friends. The U.S. had dominated us for too long."[1]

Furthermore, the United States quickly decided that the Cuban Revolution could not be allowed to run its course and that the new regime should be removed from power, a decision that eventually led to the failed Bay of Pigs Invasion in April 1961. This course of action resulted not just from fears over American economic investments in the island and disapproval at what Washington perceived as the summary executions of old regime officials. It also developed from the Cold War setting in which these events played out — at the time it appeared that Washington was losing the Cold War. China had turned communist a mere ten years previous, and in light of the reorientation of Soviet foreign policy in the aftermath of Joseph Stalin's death, concerns abounded that the Cuban Revolution was the forerunner to further communist penetration of Latin America.[2]

As a result, it was always unlikely that a close relationship between revolutionary Havana and Washington would develop, but the fact that these events took place in the late 1950s and early 1960s at the height of the Cold War was vital for the inception of Cuban-Soviet relations. Because Soviet-U.S. rivalry had produced bipolar international politics, if Cuba did not join the U.S. camp, it would have to enter the Soviet one.

Havana was drawn toward Moscow for reasons apart from the role of Washington and the bipolar nature of international relations. Many countries in the developing world that had newly gained their independence were attracted to Moscow because the Soviet development model from the 1930s had brought about rapid modernization and industrialization; and in the Western Hemisphere, Russia lacked a colonial past in the traditional sense, unlike other European powers like France, Portugal, Spain, and the United Kingdom, among others.[3] With respect to Cuba, this latter reason was valid because of the nature of Cuban-U.S. relations from 1898 to 1959. Moreover, the Cuban ruling elite may have been drawn to the Soviet political model with the presence of the avowed Marxists Raúl Castro and Che Guevara within Cuba's new leadership.[4]

The timing of these events was important for Moscow. Since the death of Stalin in 1953, the Kremlin had attempted to implement several changes in Soviet foreign policy to increase its global presence. Furthermore, Cuba's geographical location and the revolution's anti-American nature appealed to Moscow: a relationship with Havana would illustrate a growing Soviet global power to Washington while answering Chinese accusations of Soviet revisionism. In addition, the possibility of a productive Cuban-Soviet relationship, and more generally Moscow's increasing influence in the developing world, appealed greatly to Nikita Khrushchev's extrovert personality. And the personal relationship that quickly blossomed between Khrushchev and Castro only aided the bilateral relationship.[5]

As stated, the development of the Cuban-Soviet relationship may at first have been somewhat surprising, but it was mutually beneficial to both governments. However, other pressures quickly appeared that further underpinned the relationship, not least Castro's proclaiming of himself, and thus the Cuban Revolution, as Marxist-Leninist in December 1961.[6] In light of unabated U.S. aggression, it appears that the motives for this decision were to elicit increased security guarantees from Moscow — as the Kremlin could not allow a fellow Marxist-Leninist regime to fail, especially one in such a significant geostrategic location — and to undercut continuing criticisms from China. The outcome was a further increase in pressure on Moscow with regard to its relationship with Havana. The Soviet leadership added to this pressure. The levels of aid and trade that had been invested in Cuba made a possible termination of the relationship unlikely; but if relations broke off, the money would simply have been wasted. This pressure only increased in significance as the levels of trade and aid grew dramatically over time.

The honeymoon period in the relationship is often perceived as having ended with the conclusion of the October 1962 Cuban missile crisis, a result of the acute offense to Cuban nationalism from being omitted from the talks that brought a resolution to the crisis.[7] Yet the last two weeks of October 1962 only put further pressure on the Kremlin with regard to its relationship with Havana and made a schism with Castro's government more unlikely. The visibility with which its missiles left the Caribbean had humiliated the Soviet Union, and its prestige would have been further dented had the Cuban Revolution failed — Cuban security had partly justified the missile deployment. As a result of both the Cold War setting and Sino-Chinese split, the scenario of a failed Revolution was one that the Kremlin could not allow to develop.[8] Soviet Russian support for the revolution continued and expanded.

By the mid-1970s, any tension that might have existed in Cuban-Soviet relations was long since dead: not only had the island gained membership in the Council of Mutual Economic Assistance in the summer of 1972, but also, from 1975, Cuba was involved in joint actions with the Soviets in Africa. This situation led to the emergence of Cuban leverage in Moscow, as the Caribbean island wanted payment for deploying its personnel in Africa. Soviet aid continued and expanded. Both the signing of a twenty-five-year agreement on friendship and cooperation in November 1984 and Soviet Russian delivery of some of the most advanced military hardware in the early 1980s illustrated this success in Cuban foreign policy.[9]

Moreover, in the 1980s, many of the original pressures, but augmented by others, had not abated, which continued to make a possible schism in the relationship unlikely. These included a twenty-year history, a shared ideology, and levels of aid and trade that continued to multiply — by 1985, Soviet-Cuban trade amounted to 9.85 billion pesos, or more than thirteen times than that of 1965, the first year of the original Cuban-Soviet five-year plan. As in the 1960s, if the relationship came to an end, Soviet investment would have been wasted, something that Moscow could not afford to do.[10] Furthermore, Cuba remained an important propaganda tool for the Soviet Union in the Cold War, which had taken a dramatic turn in the late 1970s and early 1980s because of increased U.S.-Soviet tensions in Afghanistan and Africa.[11]

In 1985, the rise of Mikhail Gorbachev as the leader of Soviet Russia proved a watershed in the communist world, including Cuba. The implementation of the campaign to rectify errors in Cuba and the advent of perestroika, glasnost, and "new thinking" in Soviet foreign policy meant that Gorbachev had to contend with a number of new explosive pressures in the relationship that no previous general secretary had faced.[12] It may have taken some time for the differences in the reforms to appear, but they became increasingly public starting in 1989. A debate in the Soviet Union about Cuban-Soviet relations and about the Cuban Revolution itself commenced as a result of glasnost, and Gorbachev could not ignore the debate as his predecessors had done.[13] Furthermore, Cuban aversion to Soviet reforms became clear when Castro introduced Gorbachev to the National Congress of People's Deputies on April 5, 1989, and outlined why Cuba did not need Soviet-style reforms.[14] Castro's position undoubtedly increased pressure on Gorbachev, as it became increasingly awkward for Moscow to support an unreformed Cuba.[15]

Yet during the Gorbachev era, the relationship was reformed with a 1991 trade agreement that was radically different from previous five-year agreements that the two countries had signed since 1964: the duration was for one year, and trade was to be conducted at world market prices.[16] Moreover, new thinking in Soviet foreign policy resulted in both the retreat of the significance of Marxism-Leninism and reduced tension between the superpowers. In effect, this reduced the geostrategic importance of the island for Moscow as the Cold War came to an end. In itself, the end of the Cold War fueled further calls in the Soviet Union to reform the relationship as many of the foundations of the association with Havana began crumbling. A major change in policy came with Gorbachev's historic statement on September 11, 1991: he announced the withdrawal of the final remaining Soviet troops from Cuba. Significantly, the failed August coup by antireformist communist hard-liners in the Soviet Union had occurred only days before; the defeat also ended the power of the Cuban lobby in the Russian government that had slowed reform of the Cuban-Russian relationship. In addition, it appeared Washington was involved in Gorbachev's announcement, as he made it during a joint press conference with the American secretary of state James Baker.[17]

Russian-Cuban Relations

The relationship between Havana and Moscow underwent fundamental changes when Gorbachev was the Soviet premier — he had had to face several new explosive pressures regarding the relationship that no previous general secretary had had to contend with. However, many other pressures, including some that had originally pushed the two countries together, remained significant and resulted in the relationship's continued existence. It was only with the disintegration of the Soviet Union in December 1991 that Cuban-Soviet Russian relations came to an abrupt end.

This 1991 break was both economic and political. In 1992, with the economic downturn, trade with Russia fell to less than $1 billion, or 90 percent below the 1988 level of almost $10 billion. The political aspect of these changes was highlighted at the UN Convention on Human Rights in Geneva, when Moscow voted against Havana from 1992 to 1994 — Cuba was chastised by the Convention, and the Kremlin had never previously voted that way.[18] The effect on the Cuban economy was enormous: total trade in 1993 reached $3.2 billion, less than a third of Cuban-Soviet trade in 1988.[19] As the island endured the so-called Special Period in an attempt to survive the loss of its socialist trading partners, many believed that the revolution would not survive.[20]

A variety of reasons explain these changes in the Cuban-Russian relationship. The complete elimination of Marxism-Leninism from Moscow's foreign policy instantly removed a cornerstone of the post-1959 Cuban-Soviet relationship. Moreover, the economic transition from socialism to capitalism that the new Russian Federation was embarking on and the Boris Yeltsin government's wish to move to a market-driven economy as quickly as possible had a negative impact on Cuban-Russian relations. Quite simply, Russian companies were not in a position to trade with Cuba, because they were struggling to survive in the transition and wanted market forces rather than political ones to decide terms of trade with the island. As the Cuban government appeared determined to preserve the socialist nature of its revolution, many Russians were delighted to no longer have to trade with a regime they perceived as an anachronism.

Russian-U.S. relations also played a part in this downturn, because improving relations with the West, and the United States in particular, was one of the Kremlin's chief foreign policy goals. This change had resulted from the victory of the liberal Westernizers in the raging debate in post-Soviet Russia on foreign policy; quite simply, it negated close relations with Havana because of the continued strained nature of Cuban-American relations.[21] In addition, the United States continued its Cold War practice of trying to get the Kremlin to alter its Cuba policy. Professor Eugenio Larin, the director of Latin American studies at the Institute of Cold War History of the Russian Academy of Sciences, wrote: "In order to improve political ties Washington demanded of B. H. Yeltsin that he must cut ties with Cuba. This course of action dominated the 1990s."[22] Changing Soviet policy was particularly illustrated in 1992, when Russia abstained on a UN vote condemning the passage of the Cuban Democracy Act, or the Torricelli bill, which further tightened the U.S. economic embargo against the island.[23]

Although the downturn in the relationship between Havana and Moscow unquestionably had dramatic adverse affects for the Caribbean island, not least for its economy, a complete schism never materialized. As a result of the nature and duration of the Cuban-Soviet relationship, the legacy from the Soviet era is not surprising, given that it was both multifaceted and of great significance for

Cuban-Russian relations in the 1990s. Many Cubans remain in Russia and Russians in Cuba who had intermarried, and Russian-made automobiles are still used on the island.[24] Moreover, in the early 1990s, the Cuban economy continued to be "powered" by Russian-made machinery, which needed repair and spare parts as it aged. Lacking alternative buyers, Russia proved a more-than-willing vendor.

Another highly significant part of the legacy was Cuba's accumulated debt to Moscow from the Soviet era, which Russia inherited on becoming the legal successor to the Soviet Union. This was an important, contentious issue between the two countries throughout the 1990s. Not only did Cuba not repay the debt; the two countries could not even reach agreement on the actual size of the debt. In late 2000, Aleksei Chichkin reported in *Rossiiskaya Gazeta*:

> Russia's Ministry of Economic Development and Trade puts Cuba's debt at £20 billion. Cuba didn't even recognise this debt until last year. And for understandable reasons, it brought a counterclaim — namely, that the sudden break-off of economic, scientific and technological ties with the USSR and Russia in 1989–1992 had cost the Cuban economy at least $15 billion (including adjustments for the subsequent "lost" years). Moreover, Havana proposed that Russia compensate for this by drastically lowering and then abolishing import duties on all Cuban goods and services. It promised to extend the same benefits to Moscow.[25]

However, because of Russia's economic situation, Moscow could not afford to cancel the debt, and if it terminated the relationship, any slim possibility that Cuba might repay the debt would evaporate. Interestingly, in September 2005, Moscow deferred payment of the debt but did not cancel it. The present Russian government appears to cling to the hope that the debt might be repaid; but the debt has been both an important aspect of the Soviet legacy and a significant reason for the relationship's continuation.[26]

Moreover, on the basis of their own commodity production, Cuba and Russia considered sugar-for-oil swaps in the early 1990s. Both countries required the swapped commodities, and it was easier and cheaper for them to swap products instead of buying them on the open market.[27] In addition, this process also dispensed with the need for expensive intermediaries and, importantly, given the acute economic situation both Cuba and Russia faced, neither country could afford the world market price. The U.S. embargo against Cuba further complicated the situation. Russia's economic transition decimated the country's agricultural output, which only increased the significance of the swaps to Russia. Russia also produces sugar, but the Cuban and Russian sugar harvests are out of sync. Thus, before 1991, sugar refineries in the Soviet Union could work all year with imported Cuban sugar; but as imports later failed to materialize, this process ceased. Reduced sugar imports made a bad situation in Russian agriculture worse because of reduced supplies of this important commodity and decreased employment in Russian sugar refineries, but it increased the significance for Russia of sugar-for-oil swaps.[28]

Despite all these significant elements of the Soviet legacy, the part that attracted most international attention, particularly in the United States, was the Kremlin's decision to keep open the electronic intelligence listening post at Lourdes on the outskirts of Havana. Officially, this was "necessary in order to maintain stable communications with our embassies in Latin America"; but the facility became an extremely contentious issue for Moscow and Washington throughout the 1990s and complicated the relationship between the two former superpowers.[29] However, the importance of the Soviet legacy cannot be overestimated in the relationship that evolved between Havana and Moscow in the post-Soviet world.

Furthermore, Cuba's economic reforms of the 1990s have also affected Cuban-Russian relations.[30] The specific goal of the reforms was not to attract Russian investment, although that has been an unpredicted result. Russians realized that they had lost their preeminent position in the island's economy because of the influx of foreign investment that occurred as a consequence of the reforms. The reforms not only helped the island recover from its acute economic problems in the immediate aftermath of the Cuban-Soviet relationship but also dramatically altered the composition of the island's trading partners. The opening of 260 joint projects from 1995 to 1997 with Cuban and foreign money highlights this transformation — only two projects were between Cuba and Russia.[31] In 2000, the journalist Stanislav Kondrashov wrote about joint ventures in *Vremya*: "In Cuba's nickel industry, Canadian capital now reigns supreme. And the Chinese dominate the consumer goods market. The Spanish, the British and the Mexicans are investing in Cuba."[32] Moreover, during his trip to Cuba in December 2000, Vladimir Putin commented: "We lost a lot of positions which were a top priority for both countries, and our Russian companies in Cuba have been replaced by Western competitors."[33]

If this situation was not bad enough, the huge Soviet-era investments had been lost, and foreign companies were using that to their advantage. In December 2000, Aleksei Chichkin wrote, "According to Cuba's Minister of Foreign Investment, more than half of the old Soviet projects on the Isle of Freedom have been taken over by foreign firms."[34] Moreover, *Moskovskiye Novosti* published a thoughtful article on this subject, part of which reads:

According to some estimates, in the course of 30 years of Soviet-Cuban cooperation, we invested more than $100 billion in the island's economy. One should also remember that no other country in the world has so many factories built with Soviet assistance and so many specialists trained in the USSR. Had we managed to preserve our dominant status in Cuba's nickel industry, Russia might have a monopoly on this raw material in the world market. Today there are more than 500 joint production facilities on which all work has halted. And although relations with Cuba will never be what they once were, one thing is clear: No matter who is in power in Havana — Fidel Castro or the leaders of the Miami-based opposition — Russia will continue to have economic interests in Cuba. And for this reason the thaw in our relations can only be welcomed.[35]

This analysis illustrated not only concern about the Soviet legacy in Cuba but also the long-term future of Cuban-Russian relations, which could even outlive Fidel Castro given the two countries' shared history.

The Russian recovery from the economic transition only aided improved relations between Havana and Moscow. Russian companies and individuals started to invest internationally. The result was that, in 1996, Russia was remarkably Cuba's single largest trading partner. Trade just exceeded six hundred thousand pesos, a mere fraction of trade in the Soviet era, but this had most certainly not been predicted in 1992.[36] Russian companies attempting to take advantage of the Soviet-era legacy and readdress the loss of their position in the island's economy were key. Their attempts, not globalization in general, drove the upturn for the Russians; they did not repeat their success in Cuba elsewhere in Latin America. Since 1996, other countries, particularly China and Venezuela, may have superseded Russia in significance to the Cuban economy, but this does not reduce the importance of the Russian wish to "right the wrongs" of the past.[37]

Moreover, Moscow's reaction to the American Cuban Liberty and Solidarity Act, or the Helms-Burton Act — legislation passed in 1996 in an attempt to prevent third-party countries from trading with Cuba — highlighted the significance of trade with Cuba for Russia. In addition, the act illustrated yet another attempt by Washington to influence Moscow's Cuba policy, as one section concentrated solely on the Russians' use of Lourdes. However, Moscow was willing to simply ignore the legislation. The Russian Foreign Ministry declared, "We confirm our intention to develop and broaden mutually beneficial cooperation with Cuba as well as sectors of mutual interest, particularly in the commercial and economic sphere."[38]

This setback did not stop Washington from trying to persuade Moscow to close Lourdes. In March 2000, Ileana Ros-Lehtinen, one of three Cuban American congressional representatives from Florida, tried to have the US$200 million that Russia paid Cuba annually for the use of the facility added to Russia's debt with the Paris Club of creditors. When this did not work, in July 2000, the U.S. Congress stated that, as long as Lourdes remained operational, it would not reschedule the Russian debt. Russia was deeply unhappy with this policy, and Prime Minister Mikhail Kasyanov stated, "it's inappropriate to link these two things — our installation on Cuba and the debt."[39] Cuban-Soviet relations had withstood U.S. attempts to alter them, and it appeared that this ability had outlived the end of Cold War, thus illustrating the enduring nature of the relationship.[40]

The upturn in the relationship was also political, as illustrated by Moscow again voting with Cuba at the UN Convention on Human Rights from 1995 onwards; significantly, 1995 was the year that Russian involvement in the war in Chechnya increased, as did reports about human rights abuses perpetrated by Russian troops.[41] This was significant because the Kremlin wanted to avert international focus from the issue, but by a groundbreaking Russian vote against Cuba at the convention, the opposite occurred.

Furthermore, Havana and Moscow's dislike of the one-sided nature of global politics that had emerged in the 1990s aided the relationship between the two countries. Cuba's aversion to this unipolarity was not surprising given the strained nature of Cuban-American relations and Cuba's ideological dislike of neoliberal economics. The Kremlin was unhappy with issues such as expansion of the North Atlantic Treaty Organization (NATO) to the east and Western action in the former Yugoslavia, which heralded an end to Moscow's pro-Western foreign policy of the early 1990s. In addition, Moscow had not received the aid and assistance it had hoped for from the West. This is not to say it had received none, but the belief that it could have received more was evident in the Russian State Duma, which was becoming increasingly nationalistic in its outlook.[42] Moreover, increasing nationalism amplified Moscow's desire to pursue a different foreign policy, which manifested itself in Moscow wanting to reassert itself in international politics and no longer be marginalized, as it had been throughout the 1990s. Yevgeny Primakov's appointment in December 1995 as foreign minister only helped this trend, as he viewed the world very differently than his predecessors did and believed in "spheres of influence."[43]

Russia's desire to reassert itself in global politics, which has continued under both Putin and Medvedev, has been important to improved Cuban-Russian relations, as it perfectly illustrates to Washington that Moscow is again a great power and not a peripheral actor in international relations, as it had been in the early to mid-1990s. Moreover, the high price of oil at the start of the twenty-first century helped fund Russia's more assertive foreign policy.[44] The island's importance for Moscow has only increased as Russia has taken a more general interest in Latin America; and it is perfectly logical that this orientation begin with the country about which it has the most knowledge in the region. Moreover, the use of the listening post at Lourdes as a counterbalance to NATO expansion to the east and, after September 11, 2001, to U.S. military involvement in Central Asia and Afghanistan — traditionally considered in Moscow's sphere of influence — has further increased the geostrategic significance of the island for Moscow. In late 2008, the Russian newspaper *Izvestia* suggested that, in an attempt to counter the proposed U.S. nuclear shield in Europe, Russian bombers should be stationed on the island.[45]

The geostrategic significance of Cuba in Moscow's more assertive foreign policy has seen the return of global Russian naval maneuvers in the Caribbean, as in December 2008, when Russian naval vessels visited Venezuela.⁴⁶ As part of these out-of-area deployments, Russia requires "friendly" ports for docking where it can carry out refueling and maintenance. Cuba has been willing to open its ports in this manner, and the result is the return of Russian naval warships to Cuban waters. Contemporary international relations are vastly different from those at the time of the inception of the Havana-Moscow relationship, but an original reason that drew the Kremlin toward the Cuban Revolution, the geostrategic importance of the island relative to the United States, has reemerged.

There is, however, one noticeable exception to the improving relationship, something that calls into question its enduring nature: Moscow's announcement in October 2001 to close the listening post at Lourdes. Moscow stated costs as the official reason, but the Cuban government thought otherwise. *Granma* stated that the $200 million "was not an extraordinary figure if one considers that it is barely 3% of the damage to our country's economy by the disintegration of the Socialist bloc and the USSR."⁴⁷ Havana instead believed that the United States had pressured Moscow. Putin had left himself open to this accusation; he had met with President George W. Bush just weeks before the announcement was made.⁴⁸ The idea that Washington played a part in the decision received more credence in February 2008, when Putin revisited the topic of Lourdes: "We pulled out of bases in Cuba and Vietnam. And what did we get? New American bases in Bulgaria and Romania."⁴⁹

As with previous problems and tensions that had sporadically appeared between Havana and Moscow since the early 1960s, the relationship endured and those issues quickly disappeared. Because cordial Cuban-Russian relations have returned, the issue of Lourdes does seem to be a one-off. Politically, Moscow has continued to back Cuba in its various disputes with Washington, including the island's placement on the "axis of evil" list in May 2002.⁵⁰ This was important in itself for Havana and had further advantages for the Caribbean island, as Russian power attempted to counter American influence, most noticeably in a variety of UN fora. In addition, the relationship is in harmony with Cuba's foreign policy changes in the 1990s to try to increase its bilateral relationships.

Cuban-Russian relations have economically diversified in the past fifteen years, which is important given the decrease in the Cuban sugar harvest and Venezuela's replacing of Russia as the island's main source of oil. This diversity has been evident at various trade fairs held in Havana and Moscow: for instance, the Cuban purchase of Russian-made airplanes and the signing in September 2006 of a $355 million grant by the Russian prime minister Mikhail Fradkov for the Cuban purchase of Russian goods.⁵¹ Significantly, in 2007, the official publication of the Cuban Chamber of Commerce published: "In short, it can be said that the following 10 countries have been among the top countries of Cuba's foreign trade in recent years: Venezuela, Spain, China, Canada, Holland, Russia, Italy, Brazil, Mexico and France. More than 70% of the country's trade exchange is carried out with these countries."[52] Russia's inclusion in this list more than fifteen years after the end of Cuban-Soviet relationship is both remarkable and illustrates the importance of trade to the continuing relationship. Furthermore, in 2008, the Russian Norilisk Nickel Company and the truck manufacturer Kamaz have expressed a desire to expand their ties with the island, and Gazprom has shown interest in exploratory oil drilling in Cuba's Gulf of Mexico waters.[53] In January 2009, Raúl Castro, during his first visit to Moscow since 1985, demonstrated the importance of trade to the relationship: "Of particular merit are our economic ties which will become more important as a result of the global economic crisis. I am convinced that Cuban-Russian collaboration, which has new dynamism, will continue to develop successfuly."[54]

In April 2009, President Barack Obama made changes to the amount of remittances that Cuban Americans can send to family remaining on the island and to the travel restrictions they face. This action, however, has not heralded a new era in Cuban-U.S. relations. The economic embargo remains in place, and after the attempted bombing of an airplane in the United States on December 25, 2009, Washington placed Cuba on a list of states sponsoring terrorism; as a result, Cuban citizens traveling to the United States face increased security examinations.[55] In addition, in 2010, Russian-American relations have shown signs of improvement. On April 8, 2010, Obama and Medvedev signed an agreement to reduce both countries' nuclear arsenals.[56] The Kremlin has backed Obama's changes to remittances and travel restrictions for Cuban Americans but has not commented on Cuba's inclusion on the list of states that sponsor terrorism; however, it does continue to call for the end of the embargo.[57] Both Havana's and Moscow's relationships with Washington are evolving, but Cuban-Russian relations remain important for Cuba and Russia. In general, Russian interest in Cuba and Latin America is showing no signs of abating.

Conclusions

A variety of pressures have impinged on the relationship between Havana and Moscow since its inception in the late 1950s and early 1960s and through the beginning of the twenty-first century. At its creation, the relationship was very much a product of its time: Cold War geopolitics was the key in pushing the two countries together. However, other pressures quickly appeared that gave the relationship more robust foundations, including a common ideology, Soviet investment in the Cuban Revolution, and the effects of the Cuban missile crisis. The Cold War setting and the Sino-Soviet split further increased the significance of Moscow's support of Havana; to do otherwise would have resulted in a possible schism that would have been particularly problematic for the Kremlin. As the relationship matured, yet more pressures appeared that resulted in Cuban leverage in Moscow after the mid-1970s and joint action in Africa. By the mid-1980s, with the deterioration in relations between the superpowers, Cuba retained its propagandist and strategic significance for Moscow, and by this time, the two countries had a shared twenty-year history together. Moreover, levels of aid and trade between the two continued to increase, which again reduced the chances of a permanent break in the relationship.

Cuban-Soviet relations undoubtedly underwent fundamental change while Gorbachev was the Soviet premier, not least because of the number of explosive forces in the relationship as a consequence of the reform processes in both countries, some of which had not been foreseen. This process added to the number of turbulent episodes in the thirty-year relationship. Furthermore, Moscow faced repeated U.S. attempts to influence the relationship, but the Cuban-Soviet relationship survived, coming to an end only with the disintegration of the Soviet Union. As a consequence, the Cuban-Russian relationship suffered a dramatic economic and political downturn when many of its foundations disintegrated overnight. These included the disappearance of Marxism-Leninism from Moscow's policies, the dramatic decrease in the island's geostrategic importance for the Kremlin, and the effects of the Yeltsin government's enthusiastic embrace of neoliberal economic thinking.

Yet the Cuban-Russian relationship survived even that turbulent period. A colossal Soviet-era legacy was crucial to the relationship's endurance. Also crucial were Cuba's economic changes to encourage foreign investment. However, an unforeseen effect of the changes has been an increase in Russian financial and trade interests in Cuba. Russian companies not only were missing out on economic opportunities on the island but also were wasting the huge investment from the Soviet era. Russian interest in the Cuban economy increased and in 1996 Russia was the island's main trading partner, driven by the idiosyncrasies of the countries' relationship. Other countries have since overtaken Russia in importance to the Cuban economy, but Russian interests have diversified, and the bilateral economic links remain significant for both countries.

As the twentieth century drew to a close, the geostrategic significance of Cuba increased for the Kremlin. This by no means suggests that Cuba's importance is equal to that during the Cold War, but geostrategy has reemerged in the relationship. Cuba and Russia have a robust relationship that is now almost fifty years old. The relationship may have originated during the Cold War, but many other aspects are key to explaining it as well. The relationship has endured a number of turbulent episodes — none greater than that from 1992 to 1994 — and repeated attempts by Washington to alter its course. But it has continued to survive.

Havana's relationship with Washington is still likely to change considerably. This transformation will affect the island's other bilateral relationships, including Cuban-Russian relations. However, because of the enduring Cuban-Russian relationship, the relationship may not change as much as expected. If anything, the Cuban-Russian relationship has become stronger since Raúl Castro became president, which suggests that the two countries will continue to enjoy cordial relations in the foreseeable future, in no small part because of their shared history.

NOTES

1. Mervyn J. Bain, *Soviet-Cuban Relations, 1985 to 1991: Changing Perceptions in Moscow and Havana* (Lanham, MD: Lexington Books, 2007), 17–21. See also James Blight and Philip Brenner, *Sad and Luminous Days: Cuba's Struggle with the Superpowers after the Cuban Missile Crisis* (Lanham, MD: Rowman and Littlefield, 2002), 5–9; Yuri Pavlov, *Soviet-Cuban Alliance, 1959–1991* (New Brunswick, NJ: Transaction Publishers, 1994), 3–13; Wayne Smith, *The Closest of Enemies. A Personal and Diplomatic Account of U.S.-Cuban Relations since 1957* (New York: W. W. Norton, 1987), 144.

2. Blight and Brenner, *Sad and Luminous Days*, 5–10; Michael Dobbs, *One Minute to Midnight: Kennedy, Khrushchev and Castro on the Brink of Nuclear War* (New York: Alfred A. Knopf, 2008), 33–34; Morris Morley, *Imperial State and Revolution: The United States and Cuba, 1952–1986* (Cambridge: Cambridge University Press, 1987), 72–146; Don Munton and David A. Welch, *The Cuban Missile Crisis: A Concise History* (New York: Oxford University Press, 2007), 9, 20.

3. Peter Shearman, *The Soviet Union and Cuba* (London: Routledge and Kegan Paul, 1987), 5–11.

4. In January 1959, the Kremlin was much more certain of the political leanings of Guevara and Raúl Castro than those of Fidel Castro. See Nikita Khrushchev, *Khrushchev Remembers* (New York: Penguin Books, 1971), 450.

5. Hugh Thomas, *Cuba; or, The Pursuit of Freedom* (London: Eyre and Spottiswoode 1971), 1216–17.

6. *Revolución,* December 2, 1961, 1.

7. Blight and Brenner, *Sad and Luminous Days*, 35–85.

8. Shearman, *Soviet Union and Cuba*, 11–14.

9. *Pravda,* November 11, 1984, 1, 4; Piero Gleijeses, *Conflicting Missions. Havana, Washington, and Africa, 1959–1976* (Chapel Hill: University of North Carolina Press, 2002).

10. In 1965, trade was 750,889.90 pesos. Comité Estatal de Estadísticas, *Anuario estadístico de Cuba* (Havana: Comité Estatal de Estadísticas, 1970), 14, 14; *Vneshiaia Torgovliia v 1989–1990* (Moscow: Mezhdunarodnye Otnosheniia, 1991), 5.

11. Shearman, *Soviet Union and Cuba*, 57–75.

12. Mervyn J. Bain, "Cuba-Soviet Relations in the Gorbachev Era," *Journal of Latin American Studies* 37 (November 2005): 774–90.

13. The debate in the Soviet Union about Cuba and the Cuban Revolution even reached the Castro brothers' personal lives. *Moscow Komsomolskaya Pravda,* August 28, 1990, 2.

14. *Granma,* April 5, 1989, 2.

15. See *General'nogo sekretari'a TsK KPSS, Predsedateli'a'Prezidiuma Verkhovnogo Soveta SSSR M.S. Gorbacheva v Respubliku Kuba: 2–5 apreli'a'1989 goda: dokumenty i materialy* (Moscow: Mezhdunarodnye Otnosheniia, 1989).

16. *Granma,* December 31, 1990, 1.

17. Boris Pankin, the Soviet foreign minister in 1991, believed that Washington had pressured

Gorbachev over the decision. Boris Pankin, *The Last One Hundred Days of the Soviet Union* (London: IB Tauris, 1996), 71. For the repercussions of the defeat of the Cuban lobby on the relationship, see Bain, *Soviet-Cuban Relations*, 94–95.

18. International Monetary Fund, *Direction of Trade Statistics Yearbook 1997* (Washington, D.C.: International Monetary Fund, 1997), 173; *Izvestia*, March 9, 1992, 7; *Izvestia*, March 12, 1993, 7.

19. *Vneshiaia Torgovliia v 1989–1990* (Moscow: Mezhdunarodnye Otnosheniia, 1991), 5; *Vneshiaia Torgovliia v 1986* (Moscow: Mezhdunarodnye Otnosheniia, 1987), 259, 265; United Nations, *Economic Commission for Latin America and the Caribbean* [CEPAL] *1991* (Santiago, Chile: United Nations, 1991), 135; Oficina Nacional de Estadísticas, *Anuario estadístico de Cuba 2000* (La Habana, 2000), VI-5 to VI-7, http://www.camaracuba.cu/TPHabana/Estadisticas2000/estadisticas2000.htm; International Monetary Fund. *Direction of Trade Statistics*, 392.

20. For the effect on the Cuban economy, see Carmelo Mesa-Lago, "The Economic Effects on Cuba of the Downfall of Socialism in the USSR and Eastern Europe," in *Cuba after the Cold War*, ed. Carmelo Mesa-Lago (Pittsburgh, PA: University of Pittsburgh Press, 1993), 140–43; A. M. Ritter, "Cuba's Economic Strategy and Alternative Futures," in *Cuba at a Crossroads: Politics and Economics after the Fourth Party Congress*, ed. Jorge Pérez-López (Gainesville: University Press of Florida, 1994), 67; Carmelo Mesa-Lago and Jorge Pérez-López, *Cuba's Aborted Reform: Socioeconomic Effects, International Comparisons, and Transition Policies* (Gainesville: University Press of Florida, 2005), 71–130.

21. Margot Light, "Foreign Policy Thinking," in *Internal Factors in Russian Foreign Policy*, ed. Alex Pravda, Roy Alison, and Margot Light (Oxford: Oxford University Press, 1996), 33–100.

22. Eugenio A. Larin, *Politicheskaia istorii Kuba XX Veka* (Moscow: Visshaya Shkola, 2007), 164.

23. *Izvestia*, March 9, 1992, 7.

24. Mervyn J. Bain, *Russian-Cuban Relations since 1992: Continuing Camaraderie in a Post-Soviet World* (Lanham, MD: Lexington Books, 2008), 83–86.

25. Alexei Chichkin, "Mutual Interest Replaces External Friendship," *Rossiiskaya Gazeta*, December 16, 2000, 7.

26. *ITARR-TASS News Agency*, September 15, 2005.

27. Leonid Vlekhov, "Full Circle: Mr Shumeoko Finds Golden Mean in Relations with Cuba," *Sevodnya*, December 29, 1993, 3.

28. I. Glasov, G. Kara-Murza, and A. Batchikov, *El libro blanco: Las reformas neoliberales en Rusia, 1991–2004* (Havana: Editorial de Ciencias Sociales, 2007), 111. During an interview in Havana on February 14, 2008, Dr. Rodolfo Humpierre spoke of the importance of sugar to Russian agriculture.

29. *Izvestia*, November 4, 1992, 5; William Rosenau, "A Deafening Silence: U.S. Policy and the Sigint Facility at Lourdes," *Intelligence and National Security* 9 (1994): 723–34.

30. Jorge Pérez-López, "The Cuban Economy in the Age of Hemispheric Integration," *Journal of Interamerican Studies and World Affairs* 39, no. 3 (1997): 15–22.

31. S. Batchikov, "The Cuba That We Are Losing and Everyone Else Is Finding," *Nezavisimaya Gazeta*, November 14, 1997, 2.

32. Stanislav Kondrashov, "Language of Gestures in Putin's Diplomacy," *Vremya*, December 22, 2000, 3.

33. L. Newman, "Cuba, Russia Seek New Post-Cold War Relationship" (December 14, 2000), debtproblems112.blogspot.com/2005/06/debt-problems-rising-debt-problem-1.html.

34. Chichkin, "Mutual Interest," 1.

35. Alexei Bausin, "Cuban Poker: It's America's Turn," *Moskovskiye Novosti*, May 28–June 4, 2000, 12.

36. Oficina Nacional de Estadísticas, *Anuario estadístico de Cuba 2000*, VI-5 to VI-7.

37. Oficina Nacional de Estadísticas, *Anuario estadístico de Cuba 2006* La Habana, 2007), VII-4.

38. *Granma International*, April 17, 1996, 13.

39. Aleksandr Chudodeyev, "Caribbean Crisis," *Sevodnya*, July 21, 2000, 2.

40. On few occasions since the establishment of relations between Havana and Moscow has U.S. pressure on Moscow appeared to result in a change in the Kremlin's Cuba policy. It did seem to have been successful during the Cuban missile crisis; upon discovery of Soviet nuclear submarines moored at Cienfuegos in 1970; with Gorbachev's announcement on September 11, 1991, of the removal of the final Soviet soldiers from Cuba; and possibly from 1992 to 1995 over Moscow's voting behavior in various UN fora.

41. *Nezavisimaya gazeta*, May 25, 1996, 1.

42. Stephen White, *Russia's New Politics: The Management of a Postcommunist Society* (Cambridge: Cambridge University Press, 2004), 229.

43. The close personal relationship between Primakov and the Cuban ruling elite, highlighted by Fidel Castro's invitation for Primakov and his family to holiday on the island once Primakov had resigned, only helped improve the relationship. Yevgeny M. Primakov, *Minnoe pole politiki* (Moscow: Molodai Gvardii, 2006), 149–52.

44. This more assertive Russian foreign policy led Andrei Grachev to suggest the Putin doctrine, which contained Soviet features, nationalism, and anti-Western ideas. Andrei Grachev, "Putin's Foreign Policy Choices," in *Leading Russia: Putin in Perspective — Essays in Honour of Archie Brown*, ed. Alex Pravda (Oxford: Oxford University Press, 2005), 262–64. See also Dmitri Trenin, "Russia Leaves the West," *Foreign Affairs* 85 (July–August 2006): 87–98.

45. Fidel Castro wrote of Raúl's wisdom not to comment on these reports. *Granma*, July 23, 2008, 1.

46. "Russia, Venezuela Warships to Hold Live Firing Drills on Dec. 1," *RIA Novosti*, November 25, 2008, http://www.rian.ru/Russia/20081125.

47. *Granma*, October 18, 2001, 1.

48. Castro likened it to the outcome of the Cuban missile crisis when he said, "It was a fait accompli — they informed us, hoping we'd go along." Fidel Castro and Ignacio Ramonet, *Fidel Castro: My Life — A Spoken Autobiography* (New York, 2008), 49, 287.

49. Shaun Walker, "A New Phase in the Arms Race Is Unfolding," *Independent*, February 9, 2008, 2.

50. With regard to this and to U.S. accusations of Cuba carrying out biological warfare research, Russian Foreign Minister Sergey Lavrov commented: "I think that I will not exceed my powers if I say that I have never seen any hostility toward the United States on the part of Cuba during my contacts with Cuban friends." *Interfax, Russia*, September 29, 2004.

51. *ITAR-TASS*, February 27, 2005; "Rusia con pabellón absoluto en la FIHAV-2006," *El Ruso Cubano, Boletín Informativo de le Embajada de le Federación de Rusia 2006*, no. 5, November 2, 2006, 3; "Russia Banks Syndicate $203m Aircraft Loan for Cuba," *RIA Novosti*, December 22, 2006, http://rian.ru/buisness/20061222/57603049-print.html; "Russia to Grant Cuba $355m 10-Year Loan — PM Fradkov," *RIA Novosti*, September 28, 2006, http://rian.ru/russia/20060928/54353408-print.html.

52. La Cámara de Comercio de la República de Cuba, "Nuevas tendencias y alternativa del ALBA," *Cuba Foreign Trade* (official publication of the Department of Commerce of the Republic of Cuba), no. 3 (2007): 15–16.

53. "Norilsk Nickel Eyes Metals Plant Project in Cuba," *RIA Novosti*, November 20, 2008, http://www.rian/business/20081120; "Russian Truck Maker Kamaz Considering Production in Cuba," *RIA Novosti*, November 21, 2008, http://www.rian.ru/Russia/20081121; "Official: Russians Want to Search for Oil off Cuba," *Miami Herald*, November 23, 2008, http://www.miamiherald.com/news/Americas/cuba.

54. "La colaboración cubana-rusa ha cobrado un nuevo dinamismo," *Trabajadores*, January 30, 2009, http://www.trabajadores.cu/la-colaboracion-cubano-rusa.

55. "Airport Security," *New York Times*, January 6, 2010.

56. Peter Baker, "U.S. and Russia Sign Nuclear Arms Pact," *New York Times*, April 8, 2010, http://www.nytimes.com/2010/04/09/world/europe/09prexy.html?hp.

57. "Russia Hopes U.S. Fully Lifts Economic Embargo on Cuba," *RIA Novosti*, April 21, 2009, http://rian.ru/world/20090416.

DOREEN WEPPLER-GROGAN

Cultural Policy, the Visual Arts, and the Advance of the Cuban Revolution in the Aftermath of the Gray Years

ABSTRACT

This article examines the impact on the visual arts in Cuba of a period commonly referred to as the gray years, a period during the 1970s when economic and cultural practices copied from the Soviet bureaucracy had great weight. It contends that though Cuba's cultural space was restricted during the gray years, there were always artists who created points of resistance, refusing to accept either the stereotypical notions of Cuban identity that a layer of dogmatists ensconced in major cultural institutions or their bureaucratic excesses promoted. The article locates this cultural discourse in polemics that unfolded in the 1960s, when notions of socialist realism were sharply contested, and it furthermore notes how both periods of debate are providing vital reference points in contemporary discussions on cultural policy. With the demise of the Soviet Union and the introduction of the Special Period in the 1990s, artists in Cuba were forced to contend with new factors that challenged the mode of cultural production on the island, particularly the growing inroads of the capitalist market. The article explains how initiatives like the Battle of Ideas, launched in 1999, can help avoid a comparable future rupture with the Cuba's cultural policy.

RESUMEN

Este artículo examina el impacto en las artes visuales en Cuba de un período comúnmente conocido como los años grises, un período durante la década de 1970, cuando las prácticas económicas y culturales copiadas de la burocracia soviética tenían gran peso. El artículo se sostiene que, aunque el espacio cultural de Cuba se restringió durante los años grises, es incorrecto concluir que la producción artística fue tan limitada por la estrecha visión política de una parte de los funcionarios culturales, que se produjo poco digno de consideración. De hecho, siempre hubo artistas que crearon puntos de resistencia, negándose a aceptar ya sea las nociones estereotipadas de la identidad cubana promovida por una capa de dogmáticos instalados en las principales instituciones culturales o sus excesos burocráticos. Se sitúa este discurso cultural en la polémica que se desarrolló en la década de 1960 cuando se hizo pronunciada oposición a las ideas del realismo socialista, y además, el artículo nota cómo estos dos períodos de debate proporcionan puntos de referencia vitales a las discusiones contemporáneas sobre la política cultural. Con la desaparición de la Unión Soviética y la introducción del Período Espe-

143

cial en la década de 1990, los artistas en Cuba se vieron obligados a enfrentarse a nuevos factores que cuestionaron el modo de producción cultural en la isla, en particular, las crecientes incursiones del mercado capitalista. El ensayo explica cómo la Batalla de Ideas, una importante iniciativa lanzada en 1999, contribuirá a evitar una ruptura futura comparable, con la política cultural de Cuba.

Introduction

From the inception of the revolution, the Cuban leadership grouped around Fidel Castro recognized that the defense and advance of the revolution depended fundamentally on the mobilization of the Cuban people. Cultural development and, more specifically, artistic production have been viewed equally consistently as indispensable components of that mobilization. Widespread debate around cultural policy and the freest conditions of artistic expression are inevitably entailed in this perspective. The Cuban cultural scholar Graziella Pogolotti explained at a recent book fair in Havana that the cultural debate has always been part of a more fundamental question about how socialism will be built and that the revolution's cultural policy is part of a broader approach. "As Che [Guevara] said, to build socialism, you also have to develop the subject of that new history — the men and women, and also culture."[1] In his remarks to intellectuals at the famous library meetings in 1961, President Fidel Castro also pointed to the close association between culture and social change when he explained that the revolution cannot seek "to stifle art or culture, because one of the goals and one of the fundamental aims of the revolution is to develop art and culture, precisely so that art and culture truly become the patrimony of the people. And just as one wants a better life for the people in the material sense, so, too, does one want a better life for the people in a spiritual and cultural sense."[2]

However, it would be naive to suggest that the forging of the revolution's cultural policy has been without contradictions. From time to time, departures from the revolution's cultural policy have occurred — "aberrations" as the Cuban Minister of Culture Abel Prieto put it in a recent interview.[3] But during those periods when the cultural space for Cuba's artists has narrowed, a vigorous riposte also has been in evidence. This determined resistance to any encroachments on Cuba's cultural space would not have been possible without the mobilizations that have been a feature of the revolution from its earliest days: the Literacy Campaign in 1961 through the rectification process of the late 1980s and the Battle of Ideas launched in 1999. These mobilizations not only have enabled an active process of settling accounts with negative episodes but, along the way, also have led to political clarifications and deepened the revolution's cultural policy.

The Quinquenio Gris: Half a Decade of Gray Years

The most notorious rupture with the revolution's cultural policies occurred during the gray years from 1971 to 1976. The lessons of this period — and others — have for some time been under serious consideration in Cuba, with a growing recognition that this process is an essential step for advancing the goals of the revolution. A recent lively engagement with these issues occurred in the aftermath of the appearance on Cubavisión of Luis Pavón Tamayo in January 2007. Pavón was presented on television in a laudatory way, including images of him with Raúl Castro shortly after Castro assumed the presidency. However, Pavón had served as director of the National Cultural Council (Consejo Nacional de Cultura) from 1971 to 1976, and many Cubans who lived through that period consider him responsible for implementing repressive policies against artists and writers who refused to conform to a narrow, formulaic, and populist dogma that was construed as proletarian culture. Scores of Cubans began an e-mail campaign to register their disgust with the program, and they organized meetings with the Ministry of Culture.[4] The writers' and artists' union, the Unión Nacional de Escritores y Artistas de Cuba (UNEAC) discussed the matter, and Minister of Culture Abel Prieto presented the Cuban Communist Party's view that it had been an error to involve Pavón — and two other officials from the period — on the program because they were associated with a period that the political leadership viewed with "great disapproval" when the very tenets of the revolution's cultural policies were "set aside." In effect, the *pavonato,* as the cultural regime imposed by Pavón is often referred to, violated the cultural policies that the revolution had implemented in 1961 that guaranteed full freedom of artistic expression to all but open enemies of the revolution and "that brought together the cultural work of artists and writers of all tendencies, of all generations — Catholic, Communist, even non-revolutionaries who were sincere," as Prieto later explained in an interview.[5]

The UNEAC itself issued a critical statement about the television program, and when a meeting it called with 450 invited intellectuals was deemed insufficient, the magazine *Criterios* and the Hermanos Sais, an organization of young artists and writers, held a broader gathering. These discussions continued at a series of meetings that *Criterios* organized around a range of cultural disciplines that had experienced the repressive measures of the *pavónistas,* including filmmaking, theater, visual arts, and music.[6] At the 2008 Havana Book Fair, the debate continued. It is noteworthy that the sharp exchanges of the early 1960s about the aesthetic of socialist realism — and broader related issues — helped inform the current review of the experiences of the first half of the 1970s. The presentation of several titles recounting the cultural polemics of the 1960s as well as revisiting (and repudiating) the cultural policy that governed the short-lived gray years provided the focus at the fair.[7] As Ambrosio Fornet stated in his speech to the meeting of 450 intellectuals, "When evoking the Gray *Quinquenium*, I feel that we're plunging headlong into something that not only deals with the present but also projects us forcefully into the future, even if only because of what [Spanish philosopher Jorge Ruiz de] Santayana said: 'Those who don't know history are condemned to repeat it.' That danger is precisely what we're trying to conjure here."[8]

Yet despite the current consideration of the gray years in Cuba, the widespread consequences of the policies of the period remain little understood in much of the writings on this period produced outside of the island. Some authors sympathetic to the revolution simply ignore the repressive measures of officials who wielded power or consider them isolated actions that bear little consideration. In contrast, the U.S. art historian David Craven, who has done some of the most interesting critical writing on Cuban visual art outside the island, acknowledges the existence of different ideological tendencies within Cuba and documents occasions of restricted cultural space in Cuba. But his account would have been far more powerful had he treated each regrettable episode as part of a continual processes of clarification, *rupturas*, and so on, out of which the revolution's cultural policies are developed and within which a political trajectory can be traced on the basis of the ideals of José Martí, Che Guevara, Fidel Castro, Armando Hart, and others.

The more common approach is to treat each repressive measure as the work of the Cuban leadership en bloc, and doing so has equally serious deficiencies.[9] Not only does it totally erase the efforts of those intellectuals and artists, as well as the role of leaders like Armando Hart Dávalos, minister of culture since 1976, who have resisted encroachments on the nation's cultural space; it also robs the development of cultural policy and practice of its dynamic evolution. This is additionally unsatisfactory because as the cultural conflicts have unfolded, they have revealed how fundamental political issues are at the heart of these differences. The main problem is that this approach, which erases the continuity of a cultural policy forged through action and that views its development outside of the broader sociopolitical conditions, is incapable of explaining how obstacles that have periodically arisen in the cultural plane have been overcome.

The fact is that throughout the history of the revolution, the precise weight of these policies and practices have been intimately linked with the revolution's political development at that particular conjuncture. So it was that at the start of the 1970s a combination of factors quite outside the cultural domain allowed these dogmatic ideas to gain ascendancy for a time in the revolution's cultural institutions. Fundamental to Cuba's circumstances was *el bloqueo*, the continuing comprehensive embargo levied by the U.S. government since October 1960. Another key factor in 1970 was the campaign footing adopted by the nation to harvest 10 million tons of sugar. Despite the enormous efforts invested — "holidays were abandoned, Christmas abolished, schedules disrupted"[10] — the "battle for sugar" failed to reached its goal and disorganized the economy in the process. Finally, negative international factors, including setbacks in the guerrilla campaigns in Latin America and, in particular, the collapse of the Bolivian campaign and the death of Che Guevara, all provided conditions that led Cuba to seek increasingly close relations with the Soviet Union and the Eastern Bloc, including entry into the Council for Mutual Economic Assistance. These broad conditions provided fertile ground for the development of a narrow-minded and rigid approach to cultural production. But these practices were challenged and reversed when the international conjuncture became more favorable at the end of the decade. For instance, the advent of workers' and farmers' governments in Nicaragua and Grenada, the decision to send thirty-six thousand troops to fight a successful war in Angola in the interests of revolutionary internationalism, and the defeat of the United States in Vietnam all played a powerful role in decreasing the sense of isolation and in turn opened up cultural space on the island.[11]

The Quinquenio Gris exacted a heavy toll. Through a process known as *parametración,* the dogmatists ensconced in the cultural institutions scrutinized the religious beliefs, sexual orientation, relations with acquaintances and colleagues abroad, and other aspects of the personal lives of those engaged in cultural activity. Under these intrusive guidelines, homosexual artists were ostracized, influences from cultural pursuits undertaken in capitalist countries were considered ideologically unsound, and youths were discouraged from listening to the music of the Beatles.[12] It was a time when artistic parameters "similar to the inauspicious dogma of socialist realism were imposed in more or less visible fashion," according to the novelist Leonardo Padura.[13]

At a personal level, the cost is obvious. Many artists and intellectuals were simply marginalized for often-lengthy periods of their productive lives. Furthermore, the country itself paid a heavy price for the silencing of a whole range of intellectuals and artists. Visual artists like Antonia Eiríz and Umberto Pena both simply stopped painting in the 1970s.[14] Manuel Mendive continued his work, but nevertheless was sidelined because he persisted with his own personal aesthetic. Literary figures like the playwright Antón Arrufat, the writer Pablo Armando Fernández, and even musicians of the *nueva trova* movement Silvio Rodríguez and Pablo Milanés and the renowned pop artist Raúl Martínez González all came up against these dogmatic officials during the 1960s. Sometimes their work was criticized; in other cases, their sexual orientation or the company they kept was suspect. The actions taken against them varied. Often artists under scrutiny were unable to find any space where they could produce their work or else lacked opportunities to exhibit it; others found that trips abroad were no longer possible. Also ruled out were teaching and occupying technical or leadership posts in cultural institutions. Yet others like Arrufat received jobs in which they were unable to pursue their creative interests.[15]

All of these actions constituted a serious blow to the country's cultural life. Yet despite the narrowing of cultural space during this period, there were nevertheless ebbs and flows, never total closure. Obstacles to the production or exhibition of work even during the harsh Quinquenio Gris were vigorously "fought, questioned, halted, neutralized." [16] And very often, those who resisted were associated with the Casa de las Américas, the Latin American cultural center, or the Film Institute (Instituto Cubano del Arte é Industria Cinematográfica, or ICAIC). Both institutions have been viewed as defenders of the artistic freedoms promoted in Cuba's cultural policy from the revolution's earliest days, and both offered a different approach to artistic creativity based on the legacy of such heroes of the revolution such as José Martí and Che Guevara.

Some visual artists resisted and simply refused to paint yet another heroic picture of a muscular peasant or cows that held world records in milk production. It is noteworthy that Manuel Mendive, who ignored the proscriptions, did some of his best work during this period; a bit later, Flavio Garciandía turned to photorealism as an alternative, and so on. [17] Raúl Martínez González (1927–1995) was able to develop his personal interests to great effect through adopting the artistic language of pop art. He was one of several artists who were able to pursue their artistic vision in a manner in which they did not feel compromised and whose work cultural officials did not find problematic. Martínez González created some of the most iconic images of the revolution, which have become widely known as examples of Cuba's renowned poster art. In works like *Cartel Cubano*, circa 1968, his serial portraits — associated with devices used in Andy Warhol's pop art, despite the quite different aesthetic involved — bring together Cuban people of different ages, genders, and ethnic groups alongside international heroes and Cuba's revolutionary leaders to form a cheerful and inclusive vision of the Cuban nation. However, these pop-art works can be linked with Martínez González's formal artistic interests in the graphic arts (as well as his support for the revolution) rather than in any dogmatic proscription. Similarly, throughout this period, Servando Cabrera Moreno (1923–1981) continued to explore his fascination with social themes and, at a formal level, his experimentation with ethnic portraiture and the portrayal of musculature (that later transformed into erotic art). And again, his individual interests rather than any cultural formulae guided him. These are evident in his powerful *Peasant Militia* (1961) and continued to appear in his later *Youthful Days* (1973). Thus, contradictory forces were present even during the gray years.

The Cuban artist and art historian Antonio Eligio (Tonel) writes of "the defining weight of ideological and aesthetic reductionisms during those years" and comments on "the undeniable experience of rejection suffered by several very worthy artists for many years." He notes how cultural production was "directed towards the imposition of Socialist Realism — to some extent 'tropicalised' and almost never mentioned by its name in that context — as the only valid method of art and its interpretation in the island."[18] Yet as the Cuban art historian Gerardo Mosquera explains, there was — in terms of artistic language and formal qualities — a significant distance between the forms of artistic expression deemed acceptable in Cuba and the restrictions imposed in the Soviet Union, when socialist realism prevailed. In Cuba, when artists' creative output was deemed unacceptable during this period, at a purely artistic level, the issue was not so much the style in which the work was executed, although a radical expressionism was highly distasteful to the dogmatists. Rather, "a practice of culture as ideological propaganda, along with a stereotyped nationalism" was promoted. Furthermore, any work deemed overly influenced by Western artistic practices was undesirable, which consequently curtailed Cuban participation in international events like the Venice Biennial during this period.[19]

Antonia Eiríz and *Una tribuna*

An examination of Antonia Eiríz's (1929–1995) work, as well as that of several other artists who produced at different moments in Cuba's revolutionary process, helps chart the contradictory trajectory of Cuba's cultural policies. The hostile reception to a work like her *Una tribuna para la paz democrática* (*A Tribune for Democratic Peace*, 1968) is emblematic of the conditions of cultural production in Cuba that became more entrenched in the field of cultural production during the gray years.

This large canvas — today hanging prominently in the National Museum of Fine Arts in Havana — was originally the focus of fierce controversy (Figure 1). The work was submitted to the 1968 national salon and even was considered (unsuccessfully) for the first prize. Eiríz was initially surprised at the reception of her work:

When I began to hear remarks that my painting was "conflictive," I began to believe them. *The Tribune*, for example, was criticized very harshly. It was about to be awarded a prize and then there was no prize due to the criticism. One day I saw all the pictures together for the first time in many years. I said to myself: This is painting which expresses the moment in which I am living. And if a painter can do that, then he or she is a real painter. Thus I absolved myself.[20]

Regardless of how Eiríz judged her own work in later years, cultural officials at the time deemed it unacceptable, and her treatment led her to take the drastic decision to give up painting. It would be "their loss," not hers, she reasoned. The work itself is highly dramatic. In *Una tribuna*, Eiríz depicts the scene of a public meeting, with the vantage point of the viewer located behind the space allotted to the speakers, facing five microphones, placed on a podium. But once viewers position themselves as if they were the speaker, they confront a horrific scene. A red rope, which is attached to the canvas, providing the work with a third dimension, separates from the podium a crowd of disturbing skeleton-like figures. The features on the faces vary in definition — some have blank, grim mouths and others, barely perceptible skulls showing through the white paint. Attached to the dividing rope are seven leaflets printed with the unexplained letters *PCV*, "por una Paz Democrática," and the image of a star. As in her other works of the period, such as *Anunciación*, the palette is predominantly in somber shades of blacks, browns, and grays. The roughness in treatment with forceful brushstrokes imparts a similar haunting brutality to the work. The initial shock of the scene comes from the ghastly miscreants who form the body of the rally. The imagery on the canvas clashed sharply with the optimistic and cheerful pop art works by Raúl Martínez González associated with the heroic period of the revolution that celebrated *la lucha* and *la patria*. It was also incongruous with the euphoric mood of the *Salón de Mai* that the Cuban surrealist painter Wifredo Lam had organized just one year earlier, when almost a hundred artists from around the world traveled to Cuba to work on pieces they donated to the revolution and participated in the festive production of *Mural Cuba Colectiva*. The response to Eiríz's work sounded the alarm that a new mediocrity in artistic standards that began to judge works by their propagandist qualities was overtaking these early years of cultural pluralism and artistic exuberance.

But if Eiríz's work captured a reality that clashed with the preferred aesthetic, did it have any artistic merit? After all, she was a classically trained artist who graduated from the San Alejandro Academy of Fine Arts in 1957. The expressionist language Eiríz employed was associated with Francis Bacon, the Mexican José Luis Cuevas, as well as Francisco Goya (although she never considered this link accurate), and it was connected to neofigurative trends evident throughout Latin America in the 1950s and 1960s. The Columbian art historian Marta Traba portrayed these trends as a "culture of resistance" against the Americanization of Latin America and the aesthetics of a metropolitan-based "internationalism."[21] The Cuban art historian Graziella Pogolotti commented on a series of tints executed by Eiríz and noted how her caricatures — "monstruos que han perdido dimensión humana" ("monsters that had lost their human dimension") — represented a formal rebellion against the academicians and conformists. She firmly placed Eiríz in the expressionist tradition and saw her work as expressing a piercing, heart-rending scream. However, she viewed her creative output as transitional in character; situating it more broadly, Pogolotti interpreted the etchings as a condemnation of the moral and social misery of mankind.[22] All of these observations about Eiríz's work establish that a serious critical approach to her work was undoubtedly warranted.

FIGURE 1. Antonia Eiríz, *Una tribuna para la paz democrática* (*A Tribune for Democratic Peace*), 1968. Museo Nacional de Bellas Artes, Havana. Photography: Montreal Museum of Fine Arts, Christine Guest.

Yet, in contrast, the official reception to Eiríz's work at the time was of severe hostility. For those who directed cultural policy, the use of an expressionist artistic language was discomfiting, but the particular work under consideration was unacceptable on two further grounds. First, because of the subject matter depicted; second, the artist's extra-artistic associations were more than likely suspect. *Una tribuna* was schematically understood, at least by some officials, as a statement of opposition to the revolutionary process. Antonio José Portuondo, at the time vice president of UNEAC, allegedly condemned the work as "grotesque and defeatist . . . in essence counter revolutionary."[23] Others rejected the depiction of the crowd at a rally as a herd of shocking miscreants.[24] However, did these latter viewers fail to see what Portuondo may have observed more clearly? That is, in this work, the viewer becomes the speaker. The view depicted is, hence, through the eyes of the speaker at the podium, not through the viewer's own eyes or those of the artist herself. Indeed, the original and novel idea was that the work would be shown with several folding chairs arranged in front of it, to seat the viewer awaiting his or her turn to speak. Once at the podium, the official/viewer perceives the crowd as nothing more than a sea of faceless entities.

Eiríz herself was under scrutiny. Her work's "conflictive status," as it was described to her, may have been reinforced by her association with *Lunes*, the literary supplement to *Revolución* the newspaper of the July 26 Movement. Staffed by a heterogeneous group of intellectuals who had been "left behind by the radicalizing Revolution, unable and unwilling to change,"[25] the supplement's closure was bound up with the controversial PM affair.[26] Eiríz's connection with *Lunes* was probably through Raúl Martínez González, the supplement's art director from 1960. Her illustrations were used in about a dozen issues before it was closed. Furthermore, *Una tribuna* made its appearance in the aftermath of the Herberto Padilla affair.[27] And in his book, Padilla had included a poem about Eiríz, thereby implicitly associating her with an explosive episode that had developed an international dimension.

When Eiríz decided to stop painting, she did not disengage from the cultural sphere. Indeed, she became deeply involved in another artistic pursuit: she began to teach children and adults from the Committees for the Defense of the Revolution (CDRs) to make figures from papier-mâché. In effect, her efforts developed into a movement of amateur art practitioners that gained national recognition. As this progressed, the puppets were used in plays, whose theatrical sets, as well as the writing, were done by members of the CDRs. Whatever acclaim she achieved in this field, this "painter of tragedy," as the Cuban poet and essayist Roberto Fernández Retamar described her in 1964, was an "unforgivable casualty" of the period,[28] one whose work was not rescued until several decades later from the ignominy to which the anticultural officials had condemned it. During the 1980s, she received several awards for her work, and in 1989, she was awarded the country's highest distinction in the field of culture when Cuba's Council of State bestowed on her the Félix Varela Order.[29]

Several elements of Eiríz's story and others like hers are noteworthy and help us understand why the campaign for rectification and the recent Battle of Ideas were deemed vital for the survival of the revolution. For many visitors to the island throughout the years who commented on its culture — such as Eva Cockcroft, Lucy Lippard, Susan Sontag, Andrew Salkey, and even Jean-Paul Sartre, often the most outstanding feature they noted about artistic life was the absence of a dominant socialist realist aesthetic. And indeed it has been. However, although it has never been possible to impose in Cuba a bureaucratized system of state-sanctioned propagandist art, and certainly nothing resembling the type of artistic production that the First Congress of Soviet Writers decreed in Moscow in 1934, some of its ideological tenets became influential in the 1970s.[30] In the broader context, this is not surprising. After all, during this period, the Soviet-style model of economic planning became more established. Instead of the budgetary finance system that Che Guevara advanced, the center of which was the mobilization of the working class and voluntary labor, the economic accounting system was introduced. This model abjured the involvement of the working class in planning and saw the top-down administration of the plan as central, and one that, moreover, mimicked the capitalist market. The Cuban economist Carlos Tablada summarized the system in the following terms: "[E]ach production unit constitutes an enterprise . . . relations between enterprises are very similar to those that exist under capitalism; all transfers of products between state enterprises are carried out through the mechanism of buying and selling, with the result that the products of a state enterprise take on the characteristics of a commodity."[31]

The consequences of this economic model were experienced in other spheres, including the island's cultural policy. In 1975, the First Party Congress adopted a system of economic management and planning for the cultural sector.[32] Economic criteria were applied and accounting goals set. Commissioned works of art began to be treated as commodities for internal marketing purposes. However, negative side effects soon emerged. President Fidel Castro recalled in several speeches in later years the damaging impact all these measures had on the consciousness of the artistic producers. He referred to a certain "mercantilist" attitude that became apparent as social differentiations began to appear among cultural producers for the first time since the victory of the revolution.[33]

As collaboration deepened with the Soviet Union, Soviet instructors arrived at art schools and Cuban artists traveled to Moscow for their training. Soviet aesthetic and philosophical treatises became more widely available in Spanish. It is not surprising, therefore, that proponents of socialist realism — albeit in a "tropicalized" form — again raised their heads. Indeed, several personalities who were leading figures in the cultural apparatus in the 1970s had been prominent advocates of this aesthetic during the course of an intense polemical exchange during the 1960s. Although Edith Garcia Buchaca, a former leader of the Partido Socialista Popular (PSP) and prominent figure in the National Council of Culture, was no longer influential, her writings undoubtedly provided a reference point. In 1961, for instance, she authored a fifty-four-page pamphlet outlining how artists must be first and foremost politicians trained "to adopt the view of the masses," helping workers overcome their petit bourgeois habits and prejudices, and always ready "to unmask and denounce the enemy."[34] Another former PSP member and cultural official, Mirta Aguirre, also promoted a socialist realist aesthetic during the 1960s on the grounds that it was "a road to consciousness and as a weapon to transform the world . . . a way of creating that is based on scientific materialism."[35]

Of course, over the years, such views did not go unanswered. Those who replied, often associated with Casa de las Américas and the Cuban Film Institute, responded in the framework that Che Guevara had codified in his 1968 article in *La Mancha*. He forcefully argued that the socialist realist aesthetic mechanically portrayed "the ideal society, almost without conflicts or contradictions"; it was a frozen aesthetic that would limit artistic expression.[36] Furthermore, Guevara's view was that future great artists would appear according "to the degree that the field of culture and the possibilities for expression are broadened." When the former central leader of the old Moscow-oriented PSP Blas Roca wrote an editorial in a December 1963 issue of *Hoy* characterizing Federico Fellini's *La Dolce Vita* as "unwholesome entertainment for the working class," its very next issue carried a reply.[37] In his response, the filmmaker Alfredo Guevara from ICAIC rejected the populist notion that the public could be fed only "ideological pap, highly sterilised, and cooked in accordance with the recipes of socialist realism."[38]

The 1980s and the New Art of Cuba

By the 1980s, the consequences of the adaptation to the Soviet model became evident at every level of society: economic deterioration, mismanagement of resources, elements of corruption, excessive bureaucratization of the mechanisms of government, and growing demoralization and demobilization of the population.[39] In Fidel Castro's words, for several years, Cuba had been departing from its original revolutionary course and moving toward a system "worse than capitalism."[40] The campaign of rectification, launched in 1986, was designed to put the revolution back on its original course. Politically, the campaign stood in opposition to the policies of perestroika and glasnost, adopted by the Soviet Union in an effort to rescue its failing economy and, indeed, society. Central to rectification was the recuperation of Che Guevara's notion of the "new man" with voluntary labor — revitalized through minibrigades that began to take on characteristics of a social movement — and other forms of collective action at its heart. Fidel Castro explained the scope of the campaign in a speech in 1987:

What are we rectifying? We are rectifying all those things — and there are many — that strayed from the revolutionary spirit, from revolutionary work, revolutionary virtue, revolutionary effort, revolutionary responsibility; all those things that strayed from the spirit of solidarity among people. We're rectifying all the shoddiness and mediocrity that is precisely the negation of Che's ideas, his revolutionary thought, his style, his spirit and his example.[41]

Because the approach to rectification is often to revisit the so-called great economic debate of the 1960s, its cultural dimension is often neglected.[42] However, among visual artists, the break with the formulaic proscriptions of the cultural dogmatists registered as early as the strident *Volumen Uno* exhibition in 1980, composed of work made by the first generation of young artists who had benefited from the vast system of art education implemented by the revolution and who refused to continue producing empty, tired, stereotypical representations of cultural identity. The Cuban art historian Osvaldo Sánchez recounted how while the "guardians of the state's aesthetics" were "red with rage," the exhibition registered a watershed as thousands of viewers flocked to see the artwork. "It wasn't just a simple exhibition but the calling card of a generation that emerged, almost by surprise, with a sacrilegious smile and which couldn't be limited to those few 'young iconoclasts.' "[43] From the time of the exhibition, during the 1980s, a "tenuous current of renovation and expansion that would reconnect it with the tumultuous vitality of the 60s" marked the visual arts.[44] Innovation in the artistic languages employed, clashes with cultural authorities, polemical exchanges, and further clarification of the revolution's cultural policy peppered the period. And indeed this process has continued since the 1980s. Ambrosio Fornet, the foremost literary critic in Cuba who has authored one of the most thorough condemnations of the gray years (and indeed the term *Quinquenio Gris* is attributed to him) explains that, today, any cultural differences that emerge are handled in a manner quite different from the actions taken by the *pavónistas*. Indeed, as cited earlier, the official response to the opposition to the Cubavisión television program that lauded Pavón (entailing a government minister meeting with UNEAC, the organization of broader forums to discuss the subject, and so on) confirms this judgment. Obviously, cultural tensions have not disappeared. Conflicts of opinion are part and parcel of everyday life. However, Fornet insists, in contrast to the methods of the *pavónistas*, that mutual respect and a shared authentic interest in Cuba's cultural development are integral to the development of a living culture.[45]

156 : Doreen Weppler-Grogan

Juan Francisco Elso and *Por América*

The work of Juan Francisco Elso (1956–1988) and in particular his work *Por América* (*For the Americas*), clearly demonstrated that a new period had arrived in Cuba's cultural policy. Elso died of cancer at thirty-two years of age, after spending only a decade of his life as an artist. His initial fascination with the Indo-American people in his early work provided a bridge toward his eventual immersion in Afro-Cuban culture, a vital and active component of Cuba's national culture. It was also an established theme in Cuban painting especially through the work of Wifredo Lam, Cuba's foremost modernist artist with an international reputation. However, Elso's sculptures registered a spiritual engagement with his subject that was not present in Lam's work. Elso came to share with two other artists from equally modest backgrounds, José Bedia (b. 1959) and Richard Brey (b. 1955), a deep identification with the beliefs, visual forms, and rituals of Afro-Cuban culture, including those of *santería*.[46] Elso became initiated into *santería*, although he was not from an Afro-Cuban background. At a personal level, he did not see that this conflicted with his socialist views; indeed, he drew analogies at an ethical level between the two ways of viewing the world by insisting that the goal of both was the improvement of humanity.

His *Por América* (1986) is a less-than-human sized statue of Cuba's national hero, José Martí (Figure 2). It resembles the wooden effigies of saints found in colonial churches throughout Latin America. The statue has a number of darts embedded in the body, and others have presumably missed their target and lie at the feet of Martí. The darts bring to mind the canonical iconography of Saint Sebastian, and there are some parallels. Just as Sebastian was a military martyr, Martí was a soldier (in the wars of independence from Spain). Furthermore, however hard the Roman archers tried to execute Sebastian with their arrows, they were unsuccessful. It is not difficult to conclude that, similarly, the ideals and goals of Martí live on in his work. In addition, unlike the usual depictions of Saint Sebastian tied to a stake by the Romans and helplessly facing the arrows of the soldiers, the drawn sword Elso has put in Martí's hand also demonstrates his power.[47] Finally, just as Saint Sebastian brought sight to the blind and hearing to the deaf once they embraced his (Christian) beliefs, Martí is identified as opening the eyes and minds of the Cuban people with his pro-independence beliefs. The fleur-de-lis-shaped darts are painted in two different colors: red to signify blood drawn and green to stand for the "sprouts of a fertile rebirth."[48] The three-quarter-size figure is dressed in rags; the statue appears roughly hewn; the paintwork is chipped and splashed with mud. It contrasts with the often-elaborate and polished effigies of saints on display in liturgical spaces of Christianity, well out of reach of the congregation. The work was intended for exhibition with a group of three other sculptures addressing the theme of renewal that Elso was working on in his final months. The three pieces — a skull, a heart, and a hand — formed a series entitled *La transparencia de Dios* (*The Transparencies of God*), and *Por América* was meant to signify the attitude that guided the project of re-creating the world, the subject that the series addressed.

Por América is a complex work, but there are several elements that locate it firmly within the generation of the 1980s. For one, a closer examination indicates that it simply would not have been acceptable in the previous restrictive period of artistic production. Although the choice of a national hero for its subject would not have been controversial, the formal treatment of the subject indicates that the work sustains a matrix of readings beyond the obvious political statement associated with Martí. And it is here that problems would have arisen. This is because, on deeper examination, the work not only is inspired by African religious myths and symbols but also actually incorporates elements of associated rituals and practices. Elso executed the work after he became aware that he was dying, and with that knowledge, he decided to blend his own blood into the materials he used in his artwork. Furthermore, as a love pact, he encased inside the statue memorabilia relating to his partner, the Mexican artist Magali Lara. These aspects, specifically the inclusion of a cavity for the mementos inside the effigy, can be associated with certain African relics, "or receptacles of African or Afro Cuban power," "hidden symbolic-ritual elements that constitute the key to their power."[49] Viewers familiar with *santería* rituals would associate the presence of the cavity with pots in which religious practitioners deposit wood, earth, stones, leaves, and so on, in the belief that they represent deities whose sacred powers would take root in these conditions. The American curator and art historian Judith Bettelheim explains that the *nganga,* "a receptacle . . . usually a clay container, a gourd, or a tripod iron cauldron, which is kept in the backyard, in a cellar, or in the *monte* under a tree," is the "central icon" of the African religions still practiced in Cuba.[50]

On a more formal level, although the rough or "primitive" finish on the work is obviously intentional, it is also highly deceptive. According to Mosquera, "the discourse of the materials" can be associated with "the creation of an artwork structured through a process of syncretic combination of the sacralised and the symbolic."[51] As is evident with the use of the cavity, each step of the construction has precise symbolic meaning in the aesthetic of the artist. No material is used that does not have some symbolic significance. The process of art making itself thus can be understood to evoke the rituals of a religious ceremony. However, insofar as the sculpture can be associated with the carved saints present in the Christian religion, it also registers the syncretic character of santería that has evolved in Cuba whereby elements of Christianity have combined with the rituals and practice of African religions. And finally, the roughly hewn character of the work marks its distance from the fine finishes

FIGURE 2. Juan Francisco Elso, *Por América (For the Americas)*, 1986.
Hirshhorn Museum and Sculpture Garden, Smithsonian Institution, Photography: Lee Stalsworth.

158

associated with high art, thus bringing the work more closely to the artisan or even the amateur carver.

The choice of the subject matter for this work indicates that it transcends a purely spiritual reading. José Martí was identified above all as the revolutionary leader who fought (and died) for Cuban independence from Spain. An intellectual and national hero, Martí insisted in his many writings that a clear sense of national identity was a decisive ideological element in overcoming colonial domination. By combining Afro-Cuban themes with a national hero and associating both with Christian iconography — thus placing that hero's message for a united and independent nation centrally within the series of sculptures — Elso enhances the complexity of his exposition on the nature of Cuban identity. His is an inclusive vision of identity, and it is one that registers the "Afro-Latino" nature of the Cuban people, as Fidel Castro put it. The distance between the Martí that Elso presents and the formulaic bronze memorial sculptures so favored by the art officials of the gray years could not be greater. Indeed, at almost every level, this work clashes with the didactic, heroic art deemed appropriate during the gray years: including its Christian iconography, its incorporation of *santería* rituals, the choice of materials, and perhaps even the hero's less-than-human proportions.

The many layers of meanings captured in Elso's *Por América* cannot be mechanically related to the political realities of the time. It is, after all, a work of art, not a political statement. Nevertheless, its resonance with viewers may stem from the way Elso has captured many of the often-contradictory elements of the historical quest for a national identity that — as his choice of Martí as a vehicle for his artistic message suggests — will be forged through the crucible of struggle. After all, it is traces of the artist himself found in the memorabilia that is placed in the cavity of the statue (seen as the source of power) — possibly suggesting that mankind itself holds the key to the future. Yet the work's dynamic quality, its complex character, and the multiple readings it offers all constituted an anathema to those who in earlier years judged artistic expression in terms of its success as political propaganda in Cuba. And it is vital to avoid any notion that cultural clashes seen during the gray years have disappeared totally. Indeed, in the wake of the departure of many of the 1980s artists from the island, sporadic eruptions between cultural officials and artists have occurred. Yet today, each specific incident has been surrounded by lively discussions and debate that have served to further clarify the approach to artistic expression encapsulated in the Cuba's cultural policy. It can be said, therefore, that one thing that the response to the Pavón affair clarified is that, far from championing the revolution's cultural policy, the gray years actually constituted its negation.

Battle of Ideas

With the demise of the Soviet Union at the end of the 1980s and its disastrous consequences for the physical well-being and standard of living of the Cuban people, the rectification campaign was abruptly ended. At a time when many artists were more preoccupied with finding the means to feed themselves than with pursuing their artistic interests, efforts were made to preserve the revolution's cultural gains. Yet Minister of Culture Abel Prieto recalls how — even in the worst moments after the "special period in the time of peace" was declared in 1990, "including those many moments of uncertainty" — Armando Hart (minister of culture at the time) insisted on collectively discussing and analyzing the revolution's cultural policies. It is well known that throughout this period when Cuba's gross domestic product declined almost overnight by 35 percent, not a single school (or hospital) closed.[52] However, the measures the government was forced to take to obtain hard currency — from foreign investment on the island to the development of the tourist industry and even the circulation of the U.S. dollar — combined with steps taken by the U.S. government to tighten the economic blockade of Cuba had severe consequences. Prostitution, corruption, and increasing inequalities began to undermine the social cohesion of the revolutionary process. At a cultural level, a whole new set of economic parameters and ethical considerations arose for artistic practitioners as "art tourism" arrived on the scene and Cuba's artworks became some of the most desirable on the international market.[53]

Nevertheless, despite a virtual torrent of predictions in the Western press and other publications that the end of the revolution was in sight, that has not occurred. The key to its survival cannot be comprehended without a clear understanding of the Battle of Ideas, launched in 1999 by President Fidel Castro as part of the mobilizations demanding that Washington return the child Elián González to his country. Many observers of this immense campaigning effort view it as yet another "confusing," "unintelligible" phase of the Cuban Revolution.[54] Widely varying interpretations have been conjectured.[55] In essence, the *batalla* is a political response, with the cultural policy of the revolution at its center, to deepen the participation of Cuban people — particularly a new generation of youths — in the revolutionary process. Its goal is to broaden the cultural opportunities on the island and to address the social inequalities that deepened with Cuba's exposure to the capitalist market. Otto Rivero, a leader of the campaign and first secretary of the Union of Communist Youth explains its role in countering the so-called culture war that right-wing American politicians relaunched during the 1990s: the ideological drive "that promotes capitalism and its individualist 'dog-eat-dog' values."[56] Translated practically, this has entailed literally hundreds of national and local projects — from training young social workers and deploying them in community initiatives to establishing hundreds of video clubs that host lectures, debates, art shows, and musical performances; campaigning for computers in every school; planning fifteen new schools over ten years to train thirty thousand art instructors; expanding book production so that every family can have an inexpensive boxed set of twenty-five Cuban and world classics; and so on. The Battle of Ideas' scope and commitment to raising the cultural level of the Cuban people will be instrumental in deepening the nation's social cohesion and reknitting the links with the original cultural goals of the revolution, embodied in initiatives like the Literacy Campaign.

In many ways, a 1992 work by the Cuban artist Alexis Leyva Machado, known as Kcho, one of the most established Cuban artists in the international art market and an elected representative in the island's National Assembly, evokes the challenges posed in Cuba today. Titled *A los ojos de la historia* (*To the Eyes of History*), the work is of a spiral tower that is associated with the (unrealizable) model to house the Third International made in 1919–1920 by the Russian constructivist Vladimir Tatlin.[57] Tatlin's building was to be twice the height of the Empire State Building; executed in glass and iron; and constructed so that an iron framework would support three rotating shapes made of glass. These forms — a cylinder, a square, and a cone — would each accommodate different institutions and offices of the revolution. In sharp contrast, Kcho's frail assemblage is made from twigs, twine, and driftwood. In fact, neither tower would be a viable structure if actually constructed, but Kcho has humorously refashioned his into a drip coffee maker. A used coffee filter placed at its summit not only serves as a statement of national identity (in a country where the nation has been forged through the coffee and sugar industries) but also transforms the tower into a useful object. Although Kcho eschews any political interpretations of his work, he has referred to the tower as a "utopian socialist symbol that doesn't work."[58] Some have interpreted the work as recognition of the frailty of the socialist vision. However, they have missed the fact (have they not?) that, with some ingenuity and in the spirit of improvisation of the 1990s, the artist has taken the symbol and given it a new lease of life as a more functional, hence superior, object. In this reading, the goal remains; the sense of frailty of the work evokes the inroads of the capitalist market in Cuba, but the challenge lies in the renewal of the tower-goal.

As mobilizations like the Battle of Ideas continue to expand and deepen, as lessons of past periods are learned and opposition mounts "to the methods and Stalinist ideology that generated them," in the words of writer Reynaldo González, this will provide the best basis for cultural advances and will immeasurably strengthen the cultural policies of the revolution.[59] As Cuba's Minister of Culture Abel Prieto concluded after the recent discussions and analysis of the nature of the errors and what harm they had caused, today "we have a stronger unity in relation to our cultural policies."[60]

162 : Doreen Weppler-Grogan

NOTES

1. M. Koppel and B. O'Shaughnessey, "Broad Discussions on Culture, Politics Mark Havana Book Fair," *Militant* 72, no. 13 (2008), http://www.themilitant.com/2008/7213/721350.html.
2. Fidel Castro Ruz, "Words to the Intellectuals," June 30, 1961, http://archives.econ.utah.edu/archives/marxism.
3. Abel Prieto, Cuban minister of culture, interview by Arturo García Hernández, March 14, 2007, http://www.embacu.cubaminrex.cu.
4. The furor around the Pavón incident was headlined flamboyantly in the *Miami Herald* as "the first sign of internal dissent since Fidel Castro ceded power," implying that Pavón's presence on television was a government-inspired event signaling the opening of a new repressive period under Raúl Castro's leadership. See Frances Robels, "In Cuba Dissent by Invitation Only," *Miami Herald*, February 3, 2007. Prieto expressed concern at the "very aggressive reaction from Miami" when a digital magazine, financed by the right-wing National Endowment for Democracy, associated "what was a mistake, with Fidel's health and with Raúl's performance as interim president of Cuba—as if this had something to do with the function of our institutionalized culture." See Dalia Acosta, "CULTURE-CUBA: Exorcising the Ghosts of the Past," Inter Press Service, http://ipsnews.net/news.asp?idnews=36701.
5. Prieto interview.
6. In fact, discussion at the meetings covered a wide range of issues, including homophobia, racial discrimination, the state of the Cuban media, limitations on critical expression, and other matters.
7. Recent publications dealing with this theme include Graziella Pogolotti, *Polémicas culturales de los 60* (Havana: Editorial Letras Cubana, 2006); Alberto Abreu Arcia, *Los juegos de la escritura o la (re)escritura de la historia* (Havana: Premio Casa de las Américas, 2007). See also the compilation of the talks on these themes organized by the journal *Criterios*: Desiderio Navarro, ed., *La política cultural del período revolucionario: Memoria y reflexión* (January 2007), http://www.criterios.es, especially the contribution by Ambrosio Fornet. See also I. Anneris, L. García, and A. S. Fernández, "Los intelectuales y las esfera pública en Cuba: El debate sobre políticas culturales," *Temas* 56 (October–December 2008): 44–55; Martagloria Morales Garza, "Los debates de la década de los 60 en Cuba," *Temas* 55 (July–September 2008): 91–101.
8. Fornet sent the text of his speech to the *Miami Herald*, which printed this excerpt in its February 3, 2007, edition. The original is available at http://www.criterios.es/pdf/fornetquinque niogris.pdf.
9. For instance, Julie Bunck's work, *Fidel Castro*, on revolutionary culture in Cuba reveals no ideological differentiation on the island whatsoever. Indeed, every development in cultural policy, from the gray years to rectification, is attributed to one of three interchangeable agencies—the government, the party or Fidel Castro—without any notion of debate or contestations in the revolution's institutions. See Julie Marie Bunck, *Fidel Castro and the Quest for a Revolutionary Culture in Cuba* (University Park: Pennsylvania State University Press, 1994). Leslie Bethell, *Cuba: A Short History* (Cambridge: Cambridge University Press, 1993), sees the 1970s as a time when every Cuban politician "followed these PSP preferences quite consistently because they were persuaded of the wisdom of their arguments."
10. Richard Gott, *Cuba: A New History* (New Haven, CT: Yale University Press, 2004), 241.
11. Fidel Castro often referred to these countries, alongside Cuba, as the three giants.
12. The codification of this dogmatic stance was accomplished in the Declaration of the First National Congress for Education and Culture in 1971, which restricted the rights of homosexuals, portrayed art as a "weapon of the struggle," and so on. A translation is available in Scott Johnson, *The Case of the Cuban Poet Herberto Padilla* (New York: Gordon Press, 1971).
13. Leonardo Padura Fuentes, "Living and Creating in Cuba: Risks and Challenges," in *A*

Contemporary Cuban Reader, Reinventing the Revolution, ed. P. Brenner, M. R. Jiménez, J. M. Kirk, and W. M. Leogrande (Plymouth, U.K.: Rowman and Littlefield, 2008), 349.

14. According to Camnitzer, who has published the major work available in English on Cuban art in the 1980s, Pena rejects any "false myths of martyrdom" that imply that he stopped painting in the 1970s because he was not allowed to exhibit because of the shocking erotic elements in his compositions. Instead, personal considerations were involved. See Luis Camnitzer, *New Art of Cuba*, 2nd ed. (Austin: University of Texas Press, 2003), 85.

15. "I lost my job and was sent to work in a library basement for nine years tying parcels of books with rope . . . [and] was not allowed to publish for 14 years," Arrufat was quoted as saying in a January 16, 2007, interview with a Caribbean news agency, http://www.caribbeannetnews.com/cgi-script/csArticles/articles/000051/005155.htm.

16. Domingo Amuchastegui, *"Ni quinquenio gris ni decenio negro . . . ,"* http://www.walterlippman.com/docs1433.html.

17. Antonio (Tonel) Eligio, "Cuban Art: A Key to the Gulf and How to Use It," in *No Man Is An Island: Young Cuban Art*, ed. Seppälä Marketta (Pori, Finland: Pori Art Museum, 1990), 67–77 (exhibition catalog).

18. Antonio (Tonel) Eligio, "70, 80, 90 . . . Perhaps 100 Impressions of Art in Cuba," in *Cuba siglo XX: Modernidad y sincretismo*, ed. M. Lluisa and A. B. Zaya (Las Palmas de Gran Canaria: Centro Atlántico de Arte Moderno, 1996), 413–22 (exhibition catalog).

19. Gerardo Mosquera, "The New Cuban Art," in *Postmodernism and the Post Socialist Condition,* ed. Aleš Erjavec (Berkeley, CA: University of California Press, 2003), 208–46.

20. Giulio V. Blanc, "Antonia Eiríz, una apreciación," *Art Nexus* (July–September 1994): 45.

21. Alejandro Anreus, "The Road to Dystopia: The Paintings of Antonia Eiríz," *Art Journal* 63, no. 3 (2004): 4–17, http://www.jstor.org/stable/4134487.

22. Graziella Pogolotti, "Artes plásticas: Nuevo rostro en la tradición," *CUBA*, January 1969, 88.

23. From an interview with Padilla in the early 1980s by Alejandro Anreus, quoted in Anreus, "Road to Dystopia." Although Anreus labeled Portuondo "a leading defender of socialist realism" at the time, Camnitzer notes that Portuondo's essays on aesthetics have commanded respect in Cuba. See Camnitzer, *New Art*, 354–55.

24. Mosquera points to an ultraradical perspective evident at the time among Latin American left-wing art critics who also were critical of her work. He characterizes them as promoting positions related to the original *Proletkult* movement in the Soviet Union. See Mosquera's article in the July 1985 issue of *El caimán barbudo*, in Camnitzer, *New Art*, 363n65.

25. Antoni Kapcia, "Culture and Ideology in Post-Revolutionary Cuba," *Red Letters* 15 (1983): 13.

26. The decision by the Commission for the Study and Classification of Films that the film *Pasado meridiano,* or *PM* — produced in 1961 by two Cuban filmmakers, Orlando Jiménez and Sabá Cabrera — should not be shown sparked a controversy on both artistic and political levels. For details of the controversy, see Michael Chanan, *The Cuban Image, Cinema and Cultural Politics in Cuba* (Minneapolis: University of Minnesota Press, 1985), 133.

27. The poet Herberto Padilla was arrested in 1971 on unspecified charges, sparking an international protest that prominent hitherto supporters of the revolution around the world got caught up in. The author issued a public self-criticism, written in the style of the Moscow trial confessions of the 1930s.

28. Camnitzer, *New Art*, 26.

29. Nathalie Bondil, *Cuba: Art and History from 1868 to Today* (exhibition catalog) (Montreal: Montreal Museum of Fine Arts, 2008), 370. Eiríz spent the final years of her life in the United States and died in Miami in 1995.

30. In any event, it should be noted that these developments occurred in a post-Khrushchev era, when, by the 1960s, the severe-style school — with a more personal interpretation of the communist

ideal, stressing its roots in peasant life — had become dominant. Nevertheless, the structure of the art world Stalin imposed — the academy, the unions, and the Ministry of Culture — remained intact. Efforts to exhibit unofficial art were repressed. In 1974, KGB agents posing as workmen bulldozed an open-air Moscow exhibition. But even if unofficial art gained ground in later years, many of Stalin's art structures survived during the 1980s. Craven recounts several episodes during the 1960s when Fidel Castro responded to Soviet officials and delegations who still adhered to the socialist realist aesthetic. On one occasion, Castro declared to his visitors that the enemies of the revolution were "capitalists and imperialists, not abstract art." See David Craven, *Art and Revolution in Latin America, 1910–1990,* 2nd ed. (London: Yale University Press, 2006), 75.

31. Carlos Tablada, *Che Guevara: Economics and Politics in the Transition to Socialism* (Sydney: Pathfinder/Pacific and Asia, 1987), 46.

32. Pamela Maria Smorkaloff, *Readers and Writers in Cuba: A Social History of Print Culture, 1830s–1990s* (New York: Garland Publishing, 1997), 119.

33. In a 1986 speech, he recounted reports of painters mainly employed by the state who were not "Picasso or Michelangelo" with incomes of one hundred thousand or two hundred thousand pesos. See *Granma Weekly Review*, August 21, 1986.

34. Stephen Gregory, "Literary-Political Debate and the Development of Cultural Policy in Cuba during the 1960s," in *Cuba: Thirty Years of Revolution*, ed. R. H. Ireland and S. R. Niblo (Melbourne: Institute of Latin America Studies, La Trobe University, 1990), 31–52.

35. Mirta Aguirre, "Apuntes sobre la literatura y el arte," *Cuba Socialista* 3, no. 26 (1963): 62–81.

36. Che Guevara, *Socialism and Man in Cuba*, 2nd ed. (New York: Pathfinder Press, 1989), 16–18.

37. Both *Hoy* (paper of the old Moscow-oriented Communist Party, the PSP) and *Revolución* (paper of the July 26 Movement) continued to publish until *Granma* appeared in 1965 as the paper of the new Communist Party, the Communist Party of Cuba.

38. Chanan, *Cuban Image*, 179.

39. Rafael Hernández, *Looking at Cuba: Essays on Culture and Civil Society* (Gainesville: University Press of Florida, 2003), 99.

40. Fidel Ruz Castro, "Important Problems for the Whole of Revolutionary Thought," *New International* 6 (1987): 217.

41. Fidel Ruz Castro, "Che's Ideas Are Absolutely Relevant Today," October 8, 1987, in *Socialism and Man in Cuba*, 3rd ed., ed. Mary Alice Waters (New York: Pathfinder Press, 2009), 23–53.

42. The great debate of 1963–1964 centered on the revolution's economic policy, with the participation of economists from around the world. Two major approaches were presented, and although Guevara's ideas gained the most support, they were never fully implemented. Guevara stressed the centrality of the role of political participation and revolutionary consciousness as necessary for the economic organization of society and the building of socialism.

43. Osvaldo Sánchez, "Children of Utopia," in *No Man Is An Island: Young Cuban Art*, ed. Seppälä Marketta (Pori, Finland: Pori Art Museum, 1990), 57–59 (exhibition catalog).

44. Antonio (Tonel) Eligio, "Tree of Many Beaches: Cuban Art in Motion (1980s–1990s)," in *Contemporary Art from Cuba*, ed. Marilyn A. Zeitlin (New York: Arizona State University Art Museum and Delano Greenidge Editions, 1999), 39–52.

45. He states: "No es que desaparecieron definitivamente las tensiones, esos conflictos de opinión o de intereses que nunca dejan de aflorar en una cultura viva — recuerdo que todavía en 1991 nos enfrascamos en uno de ellos — , sino que las relaciones fueron siempre de respeto mutuo y de auténtico interés por el normal desarrollo de nuestra cultura, http://www.criterios.es/pdf/fornet quinqueniogris.pdf.

46. The rituals and beliefs of *santería* first arrived in Cuba with slavery in the sixteenth

century. The Cuban ethnologist Fernando Ortiz noted how the imposition of Christianity drove religious observances into a private sphere, whereas publicly its adherents were forced to follow the rituals of the Catholic Church, hence its syncretic character.

47. On a formal level, the obligatory contrapposto stance of the depictions of the saint does not extend to Elso's presentation of Martí.

48. Camnitzer, *New Art*, 56.

49. Gerardo Mosquera, "Juan Francisco Elso: Sacralisation and the 'Other' Post Modernity in New Cuban Art," *Third Text* (Winter 1997–98): 83–84.

50. Judith Bettleheim, "Palo Monte Mayombe and Its Influence on Cuban Contemporary Art," *African Arts* 34, no. 2 (2001): 36.

51. Mosquera, "Juan Francisco Elso," 82.

52. Juan Antonio Blanco, director of the Félix Varela Centre in Havana, explained: "The figures are dramatic. In 1989 we imported about 13 million tons of oil from the Soviet Union; in 1992 we could only import 6 million tons. In 1989 we imported about $8.4 billion worth of goods; by 1992 our import capacity plunged to $2.2 billion." Those figures combined with the lowest sugar harvest in thirty years. Benjamin Medea, *Cuba: Talking about Revolution: Conversations with Juan Antonio Blanco*, 2nd ed. (Melbourne: Ocean, 1997), 33.

53. A *Wall Street Journal* article noted the skyrocketing prices of Cuban art. The work of Cuban artist Tomás Sánchez, for instance, was double the asking price it had fetched five years earlier — with pieces at $700,000 — according to his dealer at Manhattan's Marlborough Gallery. The sales would surge, the article optimistically posited, if U.S. trade and travel restrictions were loosened with Barack Obama's presidential victory. It reported that a prominent American collector like Howard Farber was already adding to his collection three works a month from Havana, paying anything from $7,500 to $140,000. Farber made several million dollars in recent years from sales of his collection of new art from China. Kelly Crow, "The Cuban Art Revolution," *Wall Street Journal*, March 22, 2008, http://www.cremataﬁneart.com/news%20archive/CubanArtRevolution .pdf.

54. For instance, in his interesting analysis of the historical referent points of the campaign and his search for continuity, Kapcia locates the battle of ideas in one of many "bewildering" phases of the revolution. See Antoni Kapcia, "*Batalla de ideas*: Old Ideology in New Clothes?" in *Changing Cuba/Changing World*, ed. Mauricio A. Font (New York: Bildner Center for Western Hemisphere Studies, 2008).

55. Font outlines the various interpretations of the Battle of Ideas, ranging from it being a political operation of the state to maintain "the historic bureaucracy" in power to it being a counteroffensive to the imperialist ideological drive, a mechanism to transform evident demoralization among youths, and even a "spectacle" irrelevant to the lives of Cuban people. Mauricio A. Font, "Cuba and Castro: Beyond the 'Battle of Ideas,' " in Font, *Changing Cuba/Changing World*, 44–46.

56. The so-called culture war was initially associated with Ronald Reagan in the 1980s, but in the 1990s, Patrick Buchanan spearheaded a campaign with which politicians in both major parties began to identify as they shifted to the right.

57. A good description of Tatlin's tower is found in Camilla Gray, *The Russian Experiment in Art, 1863–1922*, 2nd ed. (London: Thames and Hudson, 1986), 225–28.

58. Kcho, "Crossings" (Ottawa, Canada: National Gallery of Art, 1998), 139–40, http:// www.germainekoh.com/content/press/koh_crossings_kcho.pdf.

59. Prieto interview.

60. Ibid.

EMILY J. KIRK AND JOHN M. KIRK

Cuban Medical Cooperation in Haiti: One of the World's Best-Kept Secrets

ABSTRACT

This article analyzes Cuba's medical role in Haiti since Hurricane Georges in 1998, with
particular emphasis on the Cuban government's response to the 2010 earthquake. The
article examines two central themes. First, it assesses the enormous impact on public
health that Cuba has made since 1998, and second, it provides a comparative analysis of
Cuba's medical role since the earthquake.

RESUMEN

Este artículo analiza la cooperación médica de Cuba en Haití desde el Huracán Georges
en 1998, y en particular se concentra en el rol del gobierno cubano después del terremoto
de 2010. El artículo analiza dos temas centrales. Primero, estudia el impacto enorme de
la cooperación médica cubana sobre la salud pública haitiana desde 1998, y luego ofrece
un análisis del papel cubano desde el terremoto, comparando su cooperación con la de
otros países.

Media coverage of Cuban medical cooperation following the disastrous recent
earthquake in Haiti was sparse indeed. International news reports usually described the Dominican Republic as the first to provide assistance, though Fox
News sang the praises of U.S. relief efforts in a report titled "U.S. Spearheads
Global Response to Haiti Earthquake" — a common theme of its extensive
coverage. Also, CNN broadcast hundreds of reports, and in fact, one focused
on a Cuban doctor wearing a T-shirt with a large image of Che Guevara but
indicated that he was a Spanish doctor. In general, then, international news
reports ignored Cuba's efforts. By March 24, CNN had 601 reports on its news
Web site regarding the earthquake in Haiti, only eighteen of which briefly
referenced Cuban assistance. Similarly, between them the *New York Times* and
the *Washington Post* had 750 posts regarding the earthquake and relief efforts,
though not a single one discussed in any detail any Cuban support. In reality,
however, Cuba's medical role was extremely important, and Cuba has been
present in Haiti since 1998.

Cuba and Haiti before the Earthquake

In 1998, Hurricane Georges struck Haiti. The hurricane caused 230 deaths, destroyed 80 percent of the country's crops, and left 167,000 people homeless.[1] Despite the fact that Cuba and Haiti had not had diplomatic relations in more than thirty-six years, Cuba immediately offered a multifaceted agreement to assist Haiti, of which the most important was medical cooperation. Cuba adopted a two-pronged public health approach to help Haiti. First, it agreed to maintain hundreds of doctors in the country for as long as necessary, and those doctors would work wherever the Haitian government posted them. This was particularly significant, as Haiti's health-care system was easily the worst in the Americas, with life expectancy of only fifty-four years in 1990, one of every five adult deaths due to AIDS, and 12.1 percent of children dying in 1990 from preventable intestinal infectious diseases.[2]

In addition, Cuba agreed to train Haitian doctors in Cuba, providing that they would later return and take the places of the Cuban doctors, a process of brain gain rather than brain drain. Significantly, the students were selected from nontraditional backgrounds and were mainly poor. It was thought that because of their socioeconomic background, they fully understood their country's need for medical personnel and would return to work where they were needed. The first cohort of students began studying in May 1999 at the Latin American School of Medicine (Escuela Latinoamericana de Medicina, or ELAM).

By 2007, significant change had already been achieved throughout the country. It is worth noting that Cuban medical personnel were estimated to be caring for 75 percent of the population.[3] Studies by the Pan American Health Organization (PAHO) indicated clear improvements in the health profile since this extensive Cuban medical cooperation began. Cuban medical personnel clearly have made a major difference to the national health profile since 1998, largely because of their proactive role in preventive medicine.

By 2010, at no cost to medical students, Cuba had trained some 550 Haitian doctors and is at present training a further 567. Moreover, since 1998, some 6,094 Cuban medical personnel have worked in Haiti. They had given more than 14.6 million consultations; carried out 207,000 surgical operations, including 45,000 vision restoration operations through the Operation Miracle program; attended 103,000 births; and taught literacy to 165,000. In fact at the time of the earthquake, there were 344 Cuban medical personnel in Haiti. All of this medical cooperation, it must be remembered, was provided over an eleven-year period before the earthquake of January 12, 2010.[4]

TABLE 8. Improvements in Public Health in Haiti, 1999–2007

Health Indicator	1999	2007
Infant Mortality, per 1,000 live births	80	33
Child Mortality under 5 per 1,000	135	59.4
Maternal mortality per 100,000 live births	523	285
Life expectancy (years)	54	61

Source: Pan American Health Organization, *Haiti*.

TABLE 9. Selected Statistics on Cuban Medical Cooperation, December 1998–May 2007

Visits to the doctor	10,682,124
Doctor visits to patients	4,150,631
Attended births	86,633
Major and minor surgeries	160,283
Vaccinations	899,829
Lives saved (emergency)	210,852

Source: Kovac, "Cuba Trains Hundreds of Haitian Doctors."

Cuba Post-Earthquake

The earthquake killed at least 220,000 people, injured 300,000, and left 1.5 million homeless.[5] Haitian Prime Minister Jean-Max Bellerive described it as "the worst catastrophe that has occurred in Haiti in two centuries."[6] International aid began flooding in. It is important to note the type of medical aid that some major international players provided. Médecins Sans Frontières (MSF), for example, an organization known for its international medical assistance, flew in 348 international staff, in addition to the 3,060 national staff it already employed. By March 12, MSF had treated some 54,000 patients and completed 3,700 surgical operations.[7]

Canada's contribution included the deployment of 2,046 Canadian Forces personnel, including 200 personnel from the Disaster Assistance Response Team (DART), which received the most media attention, as it conducted 21,000 consultations (though it should be noted that DART does not treat any serious trauma patients or provide surgical care). Indeed, among the DART personnel, only forty-five are medical staff, with others being involved in water purification, security, and reconstruction. In total, the Canadians stayed for only seven weeks.[8] The U.S. government, which received extensive positive media attention, sent the USNS *Comfort*, a thousand-bed hospital ship with a 550-person medical staff and stayed for seven weeks, in which time they treated 871 patients, performing 843 surgical operations.[9] Both the Canadian and American contributions were important — while they were there.

Lost in the media shuffle was the fact that for the first seventy-two hours following the earthquake, Cuban doctors were the main medical support for the country. Within the first twenty-four hours, the Cuban doctors had completed one thousand emergency surgeries, turned their living-quarters into clinics, and were running the principal medical centers in the country, including five comprehensive diagnostic centers (small hospitals) that they had previously built. In addition, another five centers in various stages of construction were used, and the Cubans turned their ophthalmology center into a field hospital, which treated 605 patients within the first twelve hours following the earthquake.[10]

Cuba soon became responsible for some 1,500 medical personnel in Haiti. Of those, some 344 doctors were already working in Haiti, and Cuba sent more than 350 members of the Henry Reeve Emergency Response Medical Brigade following the earthquake. In addition, 546 graduates of ELAM from a variety of countries, and 184 fifth- and sixth-year Haitian ELAM students joined, as did a number of Venezuelan medical personnel. In the final analysis, these personnel were working throughout Haiti in twenty rehabilitation centers and twenty hospitals, running fifteen operating theaters, and had vaccinated four hundred thousand people. With reason, Fidel Castro stated, "We send doctors, not soldiers."[11]

A glance at the medical role of the various key players is instructive. Compiled from several sources, these comparative data are particularly telling as they indicate the Cubans' significant — and widely ignored — medical contribution. In fact, they have treated 4.2 times the number of patients as did MSF, which has more than twice as many workers, as well as significantly more financial resources, and 10.8 times more than the Canadian DART team. (As noted, Canadian and American medical personnel had left by March 9.) Also notable is the fact that, although the Cuban medical contingent was roughly three times the size of the U.S. staff, it treated 260.7 times more patients than did the Americans. Clearly, there have been significant differences in the nature of medical assistance provided.

It is also important to note that approximately half the Cuban medical staff was working outside the capital, Port-au-Prince, where there was significant damage as well. Many medical missions could not get there, however, because of transportation issues. Significantly, the Cuban medical brigade also worked to minimize epidemics by making up thirty teams to educate communities on how to properly dispose of waste and how to minimize public health risks. The noted Cuban artist Kcho headed a cultural brigade made up of clowns, magicians, and dancers, supported by psychologists and psychiatrists, to deal with the trauma Haitian children experienced.

Perhaps most impressive, following the growing concern for the health of the country, given the poor and largely destroyed health-care system, Cuba worked with the Alianza Bolivariana para los Pueblos de Nuestra América

Table 10. Comparative Medical Contributions in Haiti by March 23

	MSF	Canada	United States	Cuba
Number of staff	3,408	45	550	1,504
Number of patients treated	54,000	21,000	871	227,143
Number of surgeries	3,700	0	843	6,499

Source: Data compiled from Gorry, "Two of the 170,000+ Cases"; "Cooperación con Haití"; "Haiti: Two Months after the Quake"; "New Services and New Concerns"; "Haiti-USNS Comfort Medical and Surgical Support"; Popplewell, "Singing Canada's Praise"; "USNS Comfort Leaves Haiti."

(ALBA) countries and presented the World Health Organization with an integral program to reconstruct the health care system of Haiti. Essentially, Cuba, supported by Brazil and the ALBA countries, is offering to rebuild the entire health-care system. Including hospitals, polyclinics, and medical schools, ALBA and Brazil will support the project, which Cubans and Cuban-trained medical staff will run. In addition, Havana has offered to increase the number of Haitian students attending medical school in Cuba. This offer of medical cooperation represents an enormous degree of support for Haiti.[12] Sadly, international media have not reported on this generous offer. But although North American media might have ignored Cuba's role, Haiti has not. Haiti's President René Préval noted, "You did not wait for an earthquake to help us."[13] Similarly, Prime Minister Bellerive has also repeatedly noted that the first three countries to help were Cuba, the Dominican Republic, and Venezuela.

Sadly, but not surprisingly, although Cuba's efforts to assist Haiti have increased, international efforts have continued to dwindle. The head of the Cuban medical mission, Dr. Carlos Alberto García, summed up the situation just two weeks after the tragedy: "many foreign delegations have already begun to leave, and the aid which is arriving now is not the same it used to be. Sadly, as always happens, soon another tragedy will appear in another country, and the people of Haiti will be forgotten, left to their own fate." He added, "However we will still be here long after they have all gone."[14] A continued Cuban presence has been the case. Canadian forces, for example, returned home and the USNS *Comfort* sailed several weeks later. By contrast, Cuban President Raúl Castro noted, "We have accompanied the Haitian people, and we will continue with them whatever time is needed, no matter how many years, with our very modest support."[15]

A representative of the World Council of Churches to the United Nations once made the telling comment that "humanitarian aid could not be human if it was only publicized for 15 days."[16] Today, Cuba, with the support of ALBA and Brazil, is working to build not just a field hospital but rather an entire health-care system. And although international efforts have been largely abandoned, the Cuban staff and Cuban-trained medical staff will remain, as they have done for the past eleven years, for as long as necessary. Cuban medical cooperation in Haiti is a story that international media have chosen not to tell, now that the television cameras have gone, but Cuba's story has been one of true humanitarianism and great success in saving lives since 1998. Moreover, in light of Cuba's achievement in providing public health care at no cost to the millions of Haitian patients, this approach to preventive, culturally sensitive, low-cost, and effective medical needs to be told. That significant contribution to this impoverished nation and Cuba's ongoing commitment to its people clearly deserve to be recognized. Until then, it will sadly remain as one of the world's best-kept secrets.

NOTES

1. U.S. Agency for International Development (USAID), *Audit of USAID/HAITI Hurricane Georges Recovery Programme*, May 15, 2001, http://www.usaid.gov/oig/public/fy01rpts/1-521-01-005-p.pdf.

2. Pan American Health Organization (PAHO), *Haiti* (Washington, D.C.: Pan American Health Organization, 2008), http://www.paho.org/english/dd.ais/cp_332.htm.

3. William Steif, "Cuban Doctors Aid Strife-Torn Haiti," *Columbia (SC) State*, April 26, 2004, http://havanajournal.com/culture/entry/cuban_doctors_aid_strife_torn_haiti/.

4. "Fact Sheet: Cuban Medical Cooperation in Haiti," *Medicc Review*, January 15, 2009, http://www.medicc.org/ns/index.php?s=104.

5. Anna Kovac, "Cuba Trains Hundred of Haitian Doctors to Make a Difference," *Medicc Review*, August 6, 2007, http://www.medicc.org/cubahealthreports/chr-article.php?&a.

6. Ibid.; "Fact Sheet: Cuban Medical Cooperation with Haiti," *Medicc Review*, January 15, 2009, http://www.medicc.org/ns/index.php?s=104; "La colaboración cubana permanecerá en Haití los años que sean necesarios," *Cubadebate*, February 24, 2010, http://www.cubadebate.cu/opinion/2010/02/24/cuba-estara-en-haiti-anos-quesean-necesarios.

7. "Haiti Earthquake: Special Coverage," March 20, 2010, http://www.cnn.com/SPECIALS/2010/haiti.quake/.

8. Canada, Foreign Affairs and International Trade, "Canada's Response to the Earthquake in Haiti: Progress to Date," March 17, 2010, http://www.international.gc.ca/humanitarian-manitaire/earthquake_seisme_haiti_effort.

9. American Forces Press Service, "USNS Comfort Completes Haiti Mission," March 9, 2010, http://www.trackpads.com/forum/defenselink/928304-usns-comfort-completes-hati-mission.

10. John Burnett, "Cuban Doctors Unsung Heroes of Haitian Earthquake," National Public Radio, January 24, 2010. http://www.npr.org/templates/story/story.php?storyId=122919202&sc=emaf.

11. José Steinsleger, "Haiti, Cuba y la ley primera," *La Jornada*, February 3, 2010. Data in this section come from the address by Ambassador Rudolfo Reyes Rodriguez in January 2010 in Geneva at the UN Human Rights Council meeting on Haiti. See "Address given by Ambassador Rodolfo Reyes Rodríguez on 27 January 2010 in Geneva at the 13th Special Session of the U.N. Human Rights Council on Haiti" ["Cuba en Ginebra: 'Ante tan difícil situación en Haití no puede haber titubeos ni indiferencia' "], *Cubadebate*, January 27, 2010, http://www.cubadebate.cu/especiales/2010/01/27/cuba-en — ginebra-sobre-reconstruccion-haiti.

12. In a March 27, 2010, meeting in Port-au-Prince between President Préval and the Cuban

and Brazilian ministers of health — José Ramón Balaguer and José Gomes — details were provided about what Balaguer called "a plot of solidarity to assist the Haitian people." Gomes added: "We have just signed an agreement — Cuba, Brazil and Haiti — according to which all three countries make a commitment to unite our forces in order to reconstruct the health system in Haiti. An extraordinary amount of work is currently being carried out in terms of meeting the most basic and most pressing needs, but now it is necessary to think about the future. . . . Haiti needs a permanent, quality healthcare system, supported by well-trained professionals. . . . We will provide this, together with Cuba — a country with an extremely long internationalist experience, a great degree of technical ability, great determination, and an enormous amount of heart. Brazil and Cuba, two nations that are so close, so similar, now face a new challenge: together we will unite our efforts to rebuild Haiti, and rebuild the public health system of this country." See "Cuba y Brasil suman esfuerzos con Haití." Translation to English provided by authors.

13. "Presidente Preval agradece a Fidel y Raúl Castro ayuda solidaria a Haití," *Cubadebate*, February 8, 2010, http://www.cubadebate.cu/noticias/2010/02/08presidente-preval-agradece-fidel-raul-castro.

14. María Laura Carpineta, "Habla el jefe de los 344 médicos cubanos instalados en Haití desde hace doce años," *Página*, February 4, 2010, available at cuba-l@lista.unm.edu.

15. Ibid.

16. United Nations, "Press Conference on Haiti Humanitarian Aid," March 23, 2004, http://www.un.org/News/briefings/docs/2004/CanadaPressCfc.doc.htm.

Reviews

Alfredo Guevara Valdés. *¿Y si fuera una huella?* **La Habana: Ediciones Autor y Festival del Nuevo Cine Latinoamericano, 2008.**

Cuando parecía que, después de cuatro libros de revelaciones personales, el escritor era ya incapaz de sorprendernos, la aparición de este libro es un aviso intempestivo de todo lo que aún falta por conocer del autor de *Tiempo de fundación*.

Los grandes escritores asombran con sus textos, pero no siempre alcanzan con estos grandes sorpresas. Como se sabe, el asombro es un rango distinto a la sorpresa. El primero es territorio de la enormidad, mientras que la segunda es lugar creado por ella misma. Los epistolarios de los grandes escritores sorprenden allí donde sus obras ya sólo consiguen asombrar. Entonces, las colecciones de cartas despiertan morbosidad: hacen las veces de memorias, y casi siempre se leen como narraciones, con sus meditaciones íntimas, crónicas de entuertos y revelaciones trágicas.

Si las cartas son de un hombre teatral, con sentido del humor y vasta cultura estas harán felices a los amantes de la literatura, esos pobres seres que experimentan sensaciones físicas ante la belleza de una frase o la desmesura de una imagen. Pero si ese hombre, además, es un gran pensador, y un auténtico revolucionario, y ha fundado empeños como el Instituto Cubano de Arte e Industria Cinematográficos (ICAIC), el movimiento del nuevo cine latinoamericano, el nuevo cartel cubano o el Grupo de Experimentación Sonora, su correspondencia puede provocar verdaderas obsesiones.

Publicar un epistolario o es un acto de valor inaudito o lo es de una cobardía total. Muchas veces, sus autores lo dejan como legado envenenado al mundo que abandonan. Dejan una cláusula áspera en el testamento: publiquen mis cartas. Es acaso la única sonrisa que disfrutan ante la proximidad de la partida: venganza personal, especie de después de mí el diluvio, queriendo que el mundo se acabe, con él, tras la batalla final entre quienes aparecen mencionados en la correspondencia del espanto.

Como hombre lúcido, Guevara sabe que no hay inteligencia interesante sin una pequeña escala diabólica. Pero no nos deja aquí, con su epistolario, alguna clase de herencia que pueda explotar en nuestras manos. Guevara es un hombre que no aprecia la prudencia ni la disciplina, pero sí la consecuencia de quien cumple deberes: renunció a hacer películas —quién sabe a dónde hubiese llegado el joven asistente de dirección de Luis Buñuel—, pero también renun-

173

ció a escribir formalmente filosofía, que sospecho es su gran pasión, incluso más que el cine, para poder dejarnos, en ese acto de valor que sólo raya con el candor, un epistolario, historia abierta de una huella.

Publicar un epistolario como este es violar la intimidad de los lectores. No es tanto el que ha escrito una carta sin imaginar que será leída cuarenta años después por un completo extraño, el que se descubre al publicarla. Es quien la lee el que se redescubre, el que siente su propia intimidad conmocionada.

Estas cartas conmocionan, sobre todo, los juicios hechos, las tesis que, repetidas, se han convertido en verdades al uso, en remiendos para cubrir nuestras vergüenzas: frasecitas que pretenden explicarlo todo y ya hace mucho no consiguen ocultar su miseria, pero han pasado, no obstante, a nuestra intimidad, a la forma en que pensamos y nos pensamos.

¿Cómo puede el acto por el cual otro se descubre mostrar nuestra propia intemperie? Somos esclavos de nuestra edad, esa ignorancia que nos acompaña. Miramos desde nuestro hoy lo que ha sido, lo que llamamos el pasado, y no hacemos otra cosa que proyectar sobre él lo que somos hoy. Ciertamente, es y será así, pero es esa una particular forma de no saber, o de saber en modo sectario. Estamos habituados a despreciar lo que ignoramos, pero también nos acostumbramos a otra brutalidad: ignorar lo que ignoramos. La necesidad de entender exige un esfuerzo mayor: exige saber, o saber verdaderamente, que es acaso comprender los sentidos que animaron las acciones, y sus significados para quienes las siguieron.

Este libro sirve a ese propósito. No quiere que sea comprendido para ser perdonado —aunque también, si lo merece— sino comprender para abarcar más, para llegar más hondo, para "alcanzar", diría Guevara, "la lucidez suficiente". Este libro nos lleva de regreso, nos hace recorrer, desaprendiendo, una historia, y nos hace avanzar por ella, paso a paso, volviendo a mirar. La ciencia, se dice, es mirar lo que todos han visto y observar lo que nadie ha distinguido o imaginado antes en ello. En cierto modo, eso lo es también el arte. O lo es también un libro, como este libro.

¿Y si fuera una huella? historia la Revolución Cubana desde la perspectiva del testigo de excepción que es Alfredo Guevara. Aparece cuando no son siquiera suficientes las historias que den cuenta con rigor historiográfico y/o testimonial del proceso histórico transcurrido en la isla después de 1959. Su énfasis recae en el itinerario político y en la evolución ideológica de la revolución —y, por consiguiente, no sólo en la historia de la política cultural—, contribuye a la reconstrucción de la complejidad de la edificación del poder revolucionario en Cuba, y de la diversidad contenida en ese proceso y, a su vez, a la contextualización histórica, socioeconómica, cultural e ideológica de los procesos ocurridos en el campo cultural, explicados tradicionalmente sin tomar en cuenta el conjunto de la vida vigente en el país en que se produjeron.

Guevara resume en sí, por haberlos vivido o interpretado desde una óptica muy particular, una parte considerable de los avatares experimentados por la Revolución Cubana, desde su génesis hasta el presente. Los procesos en los que ha estado inmerso, las posiciones que ha ocupado, su formación intelectual y política, su condición personal y su carácter, lo han llevado a estar casi siempre en el centro de eventos esenciales en la historia revolucionaria.

Guevara ha sido un singular formulador de políticas culturales para el contexto nacional y latinoamericano, sus ideas sobre cuál debe ser la relación entre los intelectuales y la política, y entre la política y la cultura, lo han hecho diferenciarse de otras tendencias sostenidas en el campo cultural cubano en el mismo lapso. Como muy pocas figuras de la revolución, Guevara representa una frontera de la relación entre la herejía del poder —la herejía que está en el poder y que es aún el poder mismo—, y el *statu quo* revolucionario, si deja de ser la ruptura el elemento fundamental del nuevo orden. Estas cartas son las pruebas de convicción: Guevara ha estado ahí, columna tenaz, para recordar precisamente que es el cambio lo que identifica la vida que merece ser vivida y que la rutina es la forma misma de la muerte.

Guevara sintetiza una cuestión básica para las filosofías revolucionarias: cómo construir y defender un proyecto común, desde la afirmación de una radical individualidad. Pierre Bourdieu afirmaba que un testimonio, si llega a ser esencialmente personal, anuncia la condición general de los seres sujetos a similares circunstancias. Es el caso de este testimonio de Guevara. Las polémicas, dudas, equivocaciones, aciertos, desavenencias y adhesiones del autor de *Revolución es lucidez* —expresadas de un modo muy individual— verifican la complejidad de la evolución ideológica de la Revolución Cubana, de la dialéctica de sus conflictividades internas y externas, del cómo y del por qué devino socialista, de qué es lo revolucionario dentro de la revolución, y de cuál es el legado inscrito por ella en la historia. Sin embargo, el cuerpo de su reflexión no es atinente sólo a Cuba y a su proceso revolucionario, o al cine cubano y latinoamericano: expande su importancia hacia el centro mismo de la teoría sobre qué es una cultura revolucionaria, o una cultura del socialismo.

Este libro gozará de la mejor de las suertes: ser citado una y otra vez en los textos que se escriban en el futuro sobre la revolución, sobre el nuevo cine, cubano y latinoamericano, sobre la cultura de la resistencia latinoamericana, pero también será leído con fervor por quienes quieran contemplar el espectáculo heroico de un ser humano que lucha por afirmar su autenticidad, que no necesariamente la diferencia, como el sentido de su vida.

La autenticidad es honestidad. Muchas de estas cartas, no son amables, más bien resultan inconvenientes para muchos implicados en ellas o afectados por el pensamiento que de ellas se desprende. Pero todas están fechadas, y no se ha suprimido una coma. Para sí mismo, esa es la herencia mayor que puede legar Alfredo Guevara: haber vivido en un torbellino durante más de medio siglo y poder publicar la historia de su vida, poniendo fechas, sin quitar comas.

Guevara hace entender que la verdadera disciplina revolucionaria no es la obsecuencia sino la lealtad. Es un hombre leal, pero está todo lo lejos que se puede estar de ser un asentidor. He aquí una lección perdurable. Por ello, no sorprende en el libro la angustia de Guevara por comunicarse con los más jóvenes, pero sí resulta poco común cuando tantas personas dan por hecho que se comunican y sólo consiguen el silencio.

Cuba es un país cuya población envejece, y que, como parte de ello, considera jóvenes a personas de avanzada edad. Es una sociedad que los sociólogos llaman adultocéntrica, con problemas para hacer comunicar a la sociedad oficial con los más jóvenes. Sin embargo, parece practicar un culto a lo nuevo, a lo improvisado, a lo creativo, expresión del desecho de la experiencia, de la ignorancia del pasado, o de la ignorancia sin más, que se achaca a la pobreza y es mucho peor y más invasiva que ella. El libro de Guevara se para, enhiesto, a restituir el valor de la experiencia vivida, de la planificación rigurosa, de la tradición que no se cierra a su crítica y proyección.

Alfredo Guevara nos ayuda a entender algo fundamental: la autenticidad es una conquista, no el producto de exclusiones, sino de agregaciones, de inclusiones, del desprejuicio con que se pueda mirar el mundo, tan ancho, y a veces tan ajeno.

Como Chéjov, que escribió 4 mil cartas en 25 años, Guevara ha escrito otras tantas. A él, la vida lo condenó a escribir epístolas. Su vida puesta en abrir caminos lo condenó a escribir esas cartas asombrosas y sorpresivas que cuentan la fundación de una revolución, de un cine, de una vida, y que resultan sagas de novelas, libros de ensayos y buenas películas.

Guevara es, ciertamente, malévolo cuando se pregunta "y si fuera una huella". Él ha escrito su correspondencia con la tinta limón de los clandestinajes: la pregunta parece dirigida a él, cuando en realidad nos interpela a nosotros. Con ese guiño socarrón, nos deja a solas con su misma pregunta: "¿y si (yo) fuera una huella?" Nos deja sus respuestas, para quedarnos nosotros con nuestras preguntas.

Julio César Guanche
Instituto Cubano del Arte y la Industria Cinematográfica

Ernesto Chávez Álvarez. *Historias contadas por Pura*. Ediciones La Memoria, Centro Cultural Pablo de la Torriente Brau, La Habana, 2008.

Al sur de la actual provincia cubana de Matanzas se encuentra la Ciénaga de Zapata, uno de los mayores humedales de las islas del Caribe. A pesar de su cercanía a ciudades como Cienfuegos y la propia capital provincial, Matanzas, y de no hallarse muy distante de La Habana, durante la mayor parte de la historia de Cuba fue un lugar inhóspito y apenas poblado por algunos carboneros y contrabandistas de todo tipo: durante los tiempos de la esclavitud, por sus costas llegaban numerosos alijos de africanos que entraban burlando los tratados internacionales que prohibían ese infame tráfico humano.

Por esas mismas costas se produjo en abril de 1961 la conocida invasión de Bahía de Cochinos organizada por el gobierno de Estados Unidos para aplastar la revolución, derrotada en menos de setenta y dos horas. Hoy la Ciénaga tiene varias instalaciones turísticas y buenas vías de comunicación terrestre, y su población ha crecido con atención médica, escuelas y una vida cultural activa.

Allí nació Pura de Armas, ochenta años antes de que el geógrafo, antropólogo y editor Ernesto Chávez diera a conocer sus recuerdos de infancia en este libro. Fue en 1924, en una finca dedicada al cultivo de la caña de azúcar. Era la tercera de siete hijos, pero la primera de las hembras, lo cual determinó su lugar en la familia: atender las múltiples tareas caseras, incluyendo la crianza de sus hermanos menores, y acompañar a su madre por los caseríos y poblados cercanos en busca de limosnas para mitigar las necesidades familiares.

Como tantos niños campesinos de su época, Pura cambió de residencia con frecuencia: sus padres buscaban la mejoría de vida que nunca llegaba o el padre se quedaba sin trabajo como carbonero y jornalero agrícola sin tierras.

Los recuerdos de aquella vida conforman este libro, que a través de catorce capítulos narra las andanzas familiares, los oficios del padre, las casa en que habitó, los juegos, la alimentación, las ropas que vestían, la medicina natural que practicaban, las creencias religiosas y los saberes y aventuras con los animales del entorno. El último capítulo cierra la obra con el momento dramático, tan frecuente en la Cuba de la primera mitad del siglo XX: el desalojo de la familia de su vivienda, a la fuerza, por la Guardia Rural. Se trata, pues, de un libro imprescindible para los estudios antropológicos del medio social cubano prerrevolucionario.

Ernesto Chávez, con inteligencia de antropólogo y finura de escritor, inicia el libro con una breve presentación en la que explica qué era la Ciénaga de Zapata y expone las líneas esenciales de su método de trabajo con la testimoniante, que buscó entregar al lector la sencillez y candidez de la comunicación infantil para ofrecer una memoria fabulada por el paso de los años, ya sin las inflexiones y locuciones propias de la cenaguera, pero veraces en su esencia, más con la poesía del habla de Pura, quien es improvisadora de décimas, versos de diez sílabas y peculiar rima empleada desde hace siglos en las zonas rurales cubanas de manera espontánea.

Véase, por ejemplo, la síntesis de la vida de Pura narrada en la primera de las décimas que Chávez sitúa al comienzo de cada capítulo:

> *Cuando nací no tenía*
> *Más amor que el de mi madre,*

Y a mi cariñoso padre
Que humildemente quería.
Yo de nada conocía,
Pues cenaguera nací,
Y solamente yo vi
Fango, montes, y lagunas,
Porque pañales ni cunas
Eso nunca conocí.

Historias contadas por Pura fue el texto ganador en el año 2006 del premio especial María Luisa Lafita, dedicado siempre al tema de la mujer, dentro del Concurso Memoria que convoca el Centro Pablo de la Torriente Brau, institución habanera de amplio perfil cultural, que desde hace muchos años busca mediante ese certamen rescatar y conservar la memoria de la vida cubana y de sus protagonistas.

Tuve la suerte de participar en el jurado que premió esta obra por unanimidad, y desde mi primera lectura, me sentí conmovido por la palabra de Pura vertida a la escritura por Ernesto Chávez. La riqueza de las imágenes; el disfrute de la vida que aquella niña tuvo en medio de condiciones tan hostiles; la significación del padre de Pura, quien casi se convierte en un personaje literario y que trasmitió a la hija el amor por el instante feliz, hacen del libro, como dice su prologuista, Sonnia Moro, un acercamiento imprescindible sobre los componentes de la identidad cubana y, además, el hermoso testimonio de la infancia de una mujer campesina que aprendió a leer y escribir malamente a los once años de edad, que se hizo a sí misma en su desempeño como asalariada doméstica en casas de ricos, y que, a pesar de contarnos acerca de un mundo repleto de privaciones y necesidades elementales insatisfechas, supo extraer momentos de felicidad, ternura y alegría, que, sin lugar a dudas, formaron su personalidad hasta su actual vejez.

Dice Ernesto Chávez que el libro fue doloroso para Pura y aleccionador para él. Para el lector probablemente también sea aleccionador conocer las historias de esta niña cenaguera referidas a un mundo, por suerte, desaparecido hace años en Cuba. También dice el autor que esperaba que las páginas de este texto que ella ayudó a escribir sirvieran a Pura para encontrar su niñez extraviada. Estoy seguro, sin embargo, que no sólo la testimoniante sino que todos los que lo leemos, encontramos esa niñez, aprendemos de ella y hasta la disfrutamos.

Pedro Pablo Rodríguez
Centro de Estudios Martianos

Ricardo Riverón Rojas. *El ungüento de la Magdalena: Humor en la medicina popular cubana.* **La Habana: Ediciones La Memoria, 2008.**

Aunque cubanos y cubanas somos en general conocidos y reconocidos por ser amantes de contar historias, sazonadas con dosis de humorismo, mentirillas (y mentirotas) y las consabidas exageraciones, la región central del país parecería ser su paraíso.

Bueno, no me acusen también a mí de exagerada, aunque a manera de disculpa, puedo esgrimir que es tierra de dos personalidades de la cultura cubana que se dedicaron a contar o a recopilar historias a partir del arsenal que les facilitaron testimoniantes mayoritariamente de Villa Clara: Onelio Jorge Cardoso,[1] y Samuel Feijóo,[2] nacidos ambos en el centro de la isla en 1914.

No es un secreto que mis compatriotas son expertos en tres áreas del conocimiento: la política (capaces de arreglar el mundo con una simple conversación de dos), la pelota (todos y cada una somos mánagers beisboleros en potencia) y sabemos más de medicina que los Premios Nobel y el médico chino.

Y es precisamente de sanaciones increíbles y recetas asombrosas sustentadas en el humor criollo de nuestro campos que el también villaclareño Ricardo Riverón Rojas (nacido en Zulueta, Villaclara, en 1949) nos ofrece una amena colección de ellas. Este libro fue presentado en el marco de la XII Feria Internacional del Libro de La Habana, que cada vez alcanza a más lectores y lectoras a lo largo y ancho del archipiélago.

Desde su subtítulo el autor nos alerta de su intención, ya que se trata de la gracia cubana, y como bien señala en el prólogo Pedro Pablo Rodríguez, — académico, y Premio Nacional de Ciencias sociales, sin dejar de ser un criollo, bromista y sandunguero— no imaginen que se trata de un catálogo de curas para muy diversas malezas aunque quizás se tropiece con algún remedio o práctica conocido o utilizada.

En las palabras preliminares el propio Riverón delata de dónde surgió su interés por esta temas y el camino que recorrieron esas historias: una parte de su niñez y adolescencia, transcurridas en el batey de un central azucarero, lo puso en contacto con personajes populares con una manera distinta de hablar y de pensar el español; la influencia de Feijóo que le indicara para uno de sus proyectos recoger estas recetas, reveladas generosamente en los vecindarios y entre sus amistades y que nunca vieron la luz. Y la responsabilidad profesional del investigador folclórico René Batista Moreno, que los conservara por más de veinte años y los depositara nuevamente en sus manos.

Y es que Riverón, ya en su madurez profesional, —además de investigador, periodista, editor y poeta— supo dar nueva vida estor relatos, fijar el aroma de su contexto, estructurarlos de forma que fluyeran sin interferencias, subrayando sus valores costumbristas y satíricos, sin importarle la validez del remedio sino la chispa humorística que los iluminaba al mismo tiempo que trasmitían el encanto de sus aristas absurdas o fantasiosa, pero llenas de sabiduría campesina.

El autor organiza sus recetas en cinco capítulos según los tipos de curas: por contactos inocuos, por contactos iatrogénicos, invasivos y crueles, por sustos, escarmientos y engaños, por ingestión de cocimientos, patentes y platos, por curas escatológicas, coprofágicas y venenosas y un sexto con las inclasificables.

Así desfilan con sus protagonistas, enfermedades y curaciones, a veces compitiendo por cuál nos hace reír o nos asombra más, con algo de racionalidad o totalmente locas, y aquellas en que, reconozcámoslo o no, alguna vez la abuela nos deshizo algún mal de ojo o hizo que brotara finalmente un sarampión rebelde, tras días de fiebre e incertidumbre o nos quitó algo pegado al estómago.

Sólo la relación de nombres y apodos de los personajes de estas historias, sonoros y rítmicos, perfectos para enriquece el estribillo de algún son montuno: El Calloso, Cojo Sunga, Everlina, Martín Garabato, Onofre, Lingollo, Arrecife, Limbania, Luis Frente de Mono, Mundo Esqueleto, Alina la de los Cocoriocos, Seso, Maracho, Tintín, Guajiro Purpulí... y así sucesivamente.

Las enfermedades o síntomas, otro tanto: La tía que no se podía tirar pedos, la *sangronencia*[3] — que es una enfermedad mental y se cura con escarmientos — las várices, que son el producto que las venas se pongan fofas por falta de ilusión, los tin nerviosos, las palpitaciones (que nublan la vista, y dan ganas de brincar, de acostarse arriba de una piedra de hielo y de pasarse una rata por las tetas).

Por su parte, las curaciones son, como se suele decir, un verdadero banquete; pero basta ya de dar avances porque lo que se impone es recomendar esta lectura, amena y enjundiosa, que satisfará a quienes busquen esparcimiento con esa parte del humor tradicional del campo cubano.

Aunque tengo la certeza que también será una valiosa fuente de información para las y los interesados en la cultura popular, la lengua y el contexto social de un mundo que tiende a desparecer, y como lo atrapó entonces Ricardo Riverón, ya no existirá jamás.

Sonnia Moro
Centro de Estudios Martianos de La Habana

NOTAS

1. Calabazar de Sagua, 1914; La Habana, 1986. Es considerado el cuentista nacional cubano.
2. San Juan de los Yeras, Las Villas, 1914; Villa Clara, 1992. Cuentista, poeta, pintor, estudioso del folclor, editor, periodista. Compiló numerosas colecciones y antologías. Tuvo a su cargo la revista *Islas,* de la Universidad Central. Trabajos suyos aparecieron en diversos órganos de prensa nacionales, entre ellos *Bohemia.*
3. En Cuba, *sangrón* es una persona impertinente, pesada.

Thelvia Marin Medero. *Ego sum qui sum: Escultura, pintura, poética.* Tenerife, Islas Canarias: Editorial CICSLU, 2009.

El libro sobre escultura, pintura, poética de la autora —artista plástica, escritora y promotora cultural cubana, alumna predilecta del escultor Teodoro Ramos Blanco, en la Academia San Alejandro de La Habana— muestra la génesis de su motivación por la experimentación constante. Así como la influencia legitimada en sus obras con audacia y contemporaneidad de la influencia académica de Leopoldo Romañach.

Ego sum qui sum ("yo soy quien soy", en castellano) es un volumen compilatorio de 179 páginas y 250 fotografías en blanco y negro y color, patrocinado y avalado por el escudo y el logotipo del Gobierno de Canarias, quien expresa el reconocimiento a obra de la autora. El libro asume con toda intención un discurso biográfico controvertido y atemporal. No es un libro de arte en su formato tradicional. Con criterio posmoderno y como lo expresa la artista, su estructura responde a la de una crónica periodística, que refleja en escultura, pintura y literatura, el convulso y contradictorio mundo del siglo XX y el transcurso del XXI en obras que abarcan de lo histórico a lo subjetivo —de lo colonizador a lo colonizado, de lo devoto a lo irreverente, de lo figurativo a lo abstracto, a nivel planetario— cuyo fin es invitar al lector a recorrerlo desde su propio camino. Detrás de este trabajo —hay que decirlo— se evidencian seis décadas de incesante laboriosidad de esta singular mujer.

Esculturas y lienzos de variados formatos expuestos en colecciones privadas e instituciones de Cuba y el mundo; conjuntos tridimensionales monumentarios, ambientales y conmemorativos emplazados en los cinco continentes; así como una pródiga literatura y composiciones musicales compuestas para diversas representaciones y *performances*, se muestran en esta crónica de arte, agrupados, en una secuencia que engloba las siguientes temáticas, bajo la clasificación de "Cabezas", "Martí", "Canarias", "Ambientales", "Monumentaria", "La Casa de Nadie", y "Pequeño y Mediano Formato", para culminar con las obras pictóricas, en natural coherencia dentro de sus páginas, junto a confesiones de la creadora y consideraciones críticas de prestigiosos intelectuales cubanos y foráneos.

A partir de los años 1950 simultánea al uso de un lenguaje figurativo con búsquedas formales más osadas y la utilización de novedosos materiales, alternando así la escayola, la terracota y la marmolina; con la piedra, el mármol, la cerámica, el bronce, el hierro y las técnicas mixtas, para la realización de piezas que involucran retratos escultóricos, fruto en su mayoría de encargos sociales sobre personajes de la vida pública como Miguel Gabriel (1950), pionero de la radio en Cuba; fundador de la radioemisora CMQ: el doctor Carlos J. Finlay (1956), descubridor del mosquito transmisor de la fiebre amarilla; el poeta Gustavo Sánchez Galárraga; y la bailarina Alicia Alonso (1957).

182 : *Reviews*

Paralelamente incursiona en el complejo mundo de las ambientaciones en exteriores, con el mural abstracto *Bailarín* para la antigua Academia Militar del Caribe (1957); el estilizado *Parcartus* (1978), de un parque en la provincia de Las Tunas y las imágenes de cultos sincréticos como *Los iremes*; y *La fuente de Yemayá* (1982), en el pueblo de Regla. En esa misma década recrea escenarios del universo marino en entornos hoteleros de la isla, donde aparece el *Hipocampo* (1985), en la villa turística habanera El Salado; *Las gaviotas* (1986), del Hotel Colony en Isla de Pinos; o *Los delfines* (1999), del Hotel Bellamar en Varadero.

Coleccionistas de Islas Baleares, Canarias, Barcelona, Japón, y Costa Rica, y museos, galerías y otros tantos espacios públicos y privados, atesoran y exhiben piezas de temas variados de la autora y formas que patentizan su dedicación hacia una poética arqueológica basada en las culturas indoamericanas y caribeñas y sobre la historia más reciente, devenida en referente de excepcional valor investigativo y estético. Entre sus esculturas, *El indio Hatuey* (1974), en la Plaza Indoamérica de Ecuador le valió la designación de Huésped Ilustre de Quito y el *Monumento a Serafín Sánchez* (1980), general de las gestas independentistas, constituyó en su momento la más grande escultura de bronce fundida en la isla. Es autora de tres obras que son monumento nacional.

En la misma vertiente cobran vida el poema escultórico-pictórico-literario-musical, *La casa de Nadie* (1987) y realiza su serie de esculturas neotaínas, junto a la publicación de sus libros sobre la misma temática, *Rezo a los cemíes* y *Entrevista con cuatro dioses* (1997), a las que se incorpora en 1998 *El mundo en la mano*, marcando un hito en el polifónico discurso creativo que anima buena parte del sustrato de su creación.

Su voluntad expresiva con contenidos sobre el amor, la mujer, la maternidad, la naturaleza y la cultura, se han manifestado en íntima relación con ese quehacer plástico, poético y narrativo que desde muy joven desarrolló con éxito: las esculturas *Mujer* (1949), *Gory* (1953), *Maternidad* (1955), *Platero y yo* (1962) o sus *Libélulas 1* y *2* (1987), son fuente de inspiración de los poemas *Razón de ser, Niña, Presencia, Danza* e *Hijo*, este último dedicado al segundo de sus hijos: el trascendental pintor cubano Rogelio ("Gory") López Marín.

Una faceta de marcado patriotismo que merece un destaque especial, es su profunda convicción martiana. Así se agrupan las diferentes obras dedicadas a José Martí a lo largo de su trayectoria artística, en los capítulos de este libro "Martí" y "Canarias", donde aparece la madre del apóstol Leonor Pérez Cabrera, en múltiples imágenes escultóricas. Pudiéramos hablar de una serie de obras martianas, abordadas desde diversos ángulos de su historia, con una indudable coherencia conceptual.

Con *Abdala* (1958), inicia esa arista de su producción en función del homenaje al apóstol en el contexto de la escultura monumentaria y la literatura, concretándose la mayor parte desde finales de la década del setenta. En 1978 realiza ocho bustos y tres cabezas destinadas a once sedes diplomáticas, y entre 1983 y 1984 ejecuta en La Habana tres murales para instituciones científicas.

A partir de 1987 y por una década la artista emprende sus obras conmemorativas de mayor envergadura y trascendencia, en tierra costarricense. Primero, realiza el *Monumento a José Martí*; y a continuación el *Monumento al trabajo, al desarme y la paz* (1989), ambos para el Campus de la Universidad para la Paz, organismo creado por las Naciones Unidas, en Costa Rica. Éste es el conjunto monumentario más grande de los cinco países de Mesoamérica y uno de los mayores del mundo dedicados a la paz. En su condición de catedrática de la Universidad Nacional de Costa Rica —como asesora del Proyecto de Investigación sobre Cosmogonías Costarricenses y del área pública de ensayos temáticos, poemas y las facultades humanísticas de las universidades mesoamericanas Consejo Superior Universitario Centroamericano, le solicitan y publican su Ensayo "Vigencia del pensamiento martiano en el siglo XXI" (1995). Como resultado de esas investigaciones, publica en Cuba el libro *Viaje al sexto sol*, sobre las profecías mayas, seleccionado el libro más innovador del año. Con igual decisión logra el rescate de la memoria histórica del general Antonio Maceo y Grajales en su centenario, con su obra escultórica inaugurada en *La mansión de Nicoya* (1996). Por su trabajo en la investigación de las tradiciones de los pueblos indígenas mesoamericanos, se hace acreedora de reconocimientos en la historiografía de la región.

La pintura de la artista recogida en la presente edición sintoniza con la disposición tridimensional de objetos, seres y auras en sus lienzos, provenientes de la espontaneidad causal. Licencia que retoma al plasmar una selección de sus cuadros, por ejemplo *Camino infinito, la madre tierra pare* y *Profundidad* (1957), reflejan *collages* sinuosos de texturas pródigas en transparencias y tonos vibrantes, emanadas del universo cual cambios astrales que llegan con los nuevos tiempos.

En los años sesenta y setenta, incorpora a sus acuarelas sobre cartulina composiciones geométricas violetas, rojas y azules girando alrededor de la órbita solar, son entes vivos que preceden sus códigos visuales de entre siglos, por ejemplo *Pescador, Bailarines* y *Gaviotas* (1960) y *Cononautas* (1978).

Por otra parte, algunas de las series pictóricas que ya venía desarrollando en etapas anteriores cobran mayor fuerza en su trabajo artístico, convirtiéndose en el eje fundamental de su poética. Las influencias del expresionismo, el cubismo, el dadaísmo, el *pop art*, el *op art* y el surrealismo, presentes en sus producciones de los años ochenta, se explicitan mucho más a partir de los noventa. Thelvia incursiona de nuevo en el *collage* y recrea las telas a partir de sus poemas y viceversa.

En el ámbito de esa copiosa producción pictórica, en 1997 nacen varias obras relacionadas con la temática del mudo espiritual. *La barca de Caronte* y *El ángel caído* son imágenes que en algunos casos sustentan caprichosos elementos arquitectónicos como arcos de medio punto, aldabas y vitrales en *Bajé al cielo*, y *Llamé al cielo y no me oyó*, junto a sus conocidos *Agua dulce, agua salá* es el paisaje tropical el que sustenta las sensuales representaciones de *Oshún*, *Yemayá*, y *Oya* (2000), esta última representada como la diosa del viento y de la entrada del cementerio.

Por su parte *Autorretrato* (1990), *Guitarra mujer* (1997) y una decena de bocetos femeninos testimonian toda la carga autorreferencial reinante en un segmento de su obra; al tiempo que el lienzo *Eólica* de 2001 inicia la serie Del Aire, resultante de estudios e investigaciones en torno a los fenómenos anómalos, la física cuántica y las complejas cosmogonías de diversas civilizaciones. que la condujeron a la ciencia poesía.

Sus telas, poemas y publicaciones, contenidos en el libro, reflejan la cosmogonía aborigen de los dioses *Bayamanaco, Cocorote, Atabey* o el *Dios del tabaco*, antecedentes directos de *Madre América* (2000), cuadro de extraordinaria belleza que resume a la madre tierra, a la *pachamama* y que es un proyecto escultórico que la autora aspira realizar, en bronce, en algún país del continente americano. Esta obra simboliza la estatua de la libertad de nuestra América, como la llamó Martí.

Nieves Leonard Pie
Profesional independiente en el sector Bellas Artes

Review Essay: *Valoración de la obra historiográfica de María del Carmen Barcia*

Por Jorge Ibarra Cuesta

Quizás todo empezó porque la profesora de historia de Cuba, María del Carmen Barcia deseaba comunicarse mejor con sus alumnos en la Universidad de La Habana. Las preguntas formuladas en el aula demandaban respuestas que iban más allá de la repetición de esquemas que aparecían en los manuales de historia. Por otra parte ella se había formado opiniones discrepantes sobre la obra de algunos historiadores cubanos y sobre ciertos criterios de sus colegas de cátedra. Por eso, la profesora debía buscar los testimonios del pasado en los archivos históricos de la ciudad que avalaran sus presupuestos e hicieran más interesantes e instructivas sus exposiciones. Era también el modo más adecuado para motivar a sus alumnos. En los archivos y bibliotecas encontró que sus presunciones sobre los juicios de los historiadores que había consultado para impartir sus clases, tenían cierto fundamento. En ocasiones debía adentrarse más tiempo del que disponía en la densa masa de documentos del período que estudiaba. Ella misma ha expuesto la relación inseparable que debe existir entre la enseñanza y la investigación:

Yo disfruto con enseñar a otros lo que he aprendido y aunque tengo una gran vocación por investigar, considero que la tarea del investigador no resulta completa hasta que no se confronta y un lugar ideal para establecer esa relación es el aula. Muchas soluciones a problemas que me he planteado las he hallado preparando mis clases o discutiendo con mis alumnos. Para instruir hay que saber explicar y ningún investigador puede convencer de sus resultados si no es capaz de exponerlos adecuadamente. Digo esto, porque en la enseñanza universitaria la relación docencia- investigación es esencial. Enseñar a pensar ha sido para mí una divisa, otra mantener una docencia, teórica y factual, actualizada y esto ha implicado un gran esfuerzo, pero también los alumnos lo agradecen.

Una revisión atenta de la obra de la profesora e historiadora, no puede obviar la relevancia que tienen las cuestiones teóricas y de método en sus investigaciones. Desde sus primeras publicaciones se observa un interés marcado en corroborar la validez de diferentes tesis y perspectivas en la *Historia de Cuba*. El título de su primera aproximación al pasado publicada en la *Revista de la Biblioteca Nacional José Martí* en 1980 lleva esa impronta: "Algunas cuestiones teóricas para el análisis del surgimiento y la crisis de la plantación esclavista". Otros artículos sobre la esclavitud, la fuerza de trabajo esclavo y el abolicionismo publicados subsiguientemente en *Islas*, en la revista *Santiago*, en la *Revista de Ciencias Sociales* se distinguen por su carácter conceptual y por el empleo de distintas hipótesis. Es este también el caso de un estudio monográfico suyo en el que destaca el carácter secundario de la esclavitud de plantaciones en América. Quizás lo más notable de esta contribución sea el amplio dominio que revela de la historiografía sobre la esclavitud de plantaciones en el Caribe y en Estados Unidos.[1] Nuestra colega no titubea en reconocer ciertas coincidencias de autores como Sweezey, Baran y Gunder Frank, académicos a los que la ortodoxia oficial soviética de la época les negaba la sal y el agua, con el pensamiento de Karl Marx. Su reconocimiento de los acercamientos de estos autores al marxismo no contradecía sus divergencias con ellos en más de un sentido.

El talante prudente con el cual la autora apreciaba las valoraciones parciales de los economistas y de otros científicos sociales sobre la esclavitud americana, evidencia la importancia que le atribuyó desde entonces a las investigaciones históricas concretas en el conocimiento de nuestras sociedades. Se trataba, ante todo, de esclarecer que los estudios de los economistas habían propiciado la estructuración de modelos, en los cuales, desde luego, las particularidades no tenían cabida. Le correspondía a los historiadores decir la última palabra en cuanto a la reconstitución de aspectos significativos del pasado. La colega consideraba también que los análisis sincrónicos y diacrónicos, de los economistas, realizados por separado, no rebasaban el análisis dialéctico. De ahí que se propusiera fusionar distintos análisis teóricos e históricos, en lo que consideraba una perspectiva dialéctica, para arribar a determinados resultados historiográficos. De acuerdo con ciertas premisas marxistas llegó a la conclusión que el sistema de plantaciones esclavista americano era un subsistema engendrado por el sistema capitalista mundial. Las relaciones esclavistas del Nuevo Mundo constituían un sistema secundario del capitalismo a escala mundial, "que el mismo genera, desarrolla y una vez agotadas todas sus posibilidades de racionalidad hace desaparecer por medio de sus propios mecanismos". Tal axioma parece cumplirse con exactitud en el caso de la esclavitud de las posesiones británicas del Caribe. Ahora bien, las medidas de Inglaterra, en tanta encarnación del capitalismo mundial, contra la trata de negros en Cuba y Brasil, parecen haber desempeñado un papel secundario, en relación con los factores internos que determinaron la desaparición de la esclavitud.

Estas primeras investigaciones sobre la plantación y la esclavitud durante la primera mitad del siglo XVIII y del XIX, van a encontrar su culminación en el importante estudio monográfico *Burguesía esclavista y abolición*. Estudiosos tan representativos de la historiografía cubana de los años cincuenta como el profesor Sergio Aguirre y el historiador Manuel Moreno Fraginals definían a los plantadores esclavistas cubanos, como una burguesía. Tal parecía como si los plantadores fueran tan sólo una ligera variante colonial de la burguesía europea. Un grupo de profesores de la Escuela de Historia, entre los que se encontraba María del Carmen Barcia, decidieron acercar más la noción de burguesía a la realidad colonial, añadiéndole el concepto de esclavista. En el caso de nuestra colega no prevalecía un espíritu ecléctico. Estaba conciente de las limitaciones del concepto por lo que expuso que aceptaba la denominación de burguesía esclavista provisoriamente "hasta tanto se encuentre otro que refleje más acertadamente las características de esta burguesía, carente en lo fundamental de proletariado".[2] Desconozco si a cuarenta años de la publicación de su libro, la profesora Barcia, siga sosteniendo el criterio que el plantador era un burgués en embrión, pero sería incurrir en el más absurdo de los nominalismos, negar la trascendencia de esta obra por el hecho que no estemos de acuerdo con su definición del plantador cubano.

Burguesía esclavista y abolición constituye una de las investigaciones más importantes realizadas sobre la esclavitud de plantaciones en el Caribe. La preferencia de la autora por el método histórico de análisis, a diferencia del método lógico definido por Engels, constituye una evidencia de su vocación historicista. Si bien en algunos capítulos de la obra se encuentran todavía huellas de la terminología del marxismo divulgativo, vigente durante los años sesenta en Cuba, la narración se atiene escrupulosamente en todo momento a las evidencias históricas.

Entre los aciertos más significativos de la obra se encuentra la exposición de aspectos cruciales de la política de clase de los plantadores y del poder colonial, que no habían sido tratados por los historiadores cubanos. Sus temas centrales son la fuerza de trabajo, el abolicionismo y la rentabilidad de la plantación. En ese último aspecto se opone al criterio generalizado en la historiografía cubana de que la crisis del sistema esclavista equivalía a la irrentabilidad de sus unidades económicas. En un estudio monográfico posterior publicado en 1980, la autora discutiría con su independencia de criterios habitual, los puntos de vista de Moreno Fraginals sobre la rentabilidad y la llamada crisis de la plantación esclavista.[3]

Participante de un proyecto de historia cuantitativa sobre la esclavitud con el profesor Laird Bernard de Lehman College de New York y la investigadora Fe Iglesias, de la Academia de Ciencias de Cuba, la profesora Barcia trabajó diversas fuentes en los archivos cubanos en los años comprendidos entre 1990 y 1994. El resultado de la investigación fue la publicación de un estudio sobre el mercado de esclavos cubano en el período 1790–1880.[4] A esos estudios acompañó una investigación sobre los proyectos de inmigración de españoles en la isla auspiciados por la Real Sociedad Económica de Amigos del País.[5]

A solicitud de la autora le fueron asignados los capítulos referidos al período 1868–1895, en el tomo sobre las luchas por la independencia nacional del Instituto de Historia de Cuba. La elección del tema era significativa.[6] Durante el decenio de 1990, se concentró en el estudio del período entre guerras, de relativa paz, de la segunda mitad del siglo XIX cubano. Hasta entonces la historiografía revolucionaria había preferido estudiar los períodos de grandes virajes y transformaciones sociales. La presencia del otro de nuestra historia colonial, o sea, de los sujetos históricos representativos o coincidentes con los intereses de la metrópoli hispánica, a duras penas atraían la atención de los estudiosos. De esa suerte los años comprendidos entre el estallido de la guerra de 1868 y el abandono de las tropas españolas de la isla en 1898, eran concebidos como un impetuoso *continuum* revolucionario, sin transiciones ni interrupciones de ningún genero. La visión lineal de cien años de lucha, sin cortes o períodos de estancamiento, no contribuía a que se tomara conciencia de los desafíos y enormes dificultades que debieron enfrentar en el pasado los hombres y mujeres que decidieron transformar la sociedad. Las actitudes retardatarias o rezagadas que se enfrentaron en el pasado encontraban su explicación con frecuencia en tradiciones y costumbres seculares sedimentadas en el inconciente colectivo.

Un examen detenido de esa otra cara del siglo XIX, demandaba una nueva perspectiva y nuevos métodos de investigación. La motivación más profunda que animaba a nuestra colega era proporcionarle un fundamento sociológico e histórico al proyecto investigativo anunciado por Juan Pérez de la Riva y Pedro Deschamp de escribir *La historia de la gente sin historia*. Los objetos concretos y los métodos de investigación de esa nueva historia debían ser aportados por quienes se decidieran a recorrer la nueva senda. La "historia en profundidad" del período entreguerras que anunciaba la historiadora en un artículo publicado en la revista *Temas*, suponía la localización de esos nuevos objetos de investigación y la implementación de esos nuevos métodos y técnicas.[7] Ya no se trataba de estudiar en detalle la vida de personajes históricos relevantes o de ensayar vastas generalizaciones a propósito de clases o naciones. Desde sus primeros ensayos investigativos la profesora Barcia se había acercado a sus temas de investigación motivada por un problema historiográfico a cuyo esclarecimiento deseaba contribuir. De ahí que el estudio del período de entreguerras constituyera un nuevo desafío a su quehacer investigativo.

La autora descubrió el objeto de su nueva investigación en el período comprendido entre 1878 y 1898, en las formas de sociabilidad, institucionales organizadas y espontáneas de grupos y capas sociales identificadas en torno a determinadas asociaciones o corporaciones.[8] Se debían reconstituir también los espacios públicos y privados en torno a los cuales los grupos y capas sociales se agrupaban y relacionaban entre sí y con las estructuras de poder político. La reconstrucción cuidadosa de las relaciones sociales presente en esas investigaciones dio pie a una crítica dogmática de acuerdo con la cual no se debía estudiar el entramado de las redes en los que se encontraban insertos los grupos y capas sociales, sino las luchas de clases. Ahora bien, los análisis realizados por la autora de las redes sociales, familiares y culturales se revela particularmente fecundo en tanto capta en sus particularidades la dialéctica de los enfrentamientos y conflictos sociales. De ese modo el estudio de las relaciones en las que se encuentran insertos los grupos y capas sociales, dista de ser una valoración estática del tejido social. Las redes sociales construyen lazos de solidaridad, que potencian la acción de los sujetos históricos. Lejos de inhibirlos o retraerlos de la participación social, los estimulan a que enfrenten los desafíos que se les presentan. Personajes históricos como Juan Gualberto Gómez, Rafael Serra y Morúa Delgado son valorados a la luz del contexto en que se movían, a través de las percepciones y el accionar de los personajes con los que se asociaban.

Los capítulos escritos por la autora para la *Historia de Cuba* del Instituto de Historia, constituyeron una visión de conjunto de algunos de los hechos políticos, sociales y culturales más relevantes del período entreguerras, que le permitieron acercarse a los sistemas de relaciones sociales de la segunda mitad del siglo XIX.

En *Élites y grupos sociales Cuba, 1878–1895*, la mirada se desplazaba hacia grupos sociales y pequeñas asociaciones, cuya función de representación y defensa de intereses colectivos más amplios, podía estudiarse empíricamente, de manera particularizada. En algunos casos sus actividades precedían históricamente a la aparición de los partidos políticos coloniales, en otros su praxis coexistía temporalmente con las funciones de representación más amplias de agrupaciones políticas de mayor predicamento. La proliferación de los grupos de presión y de interés, a partir de la instauración en 1879 de un régimen político bipartidista de libertades restringidas, daba cuenta de las dificultades que enfrentaban los partidos políticos en el ejercicio de sus actividades de representación. Por una parte, los grupos de presión substituían a los partidos políticos en la realización de determinadas funciones, por otra, ciertos estratos etnosociales y culturales, no se sentían representados por las formaciones políticas y se organizaban institucionalmente como grupos de interés de las capas populares y medias.

En cuanto a los grupos de presión la historiadora ha distinguido con exactitud la diversidad de objetivos, conductas y procedimientos del grupo de presión financiera integrado por Manuel Calvo y otros especuladores, con respecto a los grupos de interés corporativo, representativos de los designios económicos de la burguesía azucarera y tabacalera, lo que le ha permitido precisar las tendencias que se movían en torno a la política colonial. De manera parecida, el juego sutil que se establece entre el proceder de los grupos de presión financiera y los más orgánicos, de interés, por una parte, y de los partidos políticos, de otra, facilita distinguir su incidencia diversa en las decisiones de la metrópolis en cuanto a la isla. Si bien el interés de revelar como la política colonial española estaba dominada por grupos de especuladores, no por la burguesía insular, se logra a cabalidad, no sucede lo mismo en lo que respecta a la descripción del accionar de los grupos representativos de las capas populares.[9]

La conciencia de que esa ausencia debía ser reparada, se percibe en el prólogo de la historiadora a su próximo libro *Capas populares y modernidad en Cuba (1878–1939)*, en el que precisa como mientras el tiempo de las élites y de los grupos de presión, era nervioso, cambiante y creador, marcado por la impronta de la coyuntura, el de las capas populares era más lento y constante en el curso de una prolongada evolución. Una lección de método se desprendía de ese descubrimiento. La historiadora se había percatado de que "para comprender lo que cambiaba y la envergadura de esas mutaciones, era esencial observar lo que perduraba, ya que era éste el nivel en el que se inscribían las pertenencias de la sociabilidad, de las actitudes y representaciones colectivas".[10]

Entre los resultados de carácter general del estudio monográfico se encuentran las formas de sociabilidad de determinados grupos, estratos y clases, que tendían a perpetuarse a través del tiempo. Éstas se constituían a su vez en mecanismos de solidaridad interétnica, grupal, clasista y de defensa frente a otros grupos. De ahí su evolución, lenta y constante. Por otra parte, la relaciones étnicas y de género escindían a los grupos y estratos sociales y condicionaban actitudes diversas. La sociabilidad no se limita a la esfera pública formal, de carácter institucional organizativa, pues existían maneras informales y espontáneas de asociación. La sociabilidad en la esfera privada estaba íntimamente relacionada con la vida familiar y las relaciones de género.

El estudio institucional de la esfera pública donde se manifestaba la sociabilidad de los negros y mulatos comprendía la segunda mitad del siglo XIX y primeras décadas del XX.

Los conflictos más agudos que se manifiestan en este período se encuentran en la creciente competencia y rivalidad que implicaba la numerosa presencia de inmigrantes españoles en los oficios artesanales y empleos, que hasta entonces habían monopolizado los negros y mulatos. La promulgación de la Ley de Asociaciones en 1888, promovida por la coyuntura liberal de la península, motivó que las clases subalternas se agruparan en distintas sociedades. La mayor parte de las asociaciones que se registraron en el período fueron sindicatos y gremios, seguidos por sociedades de socorro mutuo, culturales, de recreación y benéficas. Tan importantes desde el punto de vista político como la fundación de veintinueve gremios que se constituyeron (entre ellos había ocho de tabaqueros y tres de carros de alquiler), fue la organización de los inmigrantes en los casinos españoles, fundados en 1868 con el propósito de nuclear a los trabajadores peninsulares frente al independentismo de los cubanos. La narración transcurre en esta primera parte del libro de acuerdo con cánones descriptivos tradicionales de hechos aportados a la historiografía de la clase obrera cubana por Rivero Muñiz y Aleida Plasencia. Se enfatizan, sin embargo, ciertos hechos que apenas han sido discutidos, como la forma en que los obreros rehusaban defender a las mujeres que compartían sus tareas en las fábricas frente a la patronal. La autora destaca también las críticas del periódico obrero *El Productor de Roig* San Martín al ñañiguismo y la negativa de los gremios a defender los derechos de los negros. La mayor parte de los gremios anarquistas se pronunciaban por el desplazamiento de los obreros criollos, blancos y negros, a favor de los obreros españoles.

La investigación de los centros regionales pone de relieve hechos que incidieron significativamente en la integración cultural y social de los inmigrantes españoles a fines del siglo XIX y principios del XX. Entre 1841 y 1892, se fundan centros de beneficencia y socorros mutuos de catalanes, asturianos, canarios, andaluces, montañeses, vascos y castellanos. Los comerciantes e industriales españoles con frecuencia presiden y forman parte de las directivas de esos centros de recreación y beneficencia. Los proyectos modernizadores de esos centros se manifestaron con la fundación de escuelas, bibliotecas y quintas de salud.

En la obra se acentúa con razón el carácter modernizador de esos proyectos y las múltiples acciones culturales que promovían. En 1929 había noventa y dos centros benéficos y de socorros mutuos. que prestaban servicios de salud y propiciaban la recreación de sus afiliados. Las familias criollas de los inmigrantes se beneficiaban de estos servicios. Esa parecía ser la única cara de los centros de beneficencia, pero ¿acaso no se alineaban la mayoría de ellos, presididos por personalidades de la burguesía española, con la política orientada por el *Diario de la Marina*, de darle las espaldas a los problemas del país?

El estudio de las sociedades de negros y mulatos destaca su proliferación. En 1887 había llegado a 139. De acuerdo con la autora, las negras y mulatas se manifestaban de una manera más liberada que las blancas, fundando sus propias asociaciones de forma independiente. ¿Acaso esa actitud guardaba relación con el hecho que sentían más la necesidad de liberarse en tanto eran más oprimidas por sus contrapartes? ¿Guardaba relación su carácter más independiente con el hecho que las blancas se encontraban más sometidas por sus parejas?, ¿o bien se trataba de una tradición de autonomía procedente de las familias matriarcales africanas? Un estudio posterior de la autora revelaba que en los cabildos de nación, las mujeres negras desempeñaban un papel mucho más activo y protagónico que las mujeres blancas en el espacio público de los siglos XVIII y primera mitad del XIX.

Como sugiere el relato los nombres de las sociedades de color en las décadas de 1880 y 1890 indicaban una orientación más progresista y patriótica que los gremios, sindicatos y sociedades de beneficencia, ya fuese de españoles o criollos blancos. Había cuatro que se denominaban *El Progreso*, tres *El Porvenir*, tres *La Igualdad* y seis *La Unión*. Otras llevaban el nombre de mambíes negros: cinco se designaban Antonio Maceo uno Guillermón Moncada, uno José Maceo y uno Juan Gualberto Gómez. No parece haber sido casual que setenta sociedades de negros y mulatos se fundieran en el Directorio Central de las Sociedades de Color y que teniendo como base las relaciones creadas entre ellos por su director, Juan Gualberto Gómez, se tejiera la red conspirativa del movimiento revolucionario que estallaría en 1895. La autora escudriñó activamente en la documentación de la época para dilucidar si el directorio fue constituido con finalidad conspirativa y encontró en la correspondencia del colaborador de Juan Gualberto, José León de Quesada evidencias en ese sentido.

En el texto se consignan las críticas de destacados dirigentes negros y mulatos progresistas, a determinadas tradiciones africanas en la décadas de 1880 y de 1900. No eran sólo los blancos racistas los que se oponían a las usanzas culturales de los negros.

Los pronunciamientos aparecidos en *La Fraternidad* y *El Nuevo Criollo*, los periódicos dirigidos respectivamente por Juan Gualberto Gómez y Rafael Serra, condenaban determinadas actitudes y expresiones de la cultura originaria y del folclore del negro en nombre del progreso y la civilización. Pudieran incluso reproducirse otras manifestaciones críticas más moderadas aparecidas en el periódico de los Independientes de Color, *Previsión*. No se muestra tampoco interés en revisar las tradiciones culturales originarias con el propósito de incorporar lo más valioso al acervo cultural del presente. Los testimonios del pensamiento negro están planteando un problema historiográfico de primer orden. ¿Se renegaba por completo de las raíces africanas?, ¿o se trataba tan sólo de ciertas manifestaciones culturales extrañas y chocantes a la nueva sensibilidad forjada en el proceso de transculturación nacional? ¿Acaso los criollos blancos no habían renunciado a ciertas tradiciones culturales hispánicas como los toros, luego de criticarlas en los términos más severos?, o bien ¿no se había alejado gran parte de la población criolla blanca en la época colonial de los sacramentos religiosos de la Iglesia para implantar en sus hogares altares de la cruz y practicar el culto a ciertos iconos religiosos transculturados? ¿No fue desde la década de 1930 que se realizaron investigaciones sociológicas y antropológicas del negro y de su acervo cultural originario con el propósito de valorar los fundamentos de la sabiduría tradicional africana?

De acuerdo con la autora se trataba de una disyuntiva que se les presentaba a los dirigentes negros del movimiento de liberación nacional, que habían luchado hombro con hombro con los patriotas blancos por treinta años para constituir una nación con todos y para el bien de todos. A los efectos de lograr la integración plena y la igualdad de derechos, era preciso el progreso cultural del negro. De acuerdo con la autora los dirigentes negros consideraban, "la enseñanza como el medio idóneo para superar a los grupos 'de color' y permitirles la movilidad social a la que aspiraban. Por esa razón fueron los primeros en criticar las costumbres y practicas ancestrales arraigadas entre los negros y mestizos más humildes, como los bailes y ceremonias africanas, cuyas expresiones más comunes consideraban una forma de atraso".[11] Desde luego la cuestión a esclarecer sería en que medida se sacrificaban las raíces culturales o sólo algunas de sus manifestaciones, en aras de lograr una integración en igualdad de condiciones entre blancos y negros. El carácter utópico del proyecto está fuera de duda, pero la posición de los dirigentes progresistas negros demanda una valoración comprensiva.

El problema historiográfico enunciado por la autora desbroza el camino a nuevas investigaciones que develen el discurso progresista en todos sus matices con respecto a las tradiciones ancestrales africanas. El mestizaje cultural al que aspiraban Juan Gualberto, Serra y Morua, sería resultado del largo proceso de transculturación nacional, más allá de sus pronunciamientos, en ocasiones fuera de tono, con relación a las manifestaciones culturales ancestrales.

El estudio de las formas de sociabilidad informal y familiar, le plantearon a la autora una diversidad de problemas que la historiografía cubana no se había propuesto investigar. Indagaciones de esa envergadura requerirían la organización institucional de equipos multidisciplinarios. No obstante, la historiadora sienta las premisas para un proyecto de investigaciones basado en determinados presupuestos de método y en los resultados alcanzados por sociólogos e historiadores consagrados al estudio de la familia.

El análisis de la estructura familiar en los censos y padrones, presenta dificultades de naturaleza distinta. La mayor parte de los inconvenientes están relacionados con las concepciones que tenían los enumeradores del censo sobre la residencia como base de la familia cubana y no las relaciones consanguíneas de parentesco. No obstante, como bien destaca nuestra colega algunos padrones anteriores al siglo XX, evidencian que la convivencia entre personas que no guardaban relaciones de consanguinidad, que comían de una misma olla y habitaban bajo un mismo techo, fue un modo de vida bastante generalizado en el caso de negros y mestizos y también debió serlo en algunos grupos de inmigrantes.

La revelación en la obra de datos apenas discutidos por los estudiosos de la familia, plantea nuevas cuestiones. Así, el hecho que de acuerdo con el un padrón de 1870 en el Barrio de San Isidro sólo el 6,15 por ciento de las familias negras y mulatas estuvieran casadas, evidencia que la iglesia católica apenas tenía influencia sobre la población negra y mulata para hacerla cumplir uno de sus principales sacramentos.[12] En una verificación posterior realizada por la propia autora en un padrón de esclavos que radicaban en extramuros, se reveló que en un total de ochenta y cuatro cedulas sólo dos estaban casados legalmente, veintidós vivían unidos consensualmente, sin hijos, veinticuatro constituían familias de tipo nuclear sobre la base de uniones consensuales y treinta y seis eran mujeres solteras que vivían solas con sus hijos, de modo que los casados legalmente por la Iglesia, constituían sólo el 2,3 por ciento del total. En ese sentido lo más significativo es que desde el siglo XVI el estado y la iglesia se habían consagrado en cuerpo y alma a la represión institucional de las uniones consensuales, o sea, de los concubinatos, a lo que se sumaba el interés eclesiástico en recaudar los derechos por concepto de casamientos. El hecho de por sí cuestiona las aseveraciones formuladas sobre una supuesta matriz religiosa católica que dominara el imaginario y las creencias de los pardos y morenos habaneros. De manera similar pone en tela de juicio la aserción de que el culto de los íconos religiosos de la iglesia por negros y mulatos, supusiera una adopción por éstos de los valores católicos.

La mirada atenta de la historiadora se desplaza por doquier para descubrir las redes de solidaridad y las actitudes de la población negra y mulata pobre ante los problemas cruciales de la supervivencia.

En su estudio del padrón de 1870 de familias del barrio de San Isidro, en La Habana, destaca cómo entre los cuarenta y seis miembros de una unidad residencial había tres núcleos familiares fácilmente identificables que tenían en total, veintidós miembros, casi la mitad de los habitantes de la casa, relacionados con los otros por la vía marital o filial. La otra mitad de los habitantes no guardaba relaciones de parentesco. De acuerdo con la historiadora, en esa cuartería se reunían familias relacionadas entre sí a partir de una estrategia de supervivencia, que constituía verdaderas redes de solidaridad entre los pobres. La situación descrita en el domicilio referido se repite en otros investigados por la autora.

Los grandes números de los censos tienden a confirmar las tendencias observada en los padrones habaneros. El promedio de personas por domicilio en La Habana fue registrado en los censos; en 1861 era de 14,8, en 1899, 11,5 y en 1907, 10,6, lo que confirmaba las amplitud de las relaciones de solidaridad que se tejían entre las familias pobres. En el censo de 1861 se dejaba sentir todavía la presencia de profusas dotaciones de esclavos en las residencias de sus amos, al lado de las cuarterías y solares donde se alojaban muchas familias extensas. El censo de 1899 siguió registrando un alto promedio de personas por domicilio. Tal hecho evidenciaba después de la abolición de la esclavitud, el predominio de familias pobres extensas, integradas por numerosos parientes consanguíneos y por afinidad.

Otros resultados valiosos de la investigación en base al estudio de los censos y padrones estuvieron relacionados con las relaciones de género, los hijos ilegítimos, el desplazamiento laboral de la población negra y mulata por la inmigración española, la temprana integración de la mujer negra en el mercado laboral y la alteración profunda que esto significó en las familias.

A María del Carmen Barcia no le gusta dejar nada en el tintero, de ahí que con frecuencia vuelva sobre sus pasos para tratar algún asunto inconcluso. Los planteamientos de método que formuló sobre la base de las relaciones de parentesco y familiares, serán puestos en práctica en una investigación sobre la familia esclava. La obra publicada bajo el título *La otra familia. Parientes, redes y descendencia de los esclavos en Cuba* fue premiada en el concurso de ensayo histórico-social de la Casa de las Américas del año 2005.

El gran tema a debatir en este estudio monográfico precursor es el de la existencia de la familia esclava, ignorada o negada con frecuencia por algunos autores. La investigación supondrá una crítica a las concepciones apresuradas y prematuras que atribuyen el surgimiento de la familia monogámica a la entrada en escena de la modernidad burguesa. Basada en las evidencias antropológicas más recientes, la historiadora sostiene que la familia conyugal o nuclear era el tipo de familia que existía en la mayor parte de las regiones de donde procedían los negros introducidos por la trata en el Nuevo Mundo. De manera parecida se adscribe al criterio que la poligamia era practicada en las familias bantúes sólo por una minoría de hombres poderosos que podían sostener a varias mujeres. La pareja monogámica era la relación conyugal más usual entre las distintas etnias africanas. El adulterio no era aceptado y nada los obligaba a vivir casados de por vida como prescribía la Iglesia Católica, pero las uniones consensuales tendían a prolongarse en el tiempo. Los vínculos podían disolverse por una variedad de motivos. No creían en la virginidad.

Otro punto de vista generalizado criticado por la autora es que el único tipo de relaciones familiares que pudo sobrevivir entre los negros y mulatos en Cuba fue el de la familia matrifocal, de padre desconocido, ausente e incapaz de sostenerla. De esa manera, esta investigación pionera da los primeros pasos en un terreno en el que apenas habían incursionado los fundadores de los estudios antropológicos en Cuba, el tema de la familia negra.

La refutación de los criterios expuestos por la historiografía esclavista en el Nuevo Mundo se llevara a cabo teniendo como base los padrones y censos de los siglos XVIII y XIX, así como diversos testimonios de la época e investigaciones antropológicas e históricas realizadas por otros autores de Estados Unidos, Brasil y el área del Caribe. Entre los mitos sobre la familia de ancestros africanos referidos por Bennet, que la autora rebate en el caso de Cuba de manera consistente, se encuentran los siguientes:

- El mito del sexo puro e incontrolado entre los negros
- El mito de que los negros llegaron de África sin sentido de moralidad y sin antecedentes de relaciones sexuales estables
- El mito de que la familia negra es producto del paternalismo de sus amos y de las normas de decencia inculcadas por los blancos,
- El mito de que la familia negra ha sido siempre matriarcal y se ha caracterizado por mujeres fuertes dominantes y por hombres débiles y ausentes
- El mito de que los hombres negros no son capaces de establecer relaciones estables de parentesco

Luego de establecer las enormes dificultades que debieron enfrentar los negros para instituir relaciones familiares, de acuerdo con los diversos patrones originales procedentes de distintas etnias africanas, la autora recogerá evidencias variadas que muestran como se estructuraron finalmente las familias en Cuba durante el período esclavista y con posterioridad.

Uno de los hechos reiterados en la documentación, es la resistencia de los esclavos y sus descendientes a aceptar de buen grado las normas culturales impuestas o sugeridas por las autoridades y sus amos que no se aviniesen con los valores centrales de sus culturas originarias. Un ejemplo paradigmático es el de los matrimonios legales impuestos por la Iglesia a los esclavos. Si bien estos debían obedecer las ordenes de sus amos, la gente de color libre declinaba con frecuencia contraer matrimonio religioso y establecía relaciones estables de tipo consensual. Así, de acuerdo con una investigación citada por la autora de 1585 a 1684, el 32,2 por ciento de los matrimonios realizados en La Habana eran de negros esclavos mientras sólo el 2,76 por ciento eran de negros horros, y un 6,18 por ciento entre negros esclavos y libres.[13] El censo de 1827 parece confirmar esa tendencia en tanto el 38 por ciento del total de matrimonios realizados en toda la isla eran llevados a cabo entre esclavos y sólo el 11 por ciento por libres de color.

Las relaciones familiares no sólo conformaban los patrones típicos de conducta y transmitían los hábitos y costumbres tradicionales de generación en generación, sino que constituían la argamasa que unía a las instituciones fundamentales de los negros y mulatos libres en la colonia: cabildos, cofradías y batallones de milicias. La autora toma nota de este hecho cuando estudia las redes de parentesco en estas instituciones de la sociedad colonial.

Ahora bien, el estudio del conjunto de las uniones conyugales establecidas por esclavos y libres, negros y mulatos, revela aun más el predominio incontestable de uniones consensuales estables, fuera de la Iglesia. De acuerdo con el censo de 1861 sólo el 6,15 por ciento de las familias libres de color estaban casadas por la iglesia. En la medida que en las plantaciones cubanas no existían registros de las familias esclavas como en las plantaciones británicas, la autora no ha podido distinguir los distintos tipos de familias esclavas integradas por hombres, mujeres e hijos de las integradas sólo por las madres y sus hijos. A los efectos de refutar los criterios sobre una poliginia desenfrenada en las plantaciones, la autora se remite a la investigación de Higman sobre las familias esclavas en Jamaica. De acuerdo con este estudio las familias de esclavos presididas por el padre representaban un 31,2 por ciento del total, mientras que las presididas por la madre, por ausencia de un padre, eran el 11,5 por ciento. Otras familias integradas por la mujer, los hijos y nietos, pudieran tratarse en algunos casos de madres que nunca constituyeron familias con un hombre o bien de viudas. Las investigaciones de Craton en Bahamas arrojan un saldo más favorable para las familias regidas por el hombre en tanto constituían el 54,1 por ciento, mientras las presididas por una mujer sin hombre, constituían sólo el 12,5 por ciento y el 11,9 por ciento a familias integradas por miembros de tres generaciones, incluyendo nietos.[14]

Pudiera argumentarse contra los criterios de la autora que la forma en que se organizaban las familias dependía de la voluntad de los amos y que los plantadores ingleses no pensaban igual que los plantadores criollos y españoles de Cuba. Ahora bien, la actitud observada por estos últimos con relación a sus dotaciones de esclavos en el período comprendido entre 1827 y 1861 pudiera ilustrarnos a propósito de la manera en que se constituían las familias de esclavos en Cuba. El hecho que durante esos años los amos no mostraran interés en casar a sus esclavos por la iglesia, a pesar de las recomendaciones de las autoridades y de los prelados en ese sentido y de que el matrimonio constituía un medio de control social efectivo, en una etapa caracterizada por las protestas esclavas, sugiere que estos a penas intervenían en el tipo de familias que constituían los esclavos. Como es sabido en ese período las relaciones entre los plantadores occidentales y sus dotaciones de esclavos estuvieron sujetas a duras pruebas. La conspiración de la Escalera, las sublevaciones de esclavos de 1844 y la represión desatada por los amos aconsejaba que se apelara a una diversidad de medios entre los que se encontraban los matrimonios, para calmar sus dotaciones.

Los datos que proporciona la historiadora a propósito de las relaciones porcentuales de matrimonios con respecto al número de esclavos, de acuerdo con los censos de 1827 y 1861, nos permite formarnos una idea de la actitud que observaron los plantadores con relación a sus siervos durante ese lapso de tiempo. De la misma manera la declinación del número de matrimonios de la población libre de color durante esos años, ilustra sobre la forma en que recusaban los valores y normas culturales de la iglesia y de sus amos. Así mientras en 1827, los esclavos contrajeron el 34 por ciento de los matrimonios, en 1860 habían descendido al 5,31 por ciento, lo que evidencia una creciente falta de interés de los amos en intervenir en sus asuntos familiares. Los negros y mulatos libres se alejaron de una manera más acentuada de los sacramentos de la iglesia. Así, mientras en 1827 un 11 por ciento de todos los matrimonios en La Habana habían sido contraídos por estos, en 1861, sólo alcanzaron un 4 por ciento del total de matrimonios efectuados ese año.

Quizás lo más significativo de los matrimonios fuera el hecho que los casados constituían probablemente una reducida minoría con relación al número total de esclavos y de gente de color libre solteros.

En 1860 se empadronaron un total de 105.404 pardos y morenos libres, varones y hembras, en la región occidental, de los cuales 17.767 de ambos sexos estaban casados por la iglesia para un 16,8 por ciento del total.

Ese mismo año se censaron un total de 301.402 esclavos, hembras y varones, de los cuales 25.405 de ambos sexos estaban casados legalmente para un 6,4 por ciento del total.[15]

Los esclavos casados por la iglesia no tenían una representación importante, por lo que suponemos que un porcentaje mayor debió haber constituido familias nucleares sobre la base de relaciones consensuales o bien familias matrifocales.

La minuciosa reconstrucción de familias de esclavos que reproduce la autora en el libro ofrece una perspectiva distinta. De veintitrés familias de esclavos reconstruidas, doce constituían familias nucleares de esclavos casados por la iglesia, siete eran familias basadas en relaciones consensuales, tres eran familias matrifocales y en uno no se consigna el tipo de conyugales existentes.

De todas formas el tipo de familia predominante en la investigación es la nuclear, bien como resultados de matrimonios legales o de relaciones consensuales. La matrifocalidad no parece constituir una relación mayoritaria en la obra, aun cuando la autora declara que "la mayor parte de las familias se consolidaban al margen de la legitimidad. La mayor parte de estos núcleos fueron matrifocales, aunque llama la atención que un número apreciable puede caracterizarse como nuclear, teniendo en cuenta la relación estable de pareja, que en algunos casos se conformaba legalmente". El origen de estas formulaciones hipotéticas deductivas será esclarecido debidamente por la autora que no deja sus asuntos pendientes.

Los resultados de la investigación cobran su verdadera dimensión cuando se pasa a fundamentar las hipótesis centrales. Su designio ha sido "valorar la continuidad de las estructuras de parentesco entre los negros y los mulatos y el papel que desempeñaron como transmisoras de valores culturales". Como se demuestra reiteradamente los vínculos familiares forjados en la sociedad esclavista crearon redes de solidaridad y afecto entre los esclavos y entre la gente de color libre que tenían su génesis con frecuencia en las tradiciones culturales africanas. Tales vínculos no tenían su fundamento sólo en las relaciones de parentesco basadas en la consanguinidad, sino también en las de afinidad, creadas por los negros para enfrentar colectivamente la difícil situación por la que atravesaban.

Un proyecto investigativo tan extenso demandaba la reconstrucción de numerosas familias de esclavos y de libres de color, a partir de los procesos judiciales, las actas de bautismo y otras fuentes, que permitieran una aproximación a lo que María del Carmen Barcia denomina "las formas destacadas de solidaridad, las estrategias de supervivencia, y las conductas que reflejan las relaciones estrechas y amorosas entre padres, hijos y hermanos y también con comportamientos reprobables".

En ese contexto tendieron a prevalecer las relaciones de cooperación y de protección mutua. La aparición de conductas criticables tenía su origen con frecuencia en la ruptura de los lazos solidarios.

Otro estigma, que los estudios sobre la esclavitud han hecho recaer sobre los esclavos y los negros y mulatos libres son las relaciones de concubinato generalizadas en que vivían. Ahora bien, este tipo de relaciones como se demuestra en la obra, no era privativo de la población de origen africano y era frecuente entre los blancos pobres y personalidades del patriciado criollo.

Sólo una mirada desprejuiciada y una voluntad obstinada podían desentrañar la densa capa de falsedades y prejuicios raciales que se acumulaban en la bibliografía y en la documentación referida a las relaciones de parentesco de los negros y mulatos.

En *Los ilustres apellidos: Negros en la Habana colonial*, el interés se concentra en los cabildos, cofradías y batallones de milicias de pardos y morenos en la sociedad colonial. En el relato no se recogen los hechos con el designio de tejer un recuento sucesivo, ascendente, de ocurrencias, que nos conduzca de la mano hasta la modernidad. No vale la pena relatar como transcurrían esos hechos, si no se esclarecía cómo se relacionaban de una manera significativa. De lo que se trataba era de reconstituir la vida asociativa e institucional de los negros y mulatos libres en la colonia. De ahí la necesidad de reconstruir la manera en que se vinculaban entre sí, cómo evolucionaban sus relaciones, qué sentido tenía en la época el reconocimiento social de los estamentos subalternos, cuál era el designio colonial de abrir espacios públicos a los africanos libres, cómo trascendían los excluidos la segregación racial, cuáles eran sus diferendos con el poder colonial, cómo se preservaban las normas de la cultura original, cómo se asimilaban por los descendientes de africanos las normas de la cultura hispana, cómo se fusionaban las creencias religiosas africanas con el catolicismo, cómo se estructuraban las relaciones de parentesco, de genero y de estatus en los cabildos, cofradías y milicias, cuál era el imaginario de la población de color libre, qué pensaban y qué sentían.

Sólo pueden ensayarse respuestas a tales interrogantes cuando se intercambia con otras disciplinas como la antropología, la sociología, la sociolingüística. El solo hecho de enumerarlas, deja ver que nos encontramos ante uno de los proyectos más alentadores de la historiografía cubana en los últimos años.

La primera pregunta que subtiende la narración guarda relación con los distintos designios del poder colonial y del estamento de la gente libre de color en los espacios públicos. ¿Cuál fue el propósito de las autoridades coloniales cuando fundaron los cabildos de nación y las cofradías de color? Sabemos por la autora que en Sevilla desde principios del siglo XVI se habían creado por las autoridades, cabildos de nación y cofradías religiosos para que la numerosa población negra (un 7,5 por ciento del vecindario) pudiera rendir culto a sus divinidades y recrear sus actividades culturales. El experimento sevillano se transfirió al Nuevo Mundo, pero desconocemos la razón que motivó a las autoridades coloniales a recrear esas asociaciones religiosas en Cuba. ¿Acaso los africanos emancipados practicaban sus cantos, bailes y ritos religiosos de manera muy ostentosa y ruidosa? ¿Cómo prohibirles que lo hicieran si eran libres? ¿Cómo controlarlos? ¿Cómo llegar a un entendimiento con los exesclavos, que les permitiese practicar sus creencias de modo que no se pusiera en peligro la tranquilidad y seguridad pública? Esas disyuntivas debieron influir en la adopción de la institución sevillana. Ahora bien, lo que se puso de manifiesto una vez que se instituyeron los cabildos de nación y las cofradías, fue el más rígido control por parte de las autoridades. Los africanos libres debían ser estrictamente vigilados, intervenidos y separados del resto de la población esclava y criolla libre.

La autora nos lo cuenta de manera resumida: "Los cabildos fueron formas asociativas destinadas a segregar a los negros africanos de su entorno, a controlarlos y también a dividirlos entre si pues estaba regulado que se organizasen por etnias . . . "

Se prohibió el ingreso de esclavos y criollos a los cabildos, en tanto debilitaba su control y unía a los negros más allá de la rígida segregación impuesta por las autoridades entre africanos y criollos, libres y esclavos. Los cabildos podían plantearse la dirección hegemónica y representación de la gente de color frente a las autoridades. De acuerdo con la autora la presencia de criollos y esclavos y de prácticas transculturales en los cabildos de la tierra adentro se explicaba porque allí no se albergaban tantos temores con respecto a los negros. De manera parecida los cabildos sólo se podían instituir mediante licencia real. Durante la segunda mitad del siglo XVIII y el siglo XIX, se decretaron una sucesión de bandos por los capitanes generales, dictaminando la ubicación de los cabildos en la periferia de la ciudad. No se quería tener a la vista de los vecinos las reuniones de los cabildos, que si bien eran toleradas, su presencia era sufrida o soportada, nunca deseada. Por eso no se querían en las cercanías de los centros urbanos. Desde luego, el alejamiento de la mirada de los blancos favorecía la preservación de las creencias religiosas africanas. Los cabildos constituyeron para los africanos un factor cohesionador que contribuyó a la preservación de sus variados universos simbólicos. De manera parecida, se prohibían con frecuencia hacer bailes y llantos en honor de sus muertos o la de velar con fiestas el sueño final de sus parvulitos. A diferencia de los negros que pensaban que la muerte elegía a sus predilectos para evitarle una vida de miserias, por lo que debían festejar su fallecimiento, los blancos consideraban inmoral esa conducta.

Las cofradías estuvieron adscriptas a las parroquias, bajo la supervisión de sus sacerdotes desde su fundación a fines del siglo XVI. Las cofradías tenían su residencia en los templos, mientras los cabildos tenían sus propias casas En La Habana a las cofradías les estaba permitido participar en las procesiones religiosas mentras que a los cabildos les estaba prohibido desfilar. En la tierra adentro, sin embargo, los cabildos podían participar en las procesiones tanto en las calles, como asistir a las iglesias. Las cofradías podían ser de pardos y de morenos, así como de morenos solos o de pardos solos. Estas últimas estaban animadas de un espíritu segregacionista, en tanto se separaban unos con respecto a otros. No podían dejar de pagar sus derechos por ninguna causa. Para reunirse debía estar presente el sacerdote de la parroquia a la que pertenecían.

Uno de los resultados más novedosos de la investigación lo constituye la dilucidación del papel activo que desempeñaban las mujeres en los cabildos, a diferencia de las mujeres blancas en el espacio público y en las asociaciones de la población blanca. La fortaleza de los vínculos de solidaridad en esas asociaciones de la población negra y mulata es el resultado en gran medida de las gestiones de las mujeres. Las funciones referidas no parecen estar desligadas del papel que desempeñaban en las sociedades africanas de origen.

Las cuestiones que se plantearon las autoridades con respecto a los batallones de color fueron de otra naturaleza. Ya no se trataba de integrar de una manera segregada y subordinada a la población negra y mulata, para vigilarla y controlarla de acuerdo con los fines del dominio colonial. La defensa de las posesiones hispánicas del Mar Caribe frente a las asechanzas y agresiones de las potencias europeas rivales, demandaba la participación de la población de color en la protección del orden colonial. La contribución de los batallones de pardos y morenos a la preservación del poder de España frente a las amenazas externas, suponía un trato distinto a sus oficiales y soldados. La movilidad social de los pardos y morenos estuvo íntimamente relacionada con su pertenencia a las milicias. Como señala la autora: "Esa fue la vía de ascenso más generalizada para disfrutar de algunos privilegios pequeños pero importantes y la oportunidad de obtener cierto reconocimiento de la sociedad en su conjunto". De hecho las luchas por el reconocimiento social, no suponían actitudes de deferencia frente al poder colonial, aunque pudieran manifestarse. Se trataba, ante todo, de alcanzar la nivelación o igualación en el trato con los blancos. Las luchas de los negros y mulatos estaban encaminadas a mostrar que poseían iguales o parecidas cualidades a las de los que acaparaban todo el prestigio y consideración social. Como destaca la autora: "Todos estos espacios de sociabilidad se inscribían en una peculiar dialéctica de la negociación entre el poder colonial y los grupos excluidos. Para el primero, se trataba de establecer mecanismos de control. Para los segundos, se trataba de ganar minúsculos territorios de influencia, de legitimación social y, en última instancia, de prestigio".

El servicio de las armas constituía un servicio a la comunidad frente a los enemigos de España. Se servía al rey, pero, ante todo, se dispensaban servicios a la patria. Tanto la sociedad insular como la monarquía debían reconocer los méritos de los que ofrendaban las vidas por la seguridad colectiva. La pertenencia de los negros y mulatos a los batallones de milicias constituía el medio más idóneo para que éstos fueran reconocidos por todos. De acuerdo con la clasificación de Gurvitch este tipo de sociabilidad se correspondería con un tipo de sociabilidad institucional organizada basada en el criterio combinado de "servicio con vistas al interés general o con vistas al interés particular".[16]

Ahora bien, los trabajos prestados por la gente de color a la comunidad insular no se limitaban al servicio de las armas. Los servicios y bienes producidos por el artesanado, negro y mulato, constituían la base del bienestar y la estabilidad de la comunidad insular. La conservación de las posesiones hispánicas en el caribe dependía no sólo del poderío militar español y de la gestión económica rectora del patriciado criollo. La autora demuestra en que medida la gente libre de color constituyó un protagonista olvidado por la historiografía cubana.

La trascendencia de las relaciones que se anudaran en torno al artesanado y a las milicias es expuesta en el estudio cuantitativo de los oficios que tenían los oficiales de los batallones de pardos y morenos. La oficialidad de la milicia de color estaba formada íntegramente por los gremios de los carpinteros, zapateros, talabarteros, albañiles, sastres, canteros, labradores, herreros, pintores, plateros y escribientes. Los testimonios de las autoridades citados en el texto dan cuenta de la conciencia que tenía el poder colonial de la importancia estratégica de la incorporación a la milicia de la gente de color. Los batallones de color, no sólo participarán decisivamente en la defensa de la isla, en ocasión de la invasión de Vernon a la región oriental de o de la toma de La Habana por los ingleses, sino que se desempeñará en acciones militares en Nueva Orleans (1777), en Pensacola (1781), en la Isla de Providencia (1782), en Santo Domingo (1793–1796), en los Apalaches 1802 y en San Agustín en la Florida (1810–1821) y en operaciones navales en el área del Caribe.

Desde luego, el reconocimiento de la significación que tenía su participación en la defensa de la isla, no podía traducirse en una relación igualitaria para la clase subalterna. Si bien el fuero militar privilegiaba a los pardos y morenos en algunos aspectos, el trato al que eran acreedoras las milicias blancas era siempre preferencial. No sólo el salario era doble, sino que eran privilegiados en todos los aspectos de la vida militar.

La reputación social constituía en los primeros siglos de dominio colonial un capital de tanto o más valor que el capital en metálico. La importancia que tenía la militancia en la milicia se evidencia en los numerosos testimonios relativos al hecho que los pardos y morenos, preferían comprar sus uniformes a que el estado colonial se los dotase. Por real cédula de 12 de septiembre de 1818 se decretó que los individuos de color tenían derecho que se les concediesen grados en las milicias mediante gratificación, por lo que se presentaran un aluvión de solicitudes con el objeto de comprar los cargos de oficiales. Era un medio de alcanzar una posición de prestigio, lo que era considerado más importante que dispensar una cantidad elevada de dinero. Para los descendientes de los esclavos, no había un hecho que redimiera o desagraviara más a los hombres y mujeres de su condición, que las autoridades y los amos blancos tuvieran que depender de ellos para la defensa del territorio insular común. El interés de los pardos y morenos por usar charreteras e insignias de colores rutilantes distaba de ser pueril, pues los segregacionistas se indignaban por la concesión de tales reconocimientos, en tanto entendían que con ellos se igualaban a los blancos.

La reconstrucción histórica por María del Carmen Barcia de los sistemas de relaciones de las asociaciones religiosas de la gente de color ha sido posible por un estudio casuístico detallado de la legislación colonial, las disposiciones de las autoridades, las reclamaciones, solicitudes y actos legales de los cabildos. El examen acucioso de la documentación pertinente ha posibilitado la elaboración minuciosa de tablas de decenas de cabildos y cofradías de las más diversas etnias con la fechas de su fundación en los siglos XVIII y XIX y los nombres de sus capataces, matronas y miembros. La investigación entrecruzada de los nombres y apellidos de cientos de integrantes de los cabildos, cofradías, gremios y batallones de color ha permitido identificar las redes que se tejían entre las asociaciones religiosas, los gremios de artesanos y los batallones de color y definir la importancia corporativa de las actividades institucionales de los pardos y morenos. Eran muy pocos los oficiales de batallones de color, que no fueran a la vez, miembros de una cofradía, un cabildo o un gremio artesano. Las redes familiares constituían un factor adicional que contribuía decisivamente a la cohesión de la vida social de la gente de color. Las familias negras acaudaladas habían consolidado sus fortunas a través de matrimonios bien concertados con otras familias negras de buena posición económica. Si a eso se añadían los lazos que habían trenzado sus miembros como miembros de cofradías, cabildos, gremios y milicias, nos encontramos con que se habían forjado redes muy fuertes y eficaces entre la gente principal de los estratos subalternos de color. En la obra se describen las actividades de decenas de familias a los efectos de destacar las relaciones de parentesco y las estrategias más frecuentes que ponían en práctica. La endogamia tendía a fusionar aún más a distintas familias dentro de una misma etnia. En todo caso, las redes que pautaban la vida asociativa de los pardos y morenos, constituían relaciones de poder políticos trenzadas por la clase subalterna de color a los efectos de establecer sus intereses y trazar límites muy precisos y definidos al ejercicio de la autoridad de los funcionarios coloniales y del patriciado criollo.

El sentimiento de patria enraizado en la gente de color desde el siglo XVII, conjuntamente con su aspiración a ascender socialmente, acompañaba a los valores religiosos y monárquicos que les habían sido inculcados por las autoridades coloniales. De acuerdo con la autora la consigna "morir por el Rey, la religión y la patria" colocada bajo la cruz de borgoña de la bandera de los batallones de color representaban los valores compartidos por estos y los blancos durante un período histórico. Ahora bien de la misma manera que habían servido a las armas de la Corona en el área del Caribe, para lograr un reconocimiento que los acercara socialmente a los blancos, la convicción de que nunca serían aceptados en igualdad de condiciones por estos, avivada por la revolución haitiana y el creciente distanciamiento social que trajo consigo la constitución del sistema de plantaciones esclavista, los llevó de la mano a participar en numerosas conspiraciones abolicionistas e independentistas, en los años que corren entre 1789 y 1868. En el libro se le dedican unas cuantas paginas a la influencia de la Revolución Haitiana y a las conspiraciones de Aponte y Monzón. La presentación del tema debe servir para estimular el estudio en profundidad de las tramas liberadoras de la gente de color, las que fueron mucho más numerosas y abarcaron a toda la isla. El receso en las actividades conspirativas que caracterizó al período subsiguiente a la represión de la Escalera (1844–1868), no es estudiado en la obra. Deschamp tampoco se propuso ilustrar las causas de esta cesación o pausa en las actividades conspirativas. Tampoco se ha esclarecido hasta que punto estas actividades tenían no sólo un carácter abolicionista como se ha supuesto hasta hoy día, sino también un carácter independentista. A nuestro modo de ver, después de la Revolución Haitiana es muy improbable que los negros y mulatos libres involucrados en conspiraciones abolicionistas, no estuvieran convencidos de que tales actividades suponían y llevaban aparejada la lucha por la independencia.

Sólo nos queda expresar la profunda admiración, reconocimiento y respeto que merece la obra de la historiadora y profesora emérita. No creo haber hecho justicia en toda la dimensión de la palabra a sus medulares y enjundiosas investigaciones, al conjunto de implicaciones de método y de concepción histórica que suponen sus variados aportes y reflexiones. Estamos convencidos de que por la trascendencia que tiene su obra en nuestro medio será debatida en profundidad e inspirará nuevos estudios. Pensamos que sin el conocimiento que aporta sobre las redes sociales en que se encontraba insertos los negros y mulatos libres, no es posible comprender las relaciones que los ataban al poder colonial, ni las luchas que los llevaron finalmente por sus propios pies a participar en las luchas por la independencia.

NOTAS

1. María del Carmen Barcia "La esclavitud de las plantaciones una relación secundaria", en *Temas acerca de la esclavitud* (La Habana: Editorial de Ciencias Sociales, 1986), 54–61.

2. Maria del Carmen Barcia, *Burguesía esclavista y abolición* (La Habana: Editorial de Ciencias Sociales, 1987), 21.

3. María del Carmen Barcia "Algunas cuestiones teóricas necesarias para el análisis del surgimiento y la crisis de la Plantación esclavista", *Revista de la Biblioteca Nacional "José Martí"* 22, no. 3 (1980): 57.

4. Laird Bergad y Fe Iglesias, eds., *The Cuban Slave Market 1790–1880* (New York: Cambridge University Press, 1994); "Mercado de esclavos en Cuba: Una experiencia para la formación de investigadores", en *Revista de Historia y Ciencias Sociales*, no. 13 (1994).

5. María del Carmen Barcia, "Los proyectos de población blanca y la Real Sociedad Económica de Amigos del País", *Espace Caraïbe, Revue Internationale de Sciences Humaines et Sociales,* no. 2 (1994): 111–30.

6. María del Carmen Barcia "El reagrupamiento social y político: Sus proyecciones (1878–1895)", 250–61, y "La sociedad cubana en el ocaso colonial: Vida y cultura,", 270–317, en *Las luchas por la independencia nacional y las transformaciones estructurales (1868–1895)*, editado por Instituto de Historia de Cuba (La Habana: Editorial Política, 1996).

7. María del Carmen Barcia, "La Historia Profunda", *Temas,* No. 12–13 (1998): 27–33.

8. La autora reconoce la importancia que tuvo para ella el conocimiento de la obra de Jürgen Habermas y Pierre Bourdieu.

9. María del Carmen Barcia, *Élites y grupos de presión: Cuba 1878–1895* (La Habana: Editorial de Ciencias Sociales, 1998).

10. Ibid., p. 142.

11. Ibid.,

12. María del Carmen Barcia, *Capas populares y modernidad en Cuba (1878–1930)* (La Habana: Editorial La Fuente Viva, 2005), 227. Jacobo de la Pezuela, *Diccionario geográfico, estadístico, histórico de la Isla de Cuba* (Madrid: Imprenta del Establecimiento de Mellado, 1863), 4:248–249.

13. La autora cita a Alejandro de la Fuente, "Los matrimonios de esclavos en la Habana (1585–1645)", 507–28, ejemplar mecanografiado en la Biblioteca del Instituto de Historia de Cuba, La Habana.

14. No obstante, la investigación en los registros de familias esclavas de Sta. Lucia, llevadas a efecto por Higman parece confirmar la frase de Moreno Fraginals, un tanto exagerada a juicio, de Barcia, sobre una "inestabilidad polígama sucesiva simultanea" en las sociedades de plantaciones esclavas y en las sociedades que le sucedieron. De acuerdo con Higman, a quien Barcia cita para refutar a Moreno, en Sta. Lucia un 32,4 por ciento de las familias eran sólo de mujeres con niños y un 10,9 por ciento por mujeres con sus hijos y nietos, mientras sólo estaba presididas por hombres un 7,4 por ciento de las familias. En otras palabras, la tendencia era a que los hombres fecundasen en una variedad de ocasiones a mujeres sin comprometerse a constituir familias con ellas. No

obstante, a partir de esa información, no puede determinarse que hubiera relaciones de poligamia generalizadas en la isla, aunque las numerosas familias matrifocales lo sugieran. En una valoración posterior de la situación de las familias de esclavos en las antillas británicas Higman, conjuntamente, con Engerman, llegó a la conclusión de que "números significativos de esclavos vivían en familias matrifocales, en residencias de familias nucleares, sin embargo, las familias extensivas y las residencias donde se practicara la poligamia eran relativamente raras". B. W. Higman, *Slave Population of the British Caribbean, 1807–1834* (Kingston, Jamaica: University of West Indies Press, 1984); Stanley L. Engerman y B. W. Higman, "The Demographic Structure of the Caribbean Slave Societies in the Eighteenth and Nineteenth Century", en *General History of the Caribbean: The Slave Societies in the Caribbean*, editado por Franklin Knight (Hong Kong: UNESCO Publishing, 1997), 2:87.

15. María del Carmen Barcia, *La otra familia: Parientes, redes y descendencia de los esclavos de Cuba* (La Habana: Colección Premio Casa de las Américas, 2003), 73–75. De la Pezuela, *Diccionario geográfico*, 4:248–249.

16. De acuerdo con Gurvitch el problema de las formas de sociabilidad constituye el objeto esencial de la microfísica social. El renombrado sociólogo destaca en otro momento que las tipos de sociabilidad mismas eran "las diferentes maneras de estar ligados en un todo y por un todo social". Gurvitch negaba, así mismo, que "unidades colectivas particulares tales como el Estado, la Nación, la clase social, el partido político... constituyan formas de sociabilidad". En esas entidades se combinaban varias formas de sociabilidad, pero en sí no constituían formas de sociabilidad. Se oponía también a que las formas de la sociabilidad se considerasen estructuras de la sociedad global. El ejército en tanto unidad organizativa de actividad en el que predomina la solidaridad mecánica del ordeno y mando no es una forma de sociabilidad, aunque en él se manifiestan formas de sociabilidad entre sus integrantes. De acuerdo con una interpretación esquemática, el concepto de ejército, aplicable a la milicia, se opondría a la decisión de Barcia de estudiar las formas de sociabilidad en los batallones de las milicias de color, en tanto estos constituían una forma de solidaridad forzada, mecánica, que excluiría la sociabilidad. Ahora bien la milicia se basa en el concepto de voluntariedad, a diferencia del ejército que se basa en la conscripción forzada, aunque en ambas instituciones de actividad prevalezca la solidaridad impuesta, mecánica. Con independencia del valor relativo que puedan tener los conceptos de Gurvitch consideró correcto que la historiadora se haya propuesto analizar las formas de sociabilidad que se manifiestan en esa unidad colectiva activa , basada en la solidaridad mecánica que es la milicia, pues de acuerdo con la colega "las formas de sociabilidad constituyen un campo de observación privilegiado para analizar las estructuras sociales y los sistemas de poder, pues, es en este contexto donde entran en contacto varios campos en los cuales se desarrolla la acción social". Georges Gurvitch, *Las formas de la sociabilidad: Ensayos de sociología* (Buenos Aires: Editorial Losada, 1942), 33 y 20. María del Carmen Barcia, *Los ilustres apellidos: Negros en a Habana colonial* (La Habana: Editorial Boloña, Oficina del Historiador de La Habana, 2009), 47.

Consuelo E. Stebbins. *City of Intrigue, Nest of Revolution: A Documentary History of Key West in the Nineteenth Century.* Gainesville: University Press of Florida, 2007. 258 pp.

Most scholarly attempts to understand Key West in the nineteenth century fit into one of two categories. The first treats the development of Key West predominantly in isolation, focusing on the development of industries — in wrecking, fishing, and later cigars — and infrastructure that set the foundations for the city's internal development into the twentieth century.[1] The second focuses on Key West from a more international perspective by examining the city's role as an émigré colony for Cubans seeking independence from Spanish rule.[2] Stebbins's study contributes significantly by bridging these two categories of scholarship, for her study suggests — it is puzzling why she does not make this connection more explicit — that Key West's economic and social development is best understood in a broader Caribbean context. The Caribbean Sea acted as a network for exchanges of all kinds, both legal and illegal, among the city, the mainland United States, and other islands, especially Cuba.

Basing her work primarily on personal translations of confidential reports, correspondence, and telegrams among Spanish consuls in Key West; the Spanish minister in Madrid; the governor-general of Cuba; the Spanish ambassador in Washington, D.C.; and local U.S. officials in Key West (all culled from the Archivo General del Ministerio de Asuntos Exteriores in Madrid), Stebbins traces a complex web of international interactions between 1842 and 1898. These sources provide the reader an intimate look at Key West's development and the growth of the émigré colony through an unusual prism: the perceptions of Spanish officials working there. In this way, Stebbins refocuses attention from the domestic (read, U.S.) influence of Key West's development to its impact on relations with the Spanish Empire. The documents reveal how laws passed in the United States enraged Spanish officials by reducing revenues for the Spanish Crown and how perceived inaction or unresponsiveness of U.S. customs officials and judges angered Spanish authorities while making Spanish consuls feel powerless. To the contrary, the sources reveal how attuned Spanish officials were — through the infiltration of insurgent groups — to plans intended to aid the overthrow of the Spanish Empire and to the inner workings of the Cuban émigré colony.

Stebbins divides the present study thematically more so than chronologically, beginning her examination with the salvage industry, which provided a significant source of income for the city during the first half of the nineteenth century. Closely related to Key West's development as a prosperous wrecking and salvage center — and treated in Stebbins's study in a subsequent chapter — was its growth as a port city. The city's unique position in the Caribbean on the outer, southwestern edge of the Straits of Florida made it a center for brief stopovers for ships transporting goods between U.S. ports or to foreign ports in Cuba, Central America, and the Caribbean. The establishment of customhouses in the port that taxed goods arriving in and leaving the port generated notable revenues for the city as well.

In addition to legal shipments of goods, Key West gained notoriety for two other industries: contraband and cigar manufacturing. These two industries, which grew markedly in the second half of the century, combined with other forces — namely growing anti-Spanish sentiments, the eruption of the Ten Years' War, and later the Guerra Chiquita — in providing an impetus for establishing Key West as a base of support for Cuban independence. The geography of the Keys, with numerous islands and inlets, made preventing goods smuggling nearly impossible. And although this decreased revenues to both the U.S. government and the Spanish Crown, it provided an avenue for supporters of Cuban independence to ship weapons and troops to Cuba. The growth of the cigar industry, in contrast, provided economic prosperity and an explosion in numbers of the émigré community, a population boom to which the uncertainty caused by the early wars of independence also contributed greatly. This network of migrants, comprising cigar-factory workers, businesspeople, and Cuban army officers, made up more than 36 percent of the city's population by 1885 and played a role in the third Cuban war for independence that began in 1895.

The remainder of Stebbins's documentary history traces a more well-trodden path. In the final chapters, she notes the blossoming of the émigré colony in Key West and its division and later unification under José Martí before concluding with a survey of various (mostly unsuccessful) independence expeditions that left from the city and other parts of Florida.

Although Stebbins's work is unique, especially in the sources it consults, the book is flawed in several respects. The text's construction is peculiar in that there is an overabundance of translated and excerpted documents embedded in the text without adequate historical context; brief transitional paragraphs and a four-page introduction do little to situate these documents and fail to demonstrate particular documents' historical significance. As such, *City of Intrigue* is neither a primary document reader in a traditional sense, with documents offset and indexed, nor a complete narrative of Key West's nineteenth-century history. It is a loose collection of archival documents centered on intriguing histories with "a cast of characters and crises . . . that no Florida noir novelist could imagine" in a city "seemingly suspended between prosperity and ruin, paradise and revolution" (xii). Because of the book's puzzling construction, this reviewer is not entirely clear as to how Stebbins intended this study to be used, whether as a supplemental text (analogous to a primary document reader) or as one that stands on its own. If the former, Stebbins's failure to provide complete documents (even in an appendix) or to posit the intentions of the consuls implies to the reader a truthfulness and authenticity of claims that is subject to criticism. If the latter, her decision to let the documents stand on their own, without proper contextualization, leaves major gaps in the city's history.

Despite these criticisms, Stebbins's work suggests that scholars interpret Key West's history more broadly. The history of Key West was not simply the history of the southernmost city and port in the nineteenth-century United

States. Rather, Key West was a site of critical importance, of interactions and exchanges that shaped the histories of Cuba, the Caribbean, and the United States.

Lance Ingwersen
Arizona State University

NOTES

1. Among others are Maureen Ogle, *Key West: History of an Island of Dreams* (Gainesville: University Press of Florida, 2003); Jefferson B. Browne, *Key West: The Old and the New* (1912; reprint, Gainesville: University of Florida Press, 1973); and L. Glenn Westfall, *Don Vicente Martinez Ybor, the Man and His Empire: Development of the Clear Havana Industry in Cuba and Florida in the Nineteenth Century* (New York: Garland Publishing, 1987), 17–54.

2. Among these, see Gerald E. Poyo, "Cuban Patriots in Key West, 1876–1886: Guardians at the Separatist Ideal," *Florida Historical Quarterly* 61, no. 1 (1982): 20–36; Gerald E. Poyo, *"With All, and for the Good of All": The Emergence of Popular Nationalism in the Cuban Communities of the United States, 1848–1898* (Durham, NC: Duke University Press, 1989). See also Louis A. Perez Jr., ed., *José Martí in the United States: The Florida Experience* (Tempe: Arizona State University Center for Latin American Studies, 1995); C. Neale Ronning, *José Martí and the Emigré Colony in Key West: Leadership and State Formation* (New York: Praeger, 1990).

Contributors

Mervyn J. Bain is a lecturer in the Department of Politics and International Relations at the University of Aberdeen. His research interests are Russian foreign policy and modern-day Latin America, but more specifically Cuba. He is the author of *Soviet-Cuban Relations 1985 to 1991: Changing Perceptions in Moscow and Havana* (2007) and *Russian-Cuban Relations since 1992: Continuing Camaraderie in a Post-Soviet World* (2008). He has published articles on Cuba's relationship with the former Soviet Union in a variety of journals, including *Journal of Latin American Studies*, and his chapter "Gorbachev's Legacy for Russian/Cuban Relations Post 1991" was included in *Redefining Cuban Foreign Policy: The Political Impact of the "Special Period"* (2006). In conjunction with Andrea Oelsner he coauthored a chapter in *Democratization* (2009). He has held research grants from the British Academy and Carnegie Trust.

Mayra P. Espina Prieto is a researcher at the Centro de Investigaciones Psicológicas y Sociológicas of Cuba (CIPS) and professor at the University of Havana. She is a member of the research council at CIPS and the Centro de Antropología, as well as a member of the editorial board for the magazine *Temas*. Espina Prieto is president of the National Liaison Committee for MOST/UNESCO in Cuba. Among her recent publications are "Cuba: Reforma Económica y Reestratificación Social," in *Cuba: Sociedad y trabajo* (2000), and "Transición y dinámica de los procesos socioculturales," in *Cuba: Construyendo futuro* (2000).

Julie Feinsilver is currently a visiting researcher at Georgetown University and an independent consultant. She previously taught Latin American politics and development at Oberlin College, Bard College, Colgate University, and Wesleyan University. Since leaving academia in 1993, she has worked for the Pan American Health Organization in Research and Technological Development and, more recently, for twelve years at the Inter-American Development Bank. She has conducted research on Cuban medical diplomacy since 1979 and is the author of the book *Healing the Masses: Cuban Health Politics at Home and Abroad* (1993), as well as numerous articles and book chapters since 1989 dealing with Cuba's medical diplomacy, biotechnology development, foreign relations, nontraditional exports, and politics of health. She was the scientific editor of and contributor to the book *Biodiversity, Biotechnology and Sustainable Development in Health and Agriculture: Emerging Connections* (1996) and is currently writing a book tentatively titled *Medical Diplomacy: Fifty Years of Cuba's Soft Power Politics*.

Emily J. Kirk received her BA (honors) in international development studies and Spanish from Dalhousie University in 2009. She studied at the University of Havana in the winter of 2008 and has presented her research on both HIV/AIDS in Cuba and Cuba's medical cooperation with Haiti at various global health conferences. She is currently studying at the University of Cambridge, completing an M.Phil. in Latin American studies.

John M. Kirk is professor of Latin American studies at Dalhousie University in Halifax, Nova Scotia, Canada. He has written several books on Cuba, the most recent of which (coauthored with Michael Erisman) is *Cuban Medical Internationalism: Origins, Evolution and Goals* (2009). He is the editor of the Contemporary Cuba series at the University Press of Florida. Currently, he is working on a new book examining the impact of Cuban medical internationalism and lessons that can be learned from that policy.

Marta Núñez-Sarmiento is a professor and a researcher at the Center for Study of International Migrations at the University of Havana. Her research has concentrated on transition projects for Cuba proposed by Cuban American and U.S. scholars, women and employment in Cuba, gender studies in Cuba, images of women in Cuban mass media, and images of Cuba in Cuban and foreign mass media. Holding a master's degree in sociology from the Latin American Faculty of Social Sciences in Santiago, Chile, and a PhD in economics from the Academy of Sciences in Moscow, Russia, she has been a visiting professor at universities in the Dominican Republic, Switzerland, Sweden, the United States, Canada, Spain, and Argentina. Working as a consultant for several agencies of the United Nations (1988–2010), the Canadian Agency for International Development, the Association of Caribbean States (1999), and several nongovernmental organizations, she has also served as expert for the Council of Mutual Economic Assistance, (Moscow, 1978–1983) and counselor for the embassy of Cuba in Russia (1993–1997). She was a visiting scholar at the David Rockefeller Center for Latin American Studies at Harvard (2010).

Lars Schoultz is the William Rand Kenan Jr. Professor of Political Science at the University of North Carolina at Chapel Hill. A student of inter-American relations, he is the author of *Human Rights and United States Policy toward Latin America* (1981); *The Populist Challenge: Argentine Electoral Behavior in the Postwar Era* (1983); *National Security and United States Policy toward Latin America* (1987); *Beneath the United States: A History of U.S. Policy toward Latin America* (1998); and *That Infernal Little Cuban Republic: The United States and the Cuban Revolution* (2009). He has also coedited four additional volumes on inter-American relations. His single-authored articles have appeared in most of the principal journals of political science. A resident fellow at the National Humanities Center (1999–2000) and the Woodrow Wilson International Center for Scholars (1994–1995), Schoultz has held research fellowships from the Ford Foundation, the Fulbright-Hays Program, the MacArthur Foundation, the Rockefeller Foundation, and the Social Science Research Council.

Jean Stubbs is associate fellow of the Institute for the Study of the Americas, School of Advanced Study, University of London; codirector of the Commodities of Empire Project, in collaboration with the Open University's Ferguson Centre for African and Asian Studies; and professor emerita of London Metropolitan University, where she formerly directed the Caribbean Studies Centre. She has published widely on Cuba, and her specialist interests span tobacco, labor, gender, and race. She coedited, with Pedro Pérez Sarduy, *Afro-Cuban Voices: On Race and Identity in Contemporary Cuba* (2000), and *AFROCUBA: An Anthology of Cuban Writing on Race, Politics and Culture* (1993, 1998). She is the coauthor of *Cuba* (1996), and the author of *Cuba: the Test of Time* (1989). She is currently working on a book provisionally titled *The Havana Cigar Universe: Transnational Migration and Commodity Production, 1860–2010,* a sequel to *Tobacco on the Periphery: A Case Study in Cuban Labour History, 1860–1958* (1985, 1989).

Sara Vega is researcher on Cuban film posters and Cuban cinema at the Cuba Film Archive and member of the Steering Committee of Young Filmmakers Festival at Havana. Cowriter of the documentary film *Poética gráfica insular* (2007), Vega Miche's writings have been published in *Coordenadas del cine cubano* I y II, *Cartel de cine cubano, Imágenes de Cine: Eduardo Muñoz Bachs,* and in magazines such as *Cuba Update, AGR,* and *Cine Cubano.* Her books include *La otra imagen del cine cubano* (1997), *Carteles son . . . carteles del ICAIC* (2006), *Historia de un gran amor: Relaciones cinematográficas entre Cuba y México, 1897–2005* (2007), and *Ciudadano cartel* (2009). Having lectured in Cuba, Italy, Turkey, Chile, Colombia, Mexico, and the United States, she has also curated Cuban posters exhibitions in Biarritz, France (1999); Istanbul (2004); New York (2001); and Havana (1997, 1999, 2002–2004, 2007–2010).

Doreen Weppler-Grogan is a PhD student in the Department of History of Art and Screen Media, School of Arts, Birkbeck College, University of London. She received her BA (honors) in art history in 2000. Her dissertation, "Contemporary Artistic Practice in Cuba, The New Art of Cuba," was awarded the national Student Dissertation Prize by the Association of Art Historians. She has recently successfully completed her M.Phil. and is in the final stages of her doctoral degree. Her research interests include Cuban cultural policy, modernist and postrevolutionary artistic practice in Cuba as sites of political action, and the impact of market relations on Cuban artistic production.